D1475631

Eric Voegelin Institute Series in Political Philosophy:
Studies in Religion and Politics

Jesus and the Gospel Movement: Not Afraid to Be Partners,
    by William Thompson-Uberuaga
Michael Oakeshott on Religion, Aesthetics, and Politics,
    by Elizabeth Campbell Corey
The Religious Foundations of Francis Bacon's Thought,
    by Stephen A. McKnight
Republicanism, Religion, and the Soul of America,
    by Ellis Sandoz

Other Books in the Eric Voegelin Series in Political Philosophy

The American Way of Peace: An Interpretation, by Jan Prybyla
Art and Intellect in the Philosophy of Étienne Gilson,
    by Francesca Aran Murphy
Augustine and Politics as Longing in the World, by John von Heyking
Eros, Wisdom, and Silence: Plato's Erotic Dialogues,
    by James M. Rhodes
*Faith and Political Philosophy: The Correspondence between Leo Strauss
    and Eric Voegelin, 1934–1964,* edited by Peter Emberley and Barry
    Cooper
*A Government of Laws: Political Theory, Religion, and the American
    Founding,* by Ellis Sandoz
Hans Jonas: The Integrity of Thinking, by David J. Levy
Lonergan and the Philosophy of Historical Existence,
    by Thomas J. McPartland
The Narrow Path of Freedom and Other Essays, by Eugene Davidson
New Political Religions, or an Analysis of Modern Terrorism,
    by Barry Cooper
Robert B. Heilman and Eric Voegelin: A Friendship in Letters, 1944–1984,
    edited by Charles R. Embry
*Transcendence and History: The Search for Ultimacy from Ancient Societies
    to Postmodernity,* by Glenn Hughes
Voegelin, Schelling, and the Philosophy of Historical Existence,
    by Jerry Day

ERIC VOEGELIN
AND THE PROBLEM OF
CHRISTIAN POLITICAL ORDER

Jeffrey C. Herndon

UNIVERSITY OF MISSOURI PRESS

COLUMBIA AND LONDON

5 4 3 2 1   11 10 09 08 07

Library of Congress Cataloging-in-Publication Data

Herndon, Jeffrey C., 1962–
    Eric Voegelin and the problem of Christian political order / Jeffrey C. Herndon.
        p. cm.—(Eric Voegelin Institute series in political philosophy)
    Summary: "Analyzes the development of Voegelin's thought regarding the origins of Christianity in the person of Jesus, the development of the church in the works of Paul, and the relationship between an immanent institutional order symbolizing the divine presence and the struggle for social and political order"—Provided by publisher.
    Includes bibliographical references and index.
    ISBN 978-0-8262-1737-0 (alk. paper)
    1. Voegelin, Eric, 1901–1985.   2. Theology, Doctrinal—History—20th century.   3. History—Religious aspects—Christianity—History of doctrines—20th century.   4. Christianity and politics.   5. Church and state.   6. Jesus Christ.   7. Paul, the Apostle, Saint—Theology.
I. Title.
    B3354.V884H47 2007
    270—dc22

                                                    2007003360

♾ This paper meets the requirements of the American National Standard for Permanence of Paper for Printed Library Materials, Z39.48, 1984.

Designer: Kristie Lee
Typesetter: BookComp, Inc.
Printer and binder: Thomson-Shore, Inc.
Typefaces: ITC Berkeley Book and Golden Cockerel

Publication of this book has been assisted by a generous contribution from the Eric Voegelin Institute, which gratefully acknowledges the generous support provided for the series by the Earhart Foundation and the Sidney Richards Moore Memorial Fund.

To Cindy, Jacob, and Ariana—
with gratitude for their faith, patience, and love

Contents

Acknowledgments ix

Abbreviations of Works by Eric Voegelin Cited in the Text xiii

Introduction 1

CHAPTER ONE
Voegelin's *History of Political Ideas* 7

CHAPTER TWO
Voegelin and the Emergence of the Christian Community 30

CHAPTER THREE
Imperium 65

CHAPTER FOUR
The Age of Confusion 97

CHAPTER FIVE
Crisis 132

Conclusion 163

Bibliography 165

Index 177

Acknowledgments

Contrary to the myth of authorship, the writing of a book is really a collective enterprise. While invariably the names of one or two people appear on the title page, my own experience leads me to believe that no book would ever be finished without the help, love, support, and some degree of gentle authoritarianism on the part of those prodding the author forward in his or her work. With this in mind, I would like to thank those people who have been instrumental in the completion of this work.

As an undergraduate at Texas State University, I made the mistake of taking a course in political theory being taught by Kenneth L. Grasso. As a result of this error, the course of my personal history was irrevocably changed. For this I am grateful to Ken and other members of the political science faculty at Texas State. It was Grasso who piqued my interest in political science generally (the first question of politics is not "who gets what, where, and when?" but rather "what is a human being?") and Eric Voegelin, in particular. I would be remiss if I did not also thank Robert Gorman, Ted Hindson (who planted the idea that graduate school might be more interesting for me than law school—it turns out he was correct), and the late Randall Bland. They offered a burgeoning scholar a nurturing environment and opened up possibilities for me that I had not considered (this was in addition to the camaraderie of Notre Dame football on Saturdays and nearly always picking up the tab at dinner).

At Louisiana State University a new world was opened up, and once again I found guidance and friendship in the Political Science Department. In this regard, I would like to thank Mark Schafer for both his creative use of modern literature in class and the experience of Thai and Indian food. Thanks also go to Wayne Parent for the Friday afternoon "discussion group."

When it began to look as if the inexorability of time was going to destroy the project before completion, several people assisted me in defeating the inevitability of deadlines. Tara Montelaro, the graduate secretary in the department, worked many long hours on my behalf to help keep me on track in terms of paperwork and time management. In addition, James Garand, the director of graduate studies for the department, went out of his way to help me with scheduling and other matters related to the calendar requirements for the dissertation and the degree.

The patience and support of my doctoral committee are much appreciated. I would like to thank Cecil Eubanks for opening the world of Greek tragedy to me in a meaningful way and for his many kind words of support. James Stoner, the department's former director of graduate studies, was helpful in both that capacity and as a teacher who gave some perspective to a scholar who needed it. This was in addition to his conversations with my wife that contributed to the "gentle authoritarianism" previously mentioned. Eugene Wittkopf helped me understand the nuances of international relations theory and its implications for the understanding of political science generally.

Deserving of special recognition is Ellis Sandoz. There is no real way to thank Dr. Sandoz for his assistance in so many areas related to this project, be it from the perspective of Voegelin scholarship generally, the management of the calendar, providing insight into problems with the research project, even down to pointing out typographical errors that somehow persisted through the process. Dr. Sandoz went out of his way to help me when I needed help and was always there to push me forward. For this I am truly grateful and appreciative.

Nancy L. Clark, dean of the LSU Honors College, Virginia Bell, Ann Holmes, Mary Sirridge, and Bob McMahon (all of the LSU Honors College) helped in ways they probably never really knew, and I appreciate their support and guidance. I would also like to recognize the many fine students with whom I was privileged to work under the auspices of the Honors College (and you know who you are). Students are ultimately the reason that academics do what we do, and it has been a great honor to know so many great young scholars and genuinely exceptional human beings.

In addition to the academic assistance, this book would not have been possible without the support and love of my family. I would like to thank my mother and father for their insistence that I finish my homework before I went outside to play. In addition, I would like to express my appreciation to my wife's parents for their help and support, especially after I had taken their daughter and grandchildren away to the wilds of Louisiana.

I would like to thank Beverly Jarrett and Jane Lago of the University of Missouri Press for their generous assistance and patience throughout the preparation of the manuscript.

Finally, and most important, I would like to thank my wife, Cindy, and our children. I am sure that my son and daughter occasionally believed that their father had left the planet. As we entered into the final phase of the project, our time together was limited by the exigencies of book writing. They were patient, however, and provided many fond memories of, and necessary diversions from, the process—all this in addition to their "help" with the organization of research materials.

At the outset, I mentioned the "gentle authoritarianism" required to put together a book manuscript. No one epitomizes this quality more than my wife and partner. This book is as much hers as it is mine; in many ways it is more hers. For this reason, this book is dedicated to her, with much gratitude and love.

Any errors or omissions in the text are my responsibility alone.

Abbreviations of Works by
Eric Voegelin Cited in the Text

CW, 2	*Race and State*
CW, 5	*Modernity Without Restraint: The Political Religions, The New Science of Politics, and Science, Politics, and Gnosticism*
CW, 6	*Anamnesis*
CW, 10	*Published Essays, 1940–1952*
CW, 11	*Published Essays, 1953–1965*
CW, 17	*Order and History,* Volume IV, *The Ecumenic Age*
CW, 19	*History of Political Ideas,* Volume I, *Hellenism, Rome, and Early Christianity*
CW, 20	*History of Political Ideas,* Volume II, *The Middle Ages to Aquinas*
CW, 21	*History of Political Ideas,* Volume III, *The Later Middle Ages*
CW, 22	*History of Political Ideas,* Volume IV, *Renaissance and Reformation*
CW, 23	*History of Political Ideas,* Volume V, *Religion and the Rise of Modernity*
CW, 24	*History of Political Ideas,* Volume VI, *Revolution and the New Science*
CW, 25	*History of Political Ideas,* Volume VII, *The New Order and the Last Orientation*
CW, 26	*History of Political Ideas,* Volume VIII, *Crisis and the Apocalypse of Man*
CW, 34	*Autobiographical Reflections*

ERIC VOEGELIN
AND THE PROBLEM OF
CHRISTIAN POLITICAL ORDER

Introduction

Western civilization owes its existence to Christianity. Yet in many ways, Christianity's success was the cause of its decline as the organizing principle of Western civilization. It is one of the ironies of history that the very qualities that enabled Christianity to expand across borders, cultures, and peoples should, in turn, be the underlying source of its undoing.

The purpose of this book is to analyze Eric Voegelin's examination of the problem of Christian political order, from the inception of Christianity in the person of Jesus of Nazareth through the convulsion of Western civilization that is the Great Reformation, as presented in the *History of Political Ideas*. Political theorists are generally familiar with Voegelin's later arguments in *The New Science of Politics* regarding the inherent weaknesses of Christianity; however, it is only with the recent publication of the *History of Political Ideas* that the tale is told in full.

The result of this study will be a clarification of Voegelin's theory of civilizational foundation, of the meaning of Christianity politically, and of Voegelin's philosophy of history with regard to Christianity and Western political order. To this end, I will focus upon a variety of issues germane to studies of Voegelin in particular as well as to the peculiar problem of modernity and the rise of ideological mass movements. With regard to Voegelin, the study will help illuminate Voegelin's position regarding the person of Jesus himself, which, even among many ardent supporters and admirers of Voegelin's scholarship, has been a matter of some consternation. The *History of Political Ideas* contains the most extended treatment of Jesus found in any of Voegelin's writings; and the analysis herein of Voegelin's treatment of Jesus will help address the larger questions regarding

1

Voegelin's approach to Christianity in the later writings, most particularly as it relates to *The Ecumenic Age* and the almost complete absence of Jesus in that work.

More important, however, in terms of the larger question of the influence of Christianity upon the development and decline of the distinctly Western Christian civilization, the analysis will focus upon the "Pauline compromises with the world" that made it possible for Christianity to become the instrument by which the West itself was civilized. It was the unraveling of these compromises through time that resulted in the Great Reformation of the sixteenth century. The compromises made by Saint Paul with the realities of the world into which Christianity would take its place had, as their origin, a realistic assessment of reality as it can be known to human beings—that is, the reality of human nature, the world itself, the divine, and the relationships among them. It is no exaggeration to say that in the abandonment of the compromises made by Paul, Christian civilization created the conditions for its own demise.

Furthermore, as a corollary, it is important to note that the retreat from the essential compromises made by Paul at the inception of Christianity was also representative of a retreat from a true understanding of reality itself. The consequences of this movement were, of course, the age of religious wars with the horrific violence of sectarian struggle that was released. This, in turn, was followed by the even more horrific violence that resulted from the rise of ideological mass movements that were, in fact, representative of the full retreat from the realities of human existence and became the repositories of spiritual unrest.

Running throughout the history of Christian political order is an inherent tension between the underlying sentiments and ideas embodied in Jesus' announcement of the "kingdom of God" and the realization of that idea through the institution of temporal and spiritual authorities as the representation of that order on Earth. Voegelin's most complete analysis of that tension takes place within the context of the *History of Political Ideas*. It should not be forgotten that the rather cursory examination of the problem of Christian order in *The New Science of Politics* was not directed at the problem of Christian political order per se, but was rather an instrument of explanation in the examination of the nature of modernity. The purpose of *The New Science of Politics* was to propose a radical

reorientation of political science generally and political theory in particular. The current work is not directed toward the discipline of political
science but instead attempts to explicate the problem alluded to as part
of the justification Voegelin offered for his proposed reorientation of political science.

The assault upon the Pauline compromises takes many forms and
emerges from many quarters. Not merely the expression of the disaffected,
this attack also reflects the inability of the institutional order to respond
effectively to real experiences of the human spirit as they occur in history. The analysis of Voegelin's reflections on the tensions as they occur
in history will help explain the interaction of various factors, from the
creation of the small community of the faithful around the person of Jesus
of Nazareth through the crisis of the Reformation and the terrible forces
of destruction that were unleashed as a result. Throughout the *imperium*
of the high Middle Ages, the institutional orders were able to resolve the
tensions inherent in the institutionalization of the spirit. However, even
as that occurred, changing conceptions of history and the understanding of the place of human beings in the order of the universe were creating the conditions for the assault upon civilization itself. With this in
mind, this book will trace the development of Christian political order
through the *imperium,* the confusion that resulted when the *imperium*
was dissolved, and the Great Reformation as something of an anticlimax
that resulted in the institutional realization of something that had already
occurred, i.e., the destruction of Christian *homonoia* in a universal sense.
Finally, the implications of the Great Reformation are considered in light
of the preceding analysis.

Christian *homonoia* as understood by Saint Paul was no mean achievement in history. The current study was prompted by the perception that
in the Western democracies, and the United States in particular, the community substance, as defined by shared values and a common understanding of the ends of human existence that make community life
possible, are becoming increasingly problematic. To be sure, there is cur-
rently a unity of purpose with regard to the conduct of the West toward
the terrorism brought on by fundamentalist Islam, but absent an identifiable enemy, there is some question as to whether there remains sufficient civic consciousness for the maintenance of community. It is my hope

that an analysis of the breakdown of Pauline *homonoia* might contribute to a more complete understanding of our own predicament.

Finally, the current work is based on what some might claim to be a pessimistic attitude with regard to the ideological fervor of the past and its capacity to reemerge in new forms. The tension of existence was not resolved when the Soviet Union imploded, and the capacity (it might be argued that it is a tendency) of human beings to fall into the dream world of ideological abstraction has not changed. At the edge of civilized existence there always lives the danger that the past will be born anew. While the shape of the ideological disorder of the future cannot be known, however, the inclination to fall from uncertain truth into certain untruth, as Voegelin put it, remains.

The Plan of the Work

In Voegelin's account of Christian political order in the *History of Political Ideas,* the ultimate success of the Christian community, the substructure that would allow it to encompass the Western world, is attributable to a series of "compromises" made by Paul very early in the life of the community. However, it can also be said that Christian history, the decline from the maximal level of differentiation to the political ideologies and creeds of modernity, is the history of the failure of those compromises to sustain the community through time. It is through the examination of the unraveling of these compromises that one can gain a greater appreciation of Christianity as the source of both the order and disorder that have come to characterize the existence of human beings in history.

Chapter two examines Voegelin's discussion of the emergence of the Christian community as it appears in history. As such, its primary focus will be upon the first volume of the *History.* Voegelin's analysis will be placed in the context of "historical Jesus" scholarship and followed by a discussion of Voegelin's methodological approach to the Gospel accounts of the life, death, and resurrection of Jesus and Voegelin's conclusions regarding the self-consciousness of Jesus from those accounts. The chapter culminates with an examination of the "community substance" that actually constitutes the grounding of Christian order through the experience of faith and a discussion of Paul's formulation of the constitution of the new community. This includes the critical compromises made by Paul in light of the realities of the world into which Christianity emerged. The history of Christian political order is largely connected to these compromises and their dissolution in the face of historical circumstances.

In chapter three, the analysis turns to the evocation of the *sacrum imperium* as the underlying rationale for the order of the medieval period. In this regard, the historical construction of the imperial order will be examined in addition to the tensions that existed with regard to the division of temporal and spiritual power brought about by the Gelasian doctrine and its implications for political order. Another subject of analysis will be the association between the reformist impulse that consistently forms a part of the Christian experience and the role of the monastic orders as both a civilizing influence on the general society and as conduits for reform. The chapter concludes with a discussion of the transformation in the understanding of history that creates the conditions necessary for the end of the *sacrum imperium* itself.

Chapter four begins at the beginning in a metaphorical sense. One of the primary obstacles to the vision of Saint Paul was the natural diversification of humanity. This problem reappears in the latter half of the Middle Ages and extends through the Reformation into the Enlightenment. As such, it will be the primary impetus that leads inexorably to the unleashing of the sectarian forces that ended the Catholic Church's monopoly as the representative institution of transcendent order in the West. Indeed, the church itself would help to create the conditions for its own undoing by adopting a reductionist epistemology and an increasing concern with being "in the world" to the neglect of remaining "not of the world." This institutional tension is reflective of the human experience of being "in-between," the existence in tension that would serve to inform so much of Voegelin's later work. Through its inability to balance its own existence in tension, the church committed suicide as the sole mediating institution by adopting a position that was incapable of reforming from within, leading inexorably to the Great Reformation without.

The concluding chapter will explore Voegelin's treatment of Martin Luther and John Calvin in the context of the political, social, and religious convulsion of the Great Reformation. As part of this undertaking, we will examine the implications of the spiritual forces released as a result of the

Reformation and the transformative effect that movement had upon the political and social existence of human beings. In addition, we will examine the sectarian underpinnings that resulted in the general conflagration of the Great Reformation. This will involve Voegelin's discussion of modernity found especially in *The New Science of Politics* and *Science, Politics, and Gnosticism*, the two works that have the most direct bearing upon the discussion in the *History*. Finally, we will recommend future lines of investigation to which the *History* might make significant contributions.

CHAPTER ONE

Voegelin's *History of Political Ideas*

The Background to the *History of Political Ideas*

In 1939, Eric Voegelin was contracted by Fritz Morstein Marx of the McGraw-Hill publishing house to write a "textbook of moderate size" to compete with George H. Sabine's *History of Political Theory.* Morstein Marx saw the project as a work of some "200 to 250 pages" that would recount the major thinkers and political ideas that emerged from the pre-Socratics to the present. Between 1939 and 1954, Voegelin worked in starts and stops on his *History of Political Ideas,* as the work came to be titled. While a complete history of the *History* is beyond the scope of the current study, it is important to note that in the process of devoting himself to the task, Voegelin became, as he put it, "aware of the theoretical inadequacy of my conventional preconceptions about a history of ideas" (*CW,* 34:90–91).[1]

Eventually, this awareness would lead Voegelin to propose a reformulation of the discipline of political theory itself, first, in the Walgreen Lectures at the University of Chicago in 1951, published as *The New Science of Politics,* and culminating in the publication of *Order and History.* The problem Voegelin perceived in a history of political ideas was in the confusion of the symbolization of reality through language symbols apart from the experience that engendered the use of the symbol to describe

---

1. *CW,* vol. 34, chap. 17, "From Political Ideas to Symbols of Experience," and chap. 20, "The Background of *Order and History,*" offer a more detailed examination of Voegelin's decision to abandon the *History of Political Ideas.*

it. In other words, the task of political theory, from Voegelin's perspective, was to examine the experience that gave rise to the symbol, and not the other way around. A history of political ideas, with that conceptual framework in mind, was an exercise in putting the cart before the horse. So despite the effort and time that had been invested in the *History of Political Ideas*, Voegelin abandoned the project in favor of his new exploration into the philosophy of history and his theory of consciousness.

With that said, however, the *History* is instructive in a number of ways and a suitable object for analysis. To begin with, there is the sheer scope of the project. The *History* took on a life of its own, independent of the requirements of the initial assignment. When finally published as part of *The Collected Works of Eric Voegelin* between 1997 and 1999, the 200 to 250 pages originally contracted by Morstein Marx had grown to a full eight volumes in the series, numbering nearly 2,000 pages. Rather than producing a neat biographical précis of major thinkers and their contributions to political theory proper, Voegelin had written a comprehensive examination of the cultural, political, and social forces that had shaped the modern world from the disintegration of the Hellenic polis through the modern era.

Second, there is Voegelin's conceptual breakthrough itself. Voegelin began the project with the notion that a history of political ideas was a viable approach to the problems of political order. At some point, while composing the history of political ideas, Voegelin came to the understanding that such a project did not really get to the truth of the problem of political order but was rather, in itself, a theoretical derailment. The comprehensiveness of Voegelin's approach in the *History of Political Ideas* may offer some insight into that breakthrough and Voegelin's own reevaluation of his craft and discipline. Furthermore, that same comprehensiveness served as the necessary precondition for Voegelin to begin to speculate on his own theory of consciousness and philosophy of history.

Third, and most important for the purposes of this examination, it is in the *History* that Voegelin most clearly and thoroughly examines the problem of Christian political order. Voegelin notes, "The Christian community has been, for the better part of two thousand years, the most important political force in the Western world, and the evocative acts that created it are the basis of all later political evocations that occurred in

Western history—as far as it is Christian" (*CW,* 19:164). Indeed, it is certainly arguable that the single most important element in the development of "Western civilization" was the emergence of Christianity. Christianity was a peculiar development in that it sowed the seeds of both order and disorder in the world into which it emerged. On the one hand, it kept the dream of Rome alive. On the other, it provided the complex of symbols that would characterize Voegelin's examination and explication of the ideological movements that shaped the twentieth century.

Voegelin's later approach to the question of Christianity has been viewed as somewhat problematic and the source of much critical speculation. Voegelin's *Order and History* was intended originally to encompass six volumes.[2] As with the *History of Political Ideas,* however, Voegelin became uneasy with the program he had set. After completing three volumes, Voegelin realized that he had created a problem related to the sheer size of the work. Voegelin argues, "I always ran into the problem that, in order to arrive at theoretical formulations, I had first to present the materials on which the theoretical formulations were based as an analytical result" (*CW,* 34:106–7). What this would have meant, had Voegelin followed his original plan, was not simply three more volumes, but rather six or seven to fully explore the problems that interested him.

But an even more critical issue was calling Voegelin's original program into question. As work proceeded on *Order and History,* Voegelin confronted the problem of parallel experiences that did not conform to the notion of historical progression that had served as the platform for the initial undertaking. While "there was really an advance in time from compact to differentiated experiences of reality, and, correspondingly, an advance from compact to differentiated symbols of the order of being," these occurrences did not, as Voegelin had initially assumed, occur among all peoples in a linear fashion. Ultimately, the initial "conception was untenable because it had not taken proper account of the important lines of meaning in history that did not run along lines of time" (*CW,* 17:46).

What this meant was yet another abandonment. In this instance, the three proposed volumes *Empire and Christianity, The Protestant Centuries,*

---

2. Eventually, *Order and History* was published in five volumes, available in *CW,* vols. 14–18.

and *The Crisis of Western Civilization* were scuttled in favor of *The Ecumenic Age*. For many critics, this is the source of the perceived difficulties with Voegelin's approach to the question of the role of Christianity in his analysis of the history of order and the order of history. Instead of offering an analysis of the emergence of Christianity and its influence upon the course of Western civilization, Voegelin had changed course and analyzed the concept of the *ecumene* as it emerged in two different senses. On the one hand, the concept was strictly an extension of the idea of Rome, the universal empire that is not necessarily dependent upon a shared understanding of political community among its members but is rather a system of political and social organization that rests upon the reality of power. The second notion, coterminous with the first, was born within the emergence of Christianity and consisted of the idea of a universal humanity that already exists by virtue of human existence under God. These two concepts are enigmatic in the sense that they tend to overlap, contradict, and justify each other throughout history.

Voegelin's Christian Critics

It is a maxim that discussions of religion and politics are problematic; and it should be noted that Voegelin's later work on Christianity engendered the often-violent emotions associated with such discussions. Voegelin's approach to the emergence of Christianity and the essence of Christian faith in *Order and History* left many deeply dissatisfied. The content of *The Ecumenic Age*, in particular, caused some consternation among academics who were normally sympathetic to Voegelin's scholarly pursuits. Michael P. Morrissey argues that far from being "an apologetic for Christian orthodoxy," which many people expected, *The Ecumenic Age* "appeared to be a philosophical critique of traditional Christian thought." As a result of this curious turn of events, "many" of Voegelin's "followers have become his worst adversaries. A common complaint that many of them have voiced against his work, strange as it may sound, is that he actually neglected to deal with Christianity, or more precisely, with Christian faith" or "the historicity and uniqueness of Jesus."[3]

3. Morrissey, *Consciousness and Transcendence,* 231.

The most strident criticism of Voegelin's approach to the problem of Christianity as it was revealed in *Order and History* was directed toward the choice Voegelin made to examine the emergence of Christianity through an exegesis of the experience of Saint Paul and his encounter with the risen Christ. Gerhart Niemeyer, generally a great admirer and sympathetic critic of Voegelin's undertaking, argued that in *The Ecumenic Age* the treatment of Christianity was "deeply disappointing." The reason for Niemeyer's consternation was Voegelin's emphasis upon Paul's vision on the road to Damascus instead of an examination of the historical reality of Christ himself. The primary problem, according to Niemeyer, is that "Voegelin's exegesis of St. Paul would not have to be changed if one removed Jesus Christ from it altogether." By equating the "Pauline myth" with the discovery of noetic consciousness accomplished by Plato, Niemeyer believes, Voegelin committed a most egregious error in his construction of reality itself.

The difference is in the origin of the reality prompted by the philosophical reflection on the existence of divine transcendent being and human participation and experience of divine transcendent being through the invitation of Christ. According to Niemeyer's account, the Pauline myth cannot be reconciled with the Platonic account. Niemeyer writes, "Myths and philosophical speculations are induced by the ubiquitous 'mystery of meaning' which Eric Voegelin has done more than anyone else to illuminate." However, Christianity, according to Niemeyer, "stems not from a sense of general wonderment about the world of things and the Boundless, which probably would not have been very sophisticated in simple fishermen, but rather from the question which Jesus himself put: 'Who do you say I am?'"[4] The gist of Niemeyer's argument is that Voegelin does not address the question of the incarnation of the divine presence in the person of Jesus Christ and its implications for history.

In a later essay, Niemeyer does point out "that Voegelin, at no time and no place, has ever dismissed the full reality of Jesus Christ." This, perhaps, is the reason Niemeyer also maintains that if the earlier criticism were to be rewritten it would be "somewhat milder."[5] There can be

---

4. Niemeyer, "Eric Voegelin's Philosophy and the Drama of Mankind," 34–35.
5. Niemeyer, "Christian Faith and Religion in Eric Voegelin's Work," 100.

little doubt, however, that the failure of Voegelin to deal with the historicity of Jesus was troubling for Niemeyer.

Niemeyer's willingness to reexamine his earlier critique is in sharp distinction to the most vociferous critic of Voegelin's approach to Christianity, Frederic D. Wilhelmsen. Wilhelmsen, in his *Christianity and Political Philosophy*, takes up the polemicist's pen and aims it squarely at "Professor Voegelin." To be fair to Wilhelmsen, one must also note that he is at least as vitriolic toward another great light of twentieth-century political theory, Leo Strauss. According to Wilhelmsen, Leo Strauss and his followers, the so-called "Straussian school," have actively sought to remove Christian political thought generally from the corpus of political theory. "Their books and articles, replete with references to classical antiquity, not only span Greece but they probe the modern mind from Machiavelli to Locke and beyond. We can note as well a fascination and peculiar reverence for the figure of Averroes. But very little is taught us about the contribution, if any, of Christian thought to politics."[6]

Be that as it may, however, Wilhelmsen's primary concern and scorn is not with the Straussians, but rather with Eric Voegelin and his influence on modern Christian thinkers. In the penultimate chapter of *Christianity and Political Philosophy*, Wilhelmsen writes: "If Straussianism is a danger to Christian political theory, Voegelinianism is an even more subtle danger and more dangerous because of its very attractiveness to Christians who look once but fail to look twice. Voegelin respects history and he respects the Lord of history, Christ—but Voegelin does not believe in him, or, at least, he does not believe in him as historic Christianity has believed. Hence Voegelin has not believed." The problem, the "danger" alluded to by Wilhelmsen, is that Voegelin has engaged in his own peculiar sort of reductionism. Wilhelmsen's argument echoes Niemeyer's in that through Voegelin's use of the Pauline visions of the resurrected, Voegelin has circumvented both history and faith. Wilhelmsen argues that Voegelin "represents our common Western religion through the prism of the experience of Saint Paul and almost exclusively through that prism. The historical figure of Jesus is totally bypassed by Voegelin, and the only Christ to emerge in Voegelin's pages is the resurrected Christ

6. Wilhelmsen, *Christianity and Political Philosophy*, 209.

of Paul's experience, the Christ who appeared to Paul and who transfigured his life and the life of all mankind as well." In an argument similar
to that advanced by Niemeyer, Wilhelmsen complains that Voegelin's
analysis admits of no distinction between the experience of Paul and the
noetic experiences of Plato and Aristotle. This, in turn, mitigates against
the existence of "the Church" as an essential element in "constituting man's
life in history under God." Ultimately, according to Wilhelmsen, Voegelin
has failed to grasp the significance of the Christian dispensation because
he is a "Platonist" for whom "reality does not count."[7]

A response to Wilhelmsen's criticism in particular is found in Eugene
Webb's *Eric Voegelin: Philosopher of History*. Webb notes that much of the
criticism focused on Voegelin's interpretation of Christianity does not concern itself with Voegelin's analysis of Christianity per se, but rather, especially in the case of Wilhelmsen, emanates from the perception of
Voegelin's own religious beliefs and experience of faith as understood by
his Christian critics. To be sure, Voegelin himself supplied the ammuni-
tion. As Webb observes, "An interpreter who wished to put together an
argument to the effect that Voegelin is not a Christian would be able to
find as much evidence for his position as one who argued the opposite."
This being the case does not mean that the question itself has real merit.
Webb maintains, "The most penetrating question is not whether Voegelin
is a Christian or not but what is the shape of his particular variety of
Christian thought—for that his thought is Christian in at least some sense
seems incontestable. Those of his critics who have attacked his treatment
of Christianity have in effect been arguing not that Voegelin is not a
Christian at all but that he is not a Christian by their standards."[8]

Surely Voegelin had logical reasons for choosing Paul instead of Jesus
as the founder of the Christian community. William M. Thompson observes, for example, that Voegelin was "a political theorist and philosopher
of history" who was "chiefly interested in the quest for a rightly ordered
existence." As such, "his christological studies are in the service of this larger
goal." Voegelin's work in *The New Science of Politics* and most especially in
Order and History was an exploration of human consciousness of reality.

7. Ibid., 195, 197–98, 201–2.
8. Webb, *Eric Voegelin: Philosopher of History*, 226.

In this examination, Voegelin conceived of the process of "differentiation" by which human consciousness becomes aware of reality—both divine and immanent. Furthermore, if the effort is to find an adequate theory for the experience of human beings in political society, it must do so "within the historical horizon of classical and Christian experiences" because those experiences represent the "maximum of differentiation" (*CW*, 5:152). Paul, in Voegelin's account, is archetypal in his experience of the maximal differentiation of reality experienced by human being as a result of his encounter on the road to Damascus and his ability to reflect upon it. Thompson observes, "The fact that Voegelin concentrates on the Pauline Vision of the Resurrected as the experiential center of Pauline theology is an insight that increasingly wins the approval of Pauline scholars today." Furthermore, "what . . . seems to characterize Paul, and so forcefully distinguishes him from the author of Acts, is his critical attitude toward charismatic experience." Thompson argues that it is through the work of Paul, "unlike in Plato," that "we have a clearer consciousness of the source of reality's structure (the eschatological state of perfection), and of the individual as the locus where reality's directional movement becomes luminous."[9]

Webb agrees with Thompson on the crucial point regarding Voegelin's own methodology and the requirement that it be Paul who speaks rather than Jesus. The noetic investigation of the experience of reality means that the scientist is limited by theoretical principles to the content of the experiences of those who create the symbols that describe the experience of the more completely differentiated reality. Voegelin, Webb argues, had "to investigate the revelation on the level of concrete experience." With this in mind, it was a "fundamental requirement of Voegelin's own process of noetic inquiry" that he "chose Paul rather than Jesus as his major point of focus—since Paul left writings that speak of his experience directly, whereas the experience of Jesus comes to us only through the mediating interpretations of other writers."[10] By choosing to examine the experience of Paul, Voegelin was demonstrating a preference for primary source material over secondary accounts.

The objections of Thompson and Webb notwithstanding, the idea that Voegelin was hampered in his exploration of Christianity and the per-

9. Thompson, "Voegelin on Jesus Christ," 193, 188.
10. Webb, "Eric Voegelin's Theory of Revelation," 109.

son of Jesus as the incarnation of the divine substance on Earth is a view shared by Stephen J. Tonsor. In his review of *Published Essays, 1966–1985* (*CW*, vol. 12), Tonsor argues that "the great unresolved problem in Voegelin's analysis of the experience of the soul and the articulation of order is the fact of revelation and the incarnation of God's revelation in Jesus, the Christ." The reason the problem remained unresolved, according to Tonsor, lay in the historic "conflict between Athens and Jerusalem." Tonsor argues that Voegelin "believed in the God of the philosophers and tried again and again, unsuccessfully . . . to 'put on Christ.'" Voegelin's attempt to resolve the perceived conflict between Athens and Jerusalem "by transforming revelation into noetic experience" was, in Tonsor's opinion, a failure and—in a remarkable attempt at psychological profiling— the probable source of "Voegelin's hostility to doctrinal Christianity."[11]

The meaning of the incarnation is the source of another critique of Voegelin's interpretation of the Gospel. R. Bruce Douglass, while recognizing the legitimacy of Niemeyer's concern regarding the historic Jesus, sees a more "subtle problem" in Voegelin's analysis of the Gospels. According to Douglass, "From the Christian perspective the foremost consideration in any appraisal of what Voegelin has to say must be the meaning of the Gospel—i.e., the interpretation of Jesus, his identity and significance. No issue is more central in defining Christian belief, and none is more important for the success of what Voegelin seeks to accomplish in his treatment of Christianity." However, like Niemeyer, Wilhelmsen, and Tonsor, Douglass believes that Voegelin has not met the task that he set for himself. Douglass maintains that "Voegelin's interpretation of the Gospel . . . leaves something to be desired. What is missing . . . is the sense of the Gospel as *salvation*. Or, more correctly, what is missing is the sense of the Gospel as salvation *in the specifically Christian sense*."[12]

Douglass is joined in his concern regarding Voegelin's treatment of the Gospels, most specifically in "The Gospel and Culture," in which Voegelin skirts around the edge of saying that Paul may have gone too far in his expectation of a world transformed as a result of his personal experience with the risen Christ on the Damascus road. John H. Hallowell takes issue with

---

11. Tonsor, "The God Question," 67–68, 66, 68.
12. Douglass, "A Diminished Gospel," 145, 144, 146 (emphasis in the original).

this interpretation and also questions Voegelin's general understanding of the Gospels as a tool for salvation. Hallowell writes,

> Voegelin seems to be saying that only so long as the Gospel mirrors the tension of existence is it the true Gospel. It is not clear to me what his response would be those who would say the Gospel is intended to be precisely an answer to this tension, that through the cultivation by the grace of God of the virtues of faith, hope, and charity one might be enabled better to endure the life of tension in the hope that "when the fever of life is over and our work is done, we may be granted a safe lodging and a holy rest, and peace at last." It is not clear if there is any sense in which Voegelin regards the Gospel as "good news."[13]

Elsewhere, Douglass notes that Voegelin's perception of modern ideological mass movements as gnostic deformations of Christian symbols militates against the contention that the Gospels offer a "more complete knowledge of the unknown God." According to Douglass, Voegelin's emphasis upon the gnostic deformation of Christian symbols detracts from his overall assessment of Christianity generally. Thus, "it would seem to be Voegelin's view that only the discipline of philosophical reason can effectively challenge the modern predicament."[14] As a practical matter, then, according to Douglass's interpretation of Voegelin, Christianity does not order the world but rather serves as a font of disorder. Indeed, the tension of existence is not resolved at all by Voegelin's reading of the Gospels. "In place of the biblical image of a God whose presence and purposes in history are made manifest we are given a divine flux whose direction is a mystery."[15]

Indeed, the mystery of existence lies at the heart of Marion Montgomery's critique of Voegelin's exploration of Christianity. Montgomery sees in Voegelin's analysis the "adaptation of the resurrection to his own vision." Voegelin, Montgomery argues, "takes" the resurrection "and revises it to

---

13. Hallowell, "Existence in Tension," 123.

14. Douglass, "The Gospel and Political Order: Eric Voegelin on the Political Role of Christianity," 33–37, 27.

15. Douglass, "A Diminished Gospel," 149.

the purpose of his theory of consciousness, diminishing the importance of what he has on other occasions called attention to: the particularity of the incarnation." Montgomery goes on to maintain,

> Voegelin's adaptation of the resurrection to his own vision . . . is central in the questions raised about his friendliness toward Christianity. Christ is risen only symbolically for Voegelin, it would seem—specifically in man's imitations of Jesus' radical encounters of reality in the world. . . . When we consider that history has become for Voegelin the unfolding of humanity in the context of reality, we begin to suspect an aberrational construction of the meaning of the incarnation, one which reduces the event of the incarnation and replaces it with the "larger" event of the unfolding of humanity. It is for this reason . . . that Voegelin seems more acutely interested in the event of Paul's encounter on the Road to Damascus as a transformation of Paul's consciousness and through his, ours, than in the fundamental reality of the incarnation as described by Christian dogma.

Ultimately, it is Voegelin's resistance to dogma and dogmatic assertions that Montgomery believes is the source of Voegelin's difficulty in explicating the meaning of Jesus and the Christian faith generally.

> For the Christian, as an act of faith, it is the saviour and not the poet or prophet or philosopher in whom lies the promise of our return to the lost home. But Voegelin is not prepared to make a surrender through faith to the mediator, though he honors it in others: he sees a danger that, at this point in his quest at least, such a surrender is too near the surrenders to dogma in the medieval world which prepared the ground in which modern Gnostic ideologies have flourished.

However, according to Montgomery, this opposition is in itself a form of dogmatism. Montgomery argues that "the principal dogma at the heart of Voegelin's work" is the commandment "Thou shalt not rest in conclusion lest thou fall into certitude, the unforgivable sin against openness."[16]

---

16. Montgomery, "Eric Voegelin and the End of Our Exploring," 235–36, 234, 237.

Of course, it might also be that Voegelin's critics have simply misinterpreted his exploration of the incarnation. This is the position taken by Morrissey, who maintains that those who focus upon Voegelin's apparent failure to discuss the incarnation of the divine presence are simply missing the point that Voegelin repeatedly tries to get across. Morrissey writes,

> Voegelin reminds us that the revelatory drama of the Gospel movement is situated in the larger context of the revelatory drama of Israelite history which in turn partakes in the same word of the Unknown God as does the revelatory drama of philosophy. . . . They are two parallel stories that contribute eminently to the ever-unfolding comprehensive story of the It-reality, the universal presence of the divine beyond time. Consequently, we must not dichotomize philosophy and Gospel, or Athens and Jerusalem, but, based on Voegelin's theory of equivalence and differentiation, interpret their respective dramas as unique revelations of the same divine reality in different cultural contexts. The word that emerges in each context belongs to the same human-divine *metaxy*. While each story illuminates more completely one fundamental dimension of truth over the other, they both eminently participate in the larger untold story of history. Athens and Jerusalem, philosophy and Gospel, while culturally and historically distinct, both join side by side as tensional partners in the transcendent City of God.

The concern with the historicity of Jesus is problematic to the extent that "Voegelin views the meaning of Christ as that event which reveals the depth of God's presence in our *metaxy*, but this does not by any account reduce the divine to an immanent object, the historical person of Jesus, to be fully comprehended by our consciousness"[17]—precisely what many of Voegelin's critics try to accomplish.

What all of the literature has in common, however, is a paucity of original material dealing with Christianity in the later Voegelin's work. Stephen A. McKnight laments that "Voegelin has twice proposed but failed to produce a sustained analysis of its engendering experiences and its development as an ecumenic political order." For this reason, it is still "an area

---

17. Morrissey, *Consciousness and Transcendence*, 236–37, 246.

that might receive further study." Indeed, McKnight maintains, "The lack of an extended study of Christianity is puzzling in that it, in principle, occupies the same pivotal role in the reorientation of Western thought and experience as does classical philosophy."[18] In point of fact, however, Voegelin had already explored the Christian experience in the *History of Political Ideas,* and it may well be that he was simply loath to return to the beginning. A more complete analysis of the *History* and Voegelin's reflections upon the problems of Christian political order may help to answer Voegelin's critics and open up new ground for further inquiry.

"The Crisis of Civic Consciousness"

Another reason to examine Voegelin's study of the problems of Christian political order lies in the current state of political discourse in the Western democracies generally and the United States in particular in light of what Ellis Sandoz has called "the crisis of civic consciousness."

In one of the most moving and oft-quoted passages of *The New Science of Politics,* Voegelin makes the following observation: "Human society is not merely a fact, or an event, in the external world to be studied by an observer like a natural phenomenon. Although it has externality as one of its important components, it is as a whole little world, a cosmion, illuminated with meaning from within by the human beings who continuously create and bear it as the mode and condition of their self-realization" (*CW,* 5:109). Voegelin makes this assertion as part of the ongoing debate within the discipline of political science about the way that politics ought to be studied. More important, however, Voegelin is striking at the idea that political life has some *meaning* for human beings that is an essential part of their existences. When understood in those terms, the question then becomes, From whence does that meaning derive?

One of the most elementary understandings of political societies in existence is based upon Aristotle's notion of *homonoia.* Variously translated as "concord" or "like-mindedness," *homonoia* is the transformational element that defines an aggregate of individuals into a political society. Writing in *The Politics,* Aristotle asserts that "a state cannot be made out of any and

18. McKnight, "The Evolution of Voegelin's Theory of Politics and History," 45.

every collection of people." The state, in Aristotle's conception of it, is civil and political society—a community. Furthermore, such an entity can only be said to exist among those people who share *homonoia*. This concord is not merely an intellectual agreement among a few individuals within a given polity about what ought to be done, or who gets what, where, and when, but rather it consists of a shared understanding among the populace about what it means to be a human being and what the ends of the given society or community ought to be. Aristotle maintains that "the real difference between man and other animals is that humans alone have perception of good and evil, just and unjust, etc. It is the sharing of a common view in these matters that makes a household and a state."[19]

Of course, Aristotle was not the first to make this observation. For Plato, the disorder of Athens was directly related to a spiritual malaise among its people. According to the Platonic diagnosis of the problem, human societies are reflective of the human types that compose those societies. Spiritual disorder among the members of the population and the resulting disagreements regarding the ends of political and social existence will have a deleterious effect upon the polity generally. For this reason, Plato argues, the cohesion of the community and the souls of the inhabitants must be nurtured. In *The Republic,* the cohesion of the community is secured through the use of the Phoenician Tale and "the noble lie," by which the citizens of the polis will be told of the metals that were mixed into their souls.[20] What Plato is pointing toward, in terms of the myth, is not merely an arrangement of power—a system of coercion and obedience—but rather a community of mutual interests secured through the recognition of a common spiritual core.

Since Aristotle and Plato, political thinkers from a variety of different perspectives have agreed upon the fundamental nature of the idea that the cohesion of the community is a necessary condition for the realization of human potential in political existence—although there is a great deal of disagreement regarding what term ought to be used to describe the phenomenon.

19. Aristotle, *The Politics* 304, 60.
20. Plato, *The Republic* 414b–415d. For an examination of the function of the Phoenician Tale, see Voegelin, *CW,* 16:158–62; Bloom, "Interpretive Essay," 365–69; and Strauss, *The City and Man,* 101–103.

Among Alexis de Tocqueville's many observations on the condition of human beings in political society is a reflection upon Aristotle's notion of *homonoia*. Tocqueville argues that the existence of political society is premised upon the existence of "dogmatic beliefs" held by the individual members of the community. Tocqueville asserts, "It is easy to see that no society could prosper without such belief. . . . For without ideas in common, no common action would be possible, and without common action, men might exist, but there could be no body social."[21] The existence of these dogmatic beliefs is what allows for cooperative effort that is the defining characteristic of human beings in political existence.

Voegelin's most vociferous critic, Wilhelmsen, writing with Willmoore Kendall, describes "the public orthodoxy" as "that tissue of judgments, defining the good life and indicating the meaning of human existence which is held commonly by the members of any given society, who see in it the charter of their way of life and ultimate justification of their society." Indeed, Wilhelmsen and Kendall point to the fact that while the public orthodoxy is amenable to evolutionary and revolutionary changes, the necessity for a public orthodoxy, the substance of Aristotle's *homonoia*, remains constant. "Not only can society not avoid having a public orthodoxy; even when it rejects an old orthodoxy in the name of 'enlightenment,' 'progress,' the 'pluralist society,' 'the open society,' and the like, it invents, however subtly, a new orthodoxy with which to replace the old one." Wilhelmsen and Kendall point out:

> Aristotle is always at hand to remind us, only gods and beasts can live alone; man, by nature, is a political animal whose very political life demands a politea that involves an at least implicit code of manners and a tacit agreement on the meaning of the good life, and, therefore, on the meaning of man within the total economy of existence. Without this political orthodoxy . . . and a theology sketched in at least broad outline—respect for the state withers; contracts lose their efficacy; the moral bond between citizens is loosened; the state opens itself to enemies from abroad; and the politea sheds the sacral character without which it cannot long endure.[22]

21. Tocqueville, *Democracy in America*, 433.
22. Frederick D. Wilhelmsen and Willmoore Kendall, "Cicero and the Politics of the Public Orthodoxy," in *Christianity and Political Philosophy*, 26, 35–36.

Kendall reaffirms this principle in his *Conservative Affirmation in America*. Every political society, Kendall argues, "is founded upon what political philosophers call a *consensus;* that is, a hard core of shared beliefs." This consensus has to exist if the "society" is ever going to be anything more than merely an agglomeration of atomistic individuals held together by the coercive power of the government. "Those beliefs that the people share are what defines its character as a political society, what embodies its meaning as a political society, what, above all perhaps, expresses its understanding of itself as a political society."[23] In other words, the substance of the hard core of shared beliefs that represent the consensus of the members of any given society is what gives the members of that society meaning in their political lives.

In using the language of "consensus," Kendall is following in the footsteps of John Courtney Murray. Murray maintains that a political society is born in "the constitutional consensus whereby the people acquires its identity as a people and the society is endowed with its vital form, its entelechy, its sense of purpose as a collectivity organized for action in history." According to Murray, this constitutional consensus is necessary for the existence of the polity itself because it is a necessary precondition for the "public argument" that is the essence of political society in a popular regime. Murray writes:

> This consensus is come to by the people; they become a people by coming to it. . . . The consensus is not a structure of secondary rationalizations erected on psychological data . . . or on economic data. . . . It is not simply a working hypothesis whose value is pragmatic. It is an ensemble of substantive truths, a structure of basic knowledge, an order of elementary affirmations that reflect realities inherent in the order of existence. . . . It furnishes the premises of the people's action in history and defines the larger aims that actions seek in internal affairs and in external relations.[24]

A political society in existence is thus the representational form of this constitutional consensus. The precise meaning of these "substantive truths" that provide the bedrock of any political society organized for action in

23. Kendall, *The Conservative Affirmation in America*, 74.
24. Murray, *We Hold These Truths: Catholic Reflections on the American Proposition*, 9–10.

history constitutes the core of the public argument that is political life it-self. However, debate that may occur about the meaning of these truths and their application to political and social reality, the existence of the truths themselves, provides the basic framework within which individuals are transformed into members of a community.

The substance of the constitutional consensus, dogmatic beliefs, or public orthodoxy is about more than merely the institutional arrange-ments of power within any given regime. As reflections of Aristotle's no-tion of *homonoia,* each consists of shared judgments, not about "things" generally but about "first things" in particular. This notion of shared judg-ment regarding first principles is reflected in Sandoz's reflections on the nature of "civil theology" and its relationship to political order. According to Sandoz, "Civil theology . . . consists of propositionally stated true sci-entific knowledge of the divine order. It is the theology discerned and validated through reason by the philosopher, on the one hand, and through common sense and the *logique du Coeur* evoked by the persuasive beauty of mythic narrative and imitative representations on the other hand."[25] The *homonoia* expressed through any given civil theology is thus a shared conception of reality per se. Sandoz's observation is echoed by Wilhelmsen and Kendall, who argue that the "public orthodoxy implies . . . a com-mitment to metaphysical propositions whose claim to acceptance can-not be mere political utility or historical sanction, but the very structure of this as they are in themselves."[26]

Douglass makes a similar point in his discussion of civil theology. Douglass argues that a civil theology is that "set of beliefs . . . through which the members of a political society relate their political experience to the ultimate conditions of human existence." According to Douglass, it is the mediating influence of civil theology that gives meaning to po-litical existence. It is through a civil theology that "political institutions are related to that which transcends the mundane conditions of life, and by virtue of this, they themselves acquire a measure of ultimacy. They are interpreted as being more than mere human contrivances: they also become representative . . . of transcendent order."[27]

25. Sandoz, *A Government of Laws,* 53.
26. Wilhelmsen and Kendall, "Cicero and the Politics of the Public Orthodoxy," 36.
27. Douglass, "Civil Religion and Western Christianity," 169.

In his examination of civil theology, Gerhart Niemeyer notes that it

> is multilayered. At the top we find a "We hold these truths. . .". This common perspective of consciousness renders possible a broad and deep area in which action and language symbols are commonly understood: a rich soil of taken for granted assumptions, associations, and references enabling people to communicate. . . . On this soil grow common aspirations, the "agreed upon objects of love" which Augustine pointed out. On it also develops unwritten but highly effective structures, the patterns of culture, conventional judgments, the do's and don'ts usually more strictly obeyed than written statutes. Above all, here flowers confidence, the assurance with which a person moves among his fellow beings, knowing what to expect and on what grounds to engage in cooperative effort.

The truths of any given society create the structure and meaning that are a precondition for that society to exist as a coherent entity organized for action in history. They create the conditions that allow human beings within any given polity to create the cognitive maps that allow them to move through the social and political environment that they, in turn, help to create and define. Niemeyer observes that ultimately *homonoia* is "the capacity to be of the same mind, which renders possible the making of laws and taking action in history."[28]

In the experience of the United States, just such a conception of the necessity of that shared tissue of judgments lay at the heart of the American experiment in self-government with justice. The U.S. Constitution itself is based upon an understanding that there existed a shared understanding of the broader meanings and purposes of political existence. In the second outing of "Publius," one of the few of *The Federalist Papers* written by John Jay, he notes

> that Providence has been pleased to give this one connected country, to one united people. A people descended from the same ancestors, speaking the same language, professing the same religion, attached to the same principles of government, very similar in their

---

28. Niemeyer, *Between Nothingness and Paradise,* 189–90, 197.

manners and customs, and who, by their joint counsels, arms and efforts, fighting side by side throughout a long and bloody war, have nobly established their general Liberty and Independence.[29]

As Kenneth L. Grasso argues with reference to the above passage, "The existence of this cultural capital is auspicious, because the political unity to be established by the Constitution will build upon this pre-existing cultural unity and the substantive moral consensus it reflects."[30]

The substantive moral consensus and the pre-existing cultural unity of the American experiment is to be found in the classical and Christian conceptions of what it means to be a human being and the notion of reality that is informed by those conceptions. As Sandoz notes:

> As any adequate sketch of the ground of the American founding will attest, to the extent that America stands for a coherent idea or vision of reality, it is rooted in classical and Christian philosophy of being, as filtered through the Enlightenment, which magnifies the individual human person as possessed of certain inalienable rights and properties that are God-given in an indelibly defining creaturely-Creator relationship. The human being is *imago Dei*. The political and ethical order is, thus, surmounted by a metaphysical process-structure anchored in an order of truth reaching back to Moses and the prophets in Israel and to Plato, Aristotle, and the Stoics in Hellas and Rome. Not merely the rationalistic aspects of the American idea, as (say) proclaimed in the Declaration of Independence, but also its representative habits and customs or historicity partake of this general understanding of human existence: its origin and destiny generally reflect this same vision of reality and truth. The coherence and resilience of this vision that is representatively American and in significant degree merges with the universal vision of what it is to be a human being living in truth under God have shaped American civic consciousness.[31]

29. Hamilton, Jay, and Madison, *The Federalist,* ed. Cooke, 9.

30. Grasso, "We Held These Truths: The Transformation of American Pluralism," 93–94.

31. Sandoz, "The Crisis of Civic Consciousness: Nihilism and Resistance," 127.

Unfortunately, the consensus that constitutes the *homonoia* of any given society in history, and American society in particular, is fragile to the degree that it is contingent upon human existence in history. Walter Lippmann maintains,

> The cultural heritage which contains the whole structure and fabric of the good life is acquired. It may be rejected. It may be acquired badly. It may not be acquired at all. For we are not born with it. If it is not transmitted from one generation to the next, it may be lost, indeed forgotten through a dark age, until somewhere and somehow men rediscover it, and, exploring the world again, recreate it anew.
>
> The acquired culture is not transmitted in our genes, and so the issue is always in doubt. The good life in the good society, though attainable, is never attained and possessed once and for all. So what has been attained will again be lost if the wisdom of the good life in a good society is not transmitted.[32]

The patrimony that is the shared consensus necessary for political life must be passed on, generation by generation, and there is a widespread suspicion that this may in fact be the case in the American experiment in self-government with justice. As Sandoz argues, "Like the frog placed in a pot of lukewarm water that didn't notice the increase in heat until it was too late, we can react to our social deformations and diseases by not reacting or by denying there is anything really amiss. After all, our traditions and institutions are wonderfully resilient and may, like youth itself, be immortal and indestructible. Right? Wrong. Free government is fragile and must be nurtured—by us."[33]

It is more than a little ironic that, with the defeat of the Soviet Union and the proclamation that humanity had reached the "end of history" with the triumph of liberal democracy, those same democracies would become embroiled in the more intractable problem posed by the loss of meaning felt by their own constituencies. However, it should come as no real surprise. Harold R. Isaacs observed during the relative stability imposed by the Cold War that "we are experiencing . . . not the shaping

---

32. Lippmann, *The Public Philosophy,* 75.
33. Sandoz, "The Crisis of Civic Consciousness," 125.

of new coherences but the world breaking into its bits and pieces, bursting like big and little stars from exploding galaxies, each one spinning off in its own centrifugal whirl, each one straining to hold its own small pieces from spinning off in their turn."[34]

What is remarkable about the American situation is the rapidity of the polarization that has occurred in the aftermath of the Soviet implosion. Does enough of a civic consciousness still exist in the Western democracies to stave off the disunity that lies at the heart of the malaise that seems to creep into the political life of democratic societies in the absence of an external threat, of a clearly definable "other"? The so-called "culture war" is merely an extension of the nihilism that seems to be the final thread to be broken with the defeat of the totalitarianisms of the past.

If the way out of the current difficulty is to be found in the recovery of the experiences of order, then an examination of Voegelin's contributions toward the understanding of Christian political order may serve a therapeutic function. This is especially true if we accept Sandoz's thesis regarding the roots of American order in the combination of an inherited tradition that embodies both classical and Christian elements that have somehow been driven from public discourse. Ultimately, the foundations of republican democracy are rooted in an understanding of human nature that stems from the Christian understanding of what it means to be a human being, and an analysis of the changing perception of human nature in the experience of Christian political order is thus an ongoing enterprise that helps revive the roots of American order. And since Jean Bethke Elshtain is undoubtedly correct in her assertion that the "trials and tribulations of the American Republic have a way of setting the agenda for other democratic societies," the undertaking takes on a broader significance.[35]

The Relationship of the *History of Political Ideas* to Voegelin's Later Work

But even beyond the therapeutic implications of an examination of Voegelin's analysis of the problem of Christian political order, there are other reasons why an examination of the *History* is required.

34. Isaacs, *Idols of the Tribe,* 11.
35. Elshtain, *Democracy on Trial,* 1.

To begin with, there is its status as the "lost fragment" of Voegelin's political thought. While portions of the *History* have been edited and published by Hallowell as *From Enlightenment to Revolution*,[36] the edition published as part of the *Collected Works of Eric Voegelin* completes the process and offers the opportunity for a more comprehensive examination of the materials that would help shape the thinking of Voegelin's later political thought. Regarding the *History*, David Walsh observes that while "it does not attain the analytic penetration of order that Voegelin achieved in *Order and History*," it does provide "one of the best points of entry into the theoretical depth of the later Voegelin. Despite the author's abrupt statement of discontinuity, of a break in his enterprise, it is a mistake to expect that this earlier effort comes from a very different mind." For this reason, "far from being a discontinuous predecessor, *History of Political Ideas* is in fundamental continuity with Voegelin's later work."[37]

In addition to illuminating the work of the later Voegelin, the specific emphasis on the *History* is recommended by the insight offered by Sandoz and Thomas A. Hollweck in their "General Introduction to the Series." Sandoz and Hollweck argue, "Christianity is the one movement in history in which the evocative reality of cosmic analogy and the philosophical freedom of the person to contemplate this evocative reality entered into a union that achieved the greatest possible balance between the two." If this is so, an examination of Voegelin's analysis of the problem of Christian order would be a contribution to "how, past Nietzsche's nihilism, we can regain reality without dogma."[38]

Finally, an analysis of the *History* is recommended because of Voegelin's particular conception of what constitutes a political "idea." In the sense of history, the idea is the evocative element in the creation of political order. It is through the attempt to realize the institution of the idea that communities and political societies come into being. Furthermore, there is a relationship between the idea itself and the degree to which it can be realized in history, given the realities of human existence in tension. This does bring up the distinction between the idea as an evocation and

36. Voegelin, *From Enlightenment to Revolution.*
37. Walsh, "Editor's Introduction," 4.
38. Hollweck and Sandoz, "General Introduction to the Series," 24, 25.

the later Voegelin's concern with the idea as the symbol of experience. However, in the context of the current work, that distinction is relatively meaningless. Whereas the later Voegelin was primarily concerned with the revelation of order in history, the *History of Political Ideas,* especially in its consideration of the problems specifically related to Christian political order, focuses upon the sources of disorder.

CHAPTER TWO

Voegelin and the Emergence of the Christian Community

Voegelin and the "Jesus of History"

The closest that Eric Voegelin ever came to exploring the "historical Jesus" was in the *History of Political Ideas*. At the outset, however, Voegelin notes a problem that is particular to understanding the Jesus of history: The Gospels, the first-person accounts of the life of Jesus, are not "history" at all. Voegelin observes, "The Gospels, and particularly the Gospel according to Saint Mark, which created the type, are admittedly not historical reports but belong to a class of literature that is generally called hagiographic—though it might be more cautious to rank the Gospels as a genus by itself. It does not seem particularly fruitful to treat a source of this type as if it were a work by Polybius or Tacitus." In other words, to treat the Gospels as if they represent a historical rendering of the events they recount is an exercise in missing the point. As Voegelin maintains on the question of interpreting the Gospels: "I cannot see much sense in treating the Gospel text as if it were a stenographic report of events and sayings and to draw from the obvious contradictions concerning the point the conclusion that only one version can be the correct one" (*CW*, 19:152–53).

Indeed, the notion that the Gospels ought to be treated as accurate historical renderings of events is a relatively new phenomenon that has more to do with an ideological position than with a recognition of their purpose. Furthermore, there is something to be said for Voegelin's contention that they ought to be treated as a genre unto themselves.[1] Eusebius recounts Peter's ministry and describes how the first Gospel came to be written: "So brightly shone the light of true religion on the minds of Peter's hearers that, not satisfied with a single hearing or with the oral teaching of the divine message, they resorted to appeals to every kind to induce Mark . . . as he was a follower of Peter, to leave them in writing a summary of the instruction they had received by word of mouth, nor did they let him go until they had persuaded him, and thus became responsible for the writing of what is known as the Gospel according to Mark."[2] If Eusebius's account is correct, then the Gospels were intended to serve two purposes: first, to provide a "summary of instruction" for the faithful; and second, to provide theological tools for use in spreading the Christian message of "the good news."

Even if the Gospels are not first-person accounts of events witnessed, it would be a mistake to assume that one cannot gain insight into the personality of Jesus and his sense of mission through the Gospel accounts of his life, death, and life after death. The premise of "form criticism" was precisely this: that the Gospels could offer no insight into the life of Jesus because they were a continuation of an oral tradition intended to literally proclaim the good news and to establish the doctrinal authority of the early church, not to describe the life of Jesus of Nazareth. In the introduction to his *Jesus and the Word*, Rudolf Bultmann, an early proponent of form criticism, argued, "We can now know almost nothing concerning the life and personality of Jesus, since the early Christian sources show no interest in either."[3] The Gospels existed solely to promulgate the doctrines of the early Church communities.

---

1. See, for example, Shuler, "The Genre of the Gospels and the Two Gospel Hypothesis"; Shuler, *A Genre for the Gospels: The Biographical Character of Matthew;* and Talbot, *What Is a Gospel? The Genre of the Canonical Gospels.*

2. Eusebius, *Ecclesiastica Historica* 2.15.2. See also 3.24.15. On the history of the Gospels generally, see Koester, *Ancient Christian Gospels,* and Millard, *Reading and Writing in the Time of Jesus.*

3. Bultmann, *Jesus and the Word,* 8. On critical historical approaches to the Gospels, see Vorster, "Through the Eyes of a Historian"; Theissen and Merz, "The Quest for the Historical Jesus"; Dahl, "The Problem of the Historical Jesus"; and Stanton, "What Is a Gospel?" Voegelin himself had occasion to enter into a debate regarding the importance of the Old Testament to an understanding of Christianity. Bultmann held the position

The form school has an internal problem, which is found in the form of the Gospels themselves. If the intent was solely to establish the doctrinal authority of the community of the faithful, how can one account for the particular form of the medium chosen? Geza Vermes notes:

> If the evangelists were primarily preoccupied with teaching Christian doctrine, how are we to explain their choice of *biography* as the medium? They cannot have been influenced by tradition; no Jewish convention exists that the sayings of the sages should be transmitted in this way. . . .
>
> Again, if the raison d'être of the Gospels was to provide for the doctrinal needs of the churches, how are we to understand the insertion into them of sayings of Jesus, and attitudes of mind, which actually conflict with the essential teachings of primitive Christianity? The evangelists note that Jesus made disparaging comments about Gentiles. They observe that he was apparently unwilling to allow his followers to announce him as the awaited Messiah. Neither of these matters can have greatly suited the first promulgators of the Gospels, whose main task was to convince non-Jews of the truth that "Jesus is the Christ."
>
> It is consequently difficult to avoid concluding that if the evangelists chose to tell the story of Jesus's life, it was because, whatever else they may have intended, they also wished to recount history, however unprofessionally.[4]

Thus, the form of the Gospels themselves gives evidence of a primitive historiography that the form school claimed was lacking.

One of the more interesting intellectual diversions of modern times, the search for the historical Jesus, has a long history. As Charlotte Allen notes in *The Human Christ*, "During the first centuries of Christianity, the disputes among pagans, Jews, and Christians over the identity of Jesus had a curiously modern flavor. Many of the objections that Jews and pagans raised about the believability of the Gospels were exactly the same

---

that the Old Testament was theologically irrelevant. Unfortunately, Voegelin saw a "vein of gnosticism running through 'Faith and Understanding,'" the Bultmann essay. Voegelin's contribution to the debate is available in *CW*, 11:156–77.

4. Vermes, "The Gospel of Jesus the Jew," 4–5.

as those voiced by many searchers for the historical Jesus today."[5] The distinctly "modern" debate, however, has its roots in Enlightenment rationalism that reached its apex in the publication in 1906 of Albert Schweitzer's *Quest of the Historical Jesus*.[6] As Allen argues,

> Christianity's oldest and most puzzling paradox is that of the crucified man who was celebrated in song as being "in the form of God." . . . Throughout nearly 2,000 years of Christian history, his dual identity has been a source of mystery, meditation, theological investigation, and troubling inquiry. In our own theoretically post-Christian age (at least in the industrialized West), Jesus is still the *ur*-icon of civilization, the enigmatic figure who continues to fascinate our imagination. Because we live in an age when science and scholarly research is supposed to supply answers to all our questions, for the most part we are unwilling to accept such a paradox. The search for the "historical" Jesus—the human being who walked the roads of Galilee 2,000 years ago—has thus become the hallmark of modernity, an obsession that has gripped the minds of intellectuals for nearly three centuries.[7]

This may be a key to answering Gerhart Niemeyer's and Frederic Wilhelmsen's questions regarding the lack of a "historical Jesus" in Voegelin's later works. Indeed, between the composition of the *History of Political Ideas* and his subsequent work on *Order and History,* Voegelin seemed to become hostile to the notion that there could be a meaningful discussion regarding the historicity of Jesus. As Voegelin writes in *The Ecumenic Age,* "the debate about the 'historicity of Christ' is not concerned with a problem in reality; it rather is a symptom of the modern state of deculturation" (*CW,* 17:332). By *deculturation,* Voegelin was referring to the loss of openness to the experience of transcendence that lay at the

5. Allen, *The Human Christ,* 50.

6. Schweitzer, *The Quest of the Historical Jesus.* On the Enlightenment origins of the modern historical Jesus debate, see Dahl, "The Problem of the Historical Jesus," 82–83; Thiessen and Merz, "Quest for the Historical Jesus," 2–3; Kee, *Jesus in History,* 9–14; and Powell, *Jesus as a Figure in History,* 12–19. Of course there is now a "postmodern historical quest of Jesus" that began in 1985 with the first meeting of the Jesus Seminar.

7. Allen, *The Human Christ,* 4.

heart of his conception of Aristotelian *noesis,* as he describes it in *Anamnesis,* and that is also found at the core of Paul's experience of the risen Christ—which is, at the same time, the core of Voegelin's exegesis of Paul in "The Pauline Vision of the Resurrected" in *The Ecumenic Age.*[8]

In describing *The Voegelinian Revolution,* Ellis Sandoz argues that among the reasons for Voegelin's "relative obscurity" is his "revolutionary originality." Voegelin, according to Sandoz, "is (in varying degrees) at odds with all schools of thought. He does not fit any of the convenient intellectual pigeonholes." Furthermore, Sandoz notes that Voegelin "is a genuinely independent thinker. His work is strikingly free of polemics, yet it clearly entails a rejection of all the dearest idols of the Cave of modern intellectuals here and abroad."[9] And the "search for the historic Jesus" has proven itself to be remarkable in its capacity to insinuate itself into the ideological and intellectual pigeonholes of the day. As Allen observes:

> Jesus scholarship has been shaped by nearly every intellectual fashion of the past three centuries: English deism, Enlightenment rationalism, philosophical Idealism, Romanticism, Darwinism, existentialism, Marxism, and feminism. The liberal Protestant outlook of the 19th Century, the "social gospel" of the early 20th century, the "God is Dead" movement of the 1960s, and the liberation theology of the 1970s and 1980s have all cast long shadows on the search for Jesus. In 1909, the Modernist Catholic theologian George Tyrell complained that the liberal German Bible scholars of his day had reconstructed a historical Jesus who was no more than "the reflection of a liberal Protestant face, at the bottom of a deep well." In other words, the liberal searchers had found a liberal Jesus. The same can be said of Jesus-searchers of every era: the deists found a deist, the Romantics a Romantic, the existentialists an existentialist, and the liberationists a Jesus of the class struggle. Supposedly equipped with the latest critical and historical tools, the "scientific" quest for the historical Jesus has nearly always devolved into theology, ideology, and even autobiography.[10]

8. On the process of *noesis,* see "What Is Political Reality?" in *CW,* 6:341–412.
9. Sandoz, *The Voegelinian Revolution,* 11.
10. Allen, *The Human Christ,* 5.

Ultimately, however, the abandonment of the Jesus of history had more to do with the evolution of the purpose of Voegelin's scholarship. In *Order and History,* Voegelin's purpose is to explore his theory of consciousness and lay out his philosophy of history. As such, the work is an examination of the symbols of order in light of the experiences that produced them. With this in mind, the symbols cannot be separated from the experiences themselves—that is, the origin of the deformation of reality that occurs in history and culminates in the rise of ideological mass movements. As Michael P. Morrissey points out, the "meaning" of the symbols

> is moored to their source of emergence: the person who experienced, interpreted and understood the transcendent reality they objectified through their symbolic imagination. That is why, instead of focusing on the historical Jesus, Voegelin concerns himself with the *kerygmata* of a Paul, a John, or a Matthew as providing the privileged, indeed the only, access to Christ. The only "historical Jesus" we can know is the one known by the New Testament authors. The event of the *theotes* coming into revelatory luminosity in Jesus and his disciples is the significant reality behind the language that expresses the event. There would be no Christ without those who pronounced the Christ and recognized the Christ in Jesus. This event of the recognition and the symbolic representation of it cannot be separated.[11]

With that noted, however, Voegelin's purpose in the *History of Political Ideas* is somewhat different. Voegelin's analysis therein of the Jesus of history is not undertaken to explain his existence; nor is it an attempt to explain the irruption of the divine presence into immanent reality as an exercise of Christian apologetics. Rather, the analysis is done with an eye toward the community that formed around him and the ideas that serve as the evocative underpinnings of that community as a result of Jesus' existence. Voegelin does make note of the historical Jesus research, citing Charles Guignebert's *Jesus* as "the latest authoritative study"[12]; but he does so within the context of lamenting the "Insufficiency of Critical Exegesis of the Gospels" (*CW,* 19:151).

11. Morrissey, *Consciousness and Transcendence,* 233.
12. Guignebert, *Jesus.*

Guignebert concludes that Jesus lacked any sense of being the "messiah" and that his ministry on Earth had failed to accomplish its end, which was to bring about the Kingdom of God on Earth in a political sense. Furthermore, Guignebert maintains that the visions of the resurrected Christ were a result of the enthusiasm of the apostles and were not reflective of a real event. Voegelin finds Guignebert's conclusions unsatisfactory. Ultimately, Guignebert had done little to explain "what in the personality of Jesus should have been the cause for the somewhat surprising effect on the disciples after his life had ended in a black failure" (*CW*, 19:152)—at least according to Guignebert's account. To do that would require a different way of approaching the Gospel accounts of Jesus' life, death, and resurrection.

Voegelin's Approach to the Gospels

Voegelin's dissatisfaction with the critical exegesis of Gospel sources available to him stemmed from the seeming inability of the exegetes to explore "the religious personality and its effect on the disciples" (*CW*, 19:153). This lack is problematic in an analysis of the birth of the Christian community because, as Voegelin understood, "the constitution of the new community begins with the personality, the life, and the work of Jesus" (*CW*, 19:151). Thus, any attempt to understand the community must be able to increase our understanding of these elements that contributed to its constitution. To this end, Voegelin proposes

> to start from the assumption that the Gospel of the Markian type reflects the personality of Jesus, his life and work, though the details may be historically incorrect. We may agree that every single miracle report is untrustworthy and still understand the report as a whole as substantially reflecting the healing work of the Savior; we may agree that the parables and dialogue scenes have little chance of reporting correctly the pronouncements of Jesus and still be sure that he expressed himself in parables in general and that the parables as reported reflect essential features of his teaching; we may doubt the report on the baptism by John and still be sure that at some point in his life the experience must have occurred that started him on his life; and we may doubt the report on the temp-

tation and still assume the existence of the problem of temptation in his life. (*CW,* 19:153)

This method of interpretation, of course, placed Voegelin squarely at odds with the predominant school of thought at the time he wrote the early chapters on Christianity in the *History of Political Ideas.* In the approach he adopted to the critical analysis of the Gospels, Voegelin was again swimming against the tide of what was perceived as the current trend in popular scholarship.

The crucial element in understanding Jesus' personality, a question raised repeatedly in historical Jesus research, was Jesus' perception of himself as the Messiah. Voegelin describes "the question of the self-consciousness of Jesus as the Messiah" as the "most important question" in the exploration of Jesus' personality. But coupled with this assertion is the observation that "it borders sometimes on the comic to see a distinguished scholar pointing the revolver of logical consistency at the Gospel and demanding that the author make up his mind whether Jesus has said that he was the Messiah or not" (*CW,* 19:153). The situation that confronted Voegelin is further complicated by the fact that the general category of the Messianic consciousness and Jesus' self-consciousness in particular is a preoccupation that is peculiarly related to historical Jesus research.

The Messiah and the Self-Consciousness of Jesus

William Scott Green notes "the messiah as a subject of academic study derives not from ancient Jewish preoccupation, but from early Christian work-choice, theology and apologetics." At issue are the twin efforts by the authors of the New Testament to name and to describe Jesus in messianic terms. The first effort is represented by the use of the term *christos,* the Greek translation of the Hebrew word *masshiah,* as a proper surname for Jesus of Nazareth. This is closely related to the second "major achievement of the New Testament apologetics," the transformation of the Hebrew scripture "into a harbinger" of the "career, suffering, and death" of Jesus.[13] Instead, Green argues, the relative scarcity of the use

13. Green, "Messiah in Judaism," 4.

of the Hebrew noun *masshiah* in the extant texts would seem to argue against the notion of a messiah figure as an evocative category in the political and social situation confronting the people of Israel.

The problem with Green's argument, however, is that it contains its own contradiction. If the terms *christos* and *masshiah* were without meaningful content, why were they chosen? Furthermore, if the Israelitic notion of the "messiah" was not categorical in some way, how does one explain the messianic movements prevalent throughout Palestine in the century before and the century after Christ?[14] As Richard A. Horsley and John S. Hanson point out, "The scarcity of the term *messiah* in the Jewish literature of the time does not mean . . . that there was no expectation whatever of an anointed royal leader. At certain levels of Jewish society, there was indeed some anticipation of a kingly agent inspired by God to bring deliverance to the people. Besides the infrequently attested *messiah,* there were other images that expressed this particular tradition of expectation, the most prominent of which was a Davidic king."[15]

The notions of messianic expectation and the emergence of a Davidic king–like figure are relatively late developments in Judaism in the centuries before the birth of Jesus. In the original development of Jewish eschatological expectation, the covenant between God and Israel would have resulted in the direct rule of God over his people—if the people abided by the law. This oriented Israel toward expectation of the future, since it clearly had not been realized in the present. As Emil Schürer points out in *The History of the Jewish People in the Time of Jesus Christ:*

> It was . . . expected that Israel's faithfulness would be suitably rewarded in the life of both the nation and the individual. Yet it was obvious that in actual experience the reward came neither to the people as a whole, nor to individuals in the proportion anticipated. Accordingly, the more deeply this awareness penetrated into the mind of the nation and of the individual, the more they were forced to turn their eyes to the future; and of course, the worse their present state, the more lively their hope. It may therefore be said that in

14. See Horsley and Hanson, *Bandits, Prophets, and Messiahs: Popular Movements in the Time of Jesus.*

15. Ibid., 93.

later eras religious consciousness was concentrated upon hope for the future. A perfect age to come was the goal to which all other religious ideas were teleologically related. As the conduct of the Israelite was essentially observance of the Torah, so his faith was centered on awaiting God's kingdom.[16]

In the historical development of Israel, the conception of the social organization of a chosen people under God was transformed by the external pressure of other peoples and nations upon it. Voegelin notes that the constitution of the people of Israel as a religious order under God took place at a time in Israel's history and in "an environment of nomads where the tribal and clan organizations were in flux" (*CW*, 19:111) and that the initial constitution formed by the first *berith* between God and Israel placed God as the head of his united people in what Martin Buber has called a "theo-political" act.[17] Ultimately, the development of an eschatological outlook on history was, to some degree, contained in the notion of the initial covenant between God and Israel and the experience of the Exodus that culminated in the events at Mount Sinai recounted in Exodus 19. As G. R. Beasley-Murray observes: "Israel's unique achievement of an eschatology in relation to history was conditioned by the uniqueness of the revelation it experienced, the covenant into which it entered, and the history in which it was set and to which the whole complex gave rise. From the events at Sinai onward, the tribes were a group on the march under Yahweh; they were on the way to a new life in a new land, to a future that was in the hands of the Lord."[18]

Despite the uniqueness of the revelation it received and the covenant into which it entered, the exigencies of Israel's political and social existence required a social organization more in keeping with the political organization of the rival power centers that threatened Israel. As a result, Israel cried out for a king "like the other nations," despite Samuel's warnings that such an institution would cause God to turn away from his people (1 Sam. 8:4–21).

16. Schürer, *The History of the Jewish People in the Time of Jesus Christ*, 2:492.
17. Buber, *The Kingship of God*, 24.
18. Beasley-Murray, *Jesus and the Kingdom of God*, 18–19.

The institution of the Israelitic monarchy was a violation of the original covenant by which Israel was created, and it led to the rise of the prophets who challenged Israel to fulfill its share of the bargain so as to reap the rewards promised. The import of prophetic utterances moves through successive stages to reach its culmination in Ezekiel (36:26–27) and Jeremiah (31:31–34) and the promise of a "new covenant" to be "written on the hearts" of the people of Israel. But the institution of the kingship made two new formulations possible: Instead of God acting to redeem Israel, a king of Davidic origin might be the agent of supernatural transformation; and in contradistinction, the notion also arises, from the peasant countryside, "of a leader riding on an ass as did the charismatic war leaders of the pre-royal time (Deborah song, Judg. 5:10)" (*CW,* 19:109–16).

As a result of these conflicting images, there emerged what Voegelin describes as "the profound confusion of eschatological sentiment." This situation was further exacerbated by a seemingly endless series of debasements and defeats suffered by Israel. To be sure, Israel had violated its obligation under the original contract; and because of that, Israel had been, and was being, punished through its subjections to the other nations, though ultimately it would emerge victorious as God's chosen. However, as disaster piled on disaster, "it becomes increasingly difficult to maintain this position." The reason is clear: "the sinfulness of Israel, however great it may be, is not greater than that of other nations, and, furthermore, what can be the meaning of being God's chosen people if the result of the choice is endless abasement." It was against this backdrop of abasement, "out of the immense faith" of the people of Israel and their "equally profound despair" that "one of the greatest creations of mankind . . . the Suffering Servant of the Lord," emerges (*CW,* 19:116–17).

It is no wonder that, given the confusion of sentiments, the symbol of the Suffering Servant is notoriously difficult to explicate. From Voegelin's perspective, there is something of a synthesis between the idea of the people as an instrument of redemption and the appearance of a savior who will lead them to it. Voegelin maintains that the image of the Suffering Servant acted upon the Israelitic mind to explain the intense suffering endured by Israel. In the Servant Songs, the suffering of Israel is made the catalyst by which not just Israel but potentially all of humanity may experience the redemption of God. Voegelin argues that "the disproportionate suffering" of Israel "makes sense . . . only in a world plan in which the suffering becomes the means of redemption for the whole world. Under these conditions the faith can be maintained, the suffering can become bearable, and the identity of the people . . . can be preserved with the utmost tenacity" (*CW,* 19:118). It is through the Suffering Servant that Israel is elevated to the status of world redeemer, and the complex of symbols emerges that will be used to demonstrate to the world that Jesus was the fulfillment of the promise.

The image of the Suffering Servant "is still deeply embedded in the particular Israelitic experiences and sorrows," but "the image of the future Savior appears lucidly before the background of anguish." Voegelin notes the parallel language in Psalm 22:1 and Mark 15:34: "My God, my God, why hast thou forsaken me?" In his discussion, Voegelin argues that the statement from the cross is not meant as "an utterance of ultimate despair, but, as a quotation from Psalm 22," and as such "a self-interpretation and identification with the symbol of the Suffering Servant" (*CW,* 19:119). But this does not really answer the question regarding the self-consciousness of Jesus as the Messiah under the methodology employed by Voegelin. Voegelin's own answer to the question of Jesus' self-consciousness as the Messiah and primary locus in the drama of salvation is cryptic:

> If we take . . . the Gospels as the reflection of religious processes, it seems clear that the Messiah consciousness did not appear at any definite time in the life of Jesus, but that it was an experience that could become stronger at times, and at times be weakened. We may assume that the preoccupation with his quality as the Messiah was increasing toward the end of his public life when believers more strongly and in greater numbers responded to him as the Messiah; but to the end, to the prayer in Gethsemane . . . we feel the tension between the messianic and nonmessianic personality in Jesus: he, as the man, submits to the possibility of being the Messiah. (*CW,* 19:162–63)

Yet even if there was vacillation between the messianic and nonmessianic elements of Jesus' personality, there can be no doubt that the messianic consciousness had grown beyond the images of the Messiah as a war leader who would crush those who had oppressed and inflicted suffering upon Israel. Voegelin notes that Jesus' teaching "had far outgrown the cruder form of the turning of the tables; his realm was not of this world. If he was the Messiah, his fate differed widely from the images of victorious royal glory and resembled rather the Suffering Servant of Isaiah" (*CW,* 19:163). Indeed, this simple fact explains the effectiveness of Isaiah as a justification and explanation of Jesus as the Christ. Furthermore, this parallel would have been appealing, given the apparent prominence of Isaiah in rabbinic Judaism in the century preceding Jesus' birth.[19]

Mana, Metanoia, Spirit, and Faith: The Community Substance

In examining the personality of Jesus and the community that grew up around him, Voegelin focuses upon events recounted in Mark 5:25–35. As Jesus is moving through a large crowd, a woman suffering from hemorrhaging reaches out to simply touch his cloak, because she believes that by doing so she will be healed of her affliction. According to the account, upon touching Jesus' cloak, "Immediately her bleeding stopped and she felt in her body that she was freed from her suffering" (Mk. 5:29). Jesus stops and turns because he feels that some power has gone out of him. Voegelin notes: "The historicity of the incident is irrelevant; what matters is the conception of the healing process. Jesus is possessed of a mana . . . that he can communicate to other persons." However, in order for that communication to occur, there has to be a reciprocal relationship between the mana of Jesus and the faith of the believer. "The *metanoia,* the turning, the healing, the state of faith, had to spring from the soul forces of the individual; there is no sign that Jesus ever attempted to heal or convert persons who did not respond to his call" (*CW,* 19:154). Thus in life, Jesus created the conditions for the emergence of a new community based on faith, but it was to a faith that emerged in response to the call.

According to Voegelin's account, the mana of Jesus carries with it the potential for the realization of a new community. Voegelin writes, "the

---

19. On the prominence of Isaiah, see Sawyer, "Isaiah and Christian Origins," in *The Fifth Gospel: Isaiah in the History of Christianity,* 21–41, and Chilton, *A Galilean Rabbi and His Bible: Jesus' Own Interpretation of Isaiah.*

mana of Jesus and the faith of the believer are corresponding personality elements that can communicate with each other and thus constitute a kind of community substance. This interaction between Jesus and the faithful is the closest we can come through our sources to the constitution of the Christian community as a divine and at the same time historically active substance" (*CW,* 19:155). It is important to note in the descriptive passage, however, that the community as it exists under the dynamic interaction of the mana of Jesus is a community between Jesus and those who follow him. The distinctly *Christian* community of Jesus' followers does not emerge until the death of Jesus and the visions of the resurrected Christ to individuals and groups of people, some of whom had followed Jesus the man and, in the notable instance of Saint Paul, at least one who had persecuted his followers.

In the emergence of the new Christian community, it was the death and resurrection that constituted the true birth of the new community. As Voegelin notes, "The visions of the disciples in the days after the death of Jesus are the fundamental evocative acts of the Christian community" (*CW,* 19:163). It is the death and resurrection of Jesus and the witnesses of the risen Christ who testified to the occurrence that transform the potential for a new community of faith into the reality through the evocation of the visions. Voegelin argues,

> In order to understand properly the function of the visions, we have to imagine the main alternatives. If Jesus had been the Messiah according to the older Israelitic tradition, his death would have been proof of his failure, and the community of his followers would probably have dispersed. If he had been no more than a prophet, he could still have become the founder of a religion of salvation comparable to Buddhism. If his life and death had fallen under the sway of Hellenic or Roman religious forms to a larger extent than it did, he could have become a cult deity. None of these possibilities was realized. There developed, instead, the unique phenomenon of a community under the leadership of a historic personality who at the same time was a manifestation of God, so that the community of believers with the man Jesus could be continued after his death with the living divine personality of Christ. The Spirit of the Resurrected (Gk. *pneuma*) took as the community substance the place of the mana (the *dynamis*) of the living Jesus. The precondition for

this community of believers with the living God was the visionary conviction of his personal presence. (*CW,* 19:164)

While "Jesus, the man," may have died on the cross, "Christ lives, and under the guidance of his spirit the community continues to exist as it did when he was present in the flesh" (*CW,* 19:165).

While the new community is constituted by the Descent of the Spirit at Pentecost (Acts 2), the individual becomes a member of the community by responding to the call through faith. The faith in Jesus the man is transformed into faith in the risen Christ. The essence of faith in the Hebrew tradition had been oriented to the "god of history leading his people to supreme victory" (*CW,* 19:113). With the Descent of the Spirit, the element of faith is transformed into the means by which *metanoia* itself is achieved, and the individuals who experience it are taken into the community of Christ as described in the Epistle to the Hebrews. As Voegelin writes:

> The image of the indwelling of Christ, the priest, in the house of his community receives conceptual precision through the doctrine of faith. "Faith is the substance of things hoped for, the evidence of things not seen" ([Heb.] 11:1); Faith is not a subjective attitude of the individual, a belief, but the community substance itself, created by the appearance of Jesus. . . . The awakening of the faith and the consequent partaking of the Holy Ghost are, therefore, not an intellectual process but a transformation of the whole personality, the process by which man is integrated into the community substance. . . . The community is imagined as a field in which "power" circulates; faith is the process through which a man becomes a unit in this field, permeable for the circulating power substance. (*CW,* 19:167)

As with the hemorrhagic woman of Mark, the awakening of the faith requires the conscious desire of each individual human being who would take part in the community to yield to the call.

A Community for Human Existence: The Pauline Compromises

The Christian community might have remained confined as an obscure sect of Judaism in the Near East but for the genius of Paul and his capacity to conceive of an overarching community of faith that would be cognizant of the inherent weaknesses of human nature, the natural gifts of man, and the realities of the world. In the Epistle to the Hebrews, the author, who was either Paul himself or a member his circle—the authorship of the letter is a matter of some debate—notes that because Jesus "himself suffered when he was tempted, he is able to help those who are being tempted" (2:18). Paul understood the nature of human being as a fallen one that only the grace of God could redeem from his own experience and critical examination of it.

> I have the desire to do what is good, but I cannot carry it out. For what I do is not the good I want to do; no, the evil I do not want to do—this I keep on doing. . . .
> When I want to do good, evil is right there with me. For in my inner being I delight in God's law; but I see another law at work in the members of my body, waging war against the law of my mind and making me a prisoner of the law of sin at work in my members. What a wretched man I am! Who will rescue me from this body of death? Thanks be to God—through Jesus Christ our Lord!
> So then, I myself in my mind am a slave to God's law, but in the sinful nature a slave to the law of sin. (Rom. 7:18–25)

This understanding of the spiritual anthropology of human beings in which the passions, "the law of sin at work in my members," predominates and conditions Paul's speculations regarding the essence of a new community that would be a fit repository for the spirit of Christ and would prove practical as well to the existence of human beings in their lives. Voegelin notes:

> The greatness of Paul lies in his quality as a statesman that enables him to fill in the abstractions of Hebrews, and to transpose the community of the perfect with Christ into an idea that took into account the practical problems of a community that did not at all consist of perfect saints. The Epistles of Paul present the momentous step from radical perfectionism to the compromise with the realities of the Christian community in its environment. From Hebrews the path could have led to a small community of saints; Paul opens the way to imperial expansion, the way to Rome. (CW, 19:169)

These "compromises" with the realities of the world would create the conditions by which the followers of an itinerant rabbi could lay claim to the Western world. Voegelin argues, "The main function of Christianity, as far as its rise belongs in the history of political evocations, was the creation of a new community substance that would be grafted, with varying degrees of success, first on the population basis of the Roman empire, and later on the tribes of the Great Migration" (*CW,* 19:150).

This grafting was possible only because of a series of compromises made by Paul in the nascent days of Christianity. Voegelin identifies five: a compromise with history; a compromise with the weakness of human beings as realized in the differences of gifts that accrue to the members of the mystical body of Christ; the addition of the law of love to the codified law of the Old Testament; the eschatological indifference to social problems; and the compromise with authority by the acceptance of governmental authority as being ordained by God. The present study will collapse these five into three major compromises that tend to subsume the others. The eschatological indifference to social problems may be considered part of Paul's compromise with authority, and the addition of the law of love is directly related to the compromise with history. Thus, the three major headings of the compromises of Paul would be: the historical horizon, the body of Christ, and the powers that be. It is to the historical horizon that we first turn in our analysis.

The Historical Horizon

The first compromise made by Paul and identified by Voegelin is a "compromise with history." This particular compromise deals specifically with the world and the peoples in and among which Christianity emerged. The compromise with history consisted of identifying Christianity with the social world that gave it birth and that world's three realms: the pagan, the Israelitic, and the Christian. Subsumed in the limitation Paul imposes on human history by his civilizational and geographical construction are the two ideas of history as having a directional quality, as in the case of the Israelitic experience, and the periodization of history into epochs.

The second idea, strictly speaking, is also based in the experience of the people of Israel, to the degree that the myth of the metal ages first seen in Hesiod finds its place, in the book of Daniel, in the speculation upon the experience of Israel as a conquered people tossed about by a succession of empires. In interpreting the dream of Nebuchadnezzar, Daniel describes a series of empires that will dominate Israel, the fourth of which will be "a kingdom that will never be destroyed, nor will it be left to another people. It will crush all those kingdoms and bring them to an end, but it will itself endure forever" (2:31–45). This construction of history into epochs with an eschatological direction is an important element in understanding the historical justification that underlies the emergence of the Christian community.[20]

With the eschatological understanding of Israel and the periodization of history, the new Christian community was seen as the beginning of a new age. As Voegelin writes, "The new community between Christ and the faithful is not just any community that now enters the scene of history, but it is the realm of the new epoch. The epochal consciousness is fully developed: the appearance of Christ is the dividing line of world history" (*CW,* 19:168). Thus, history is now conceived of in terms of past, present, and future, with the decisive event in the center of history that imbues it with meaning. History becomes the drama of salvation. Karl Löwith observes that "the articulation of all historical time into past, present, and future reflects the temporal structure of the history of salvation. The past points to the first things, the future to the last things, and the present to a central presence which connects the past with the future through teleological succession."[21] And For the Christian, that "central presence" is the Spirit of Christ. Voegelin writes: "The idea of Hebrews envisages the aeon of Christ as the ultimate fulfillment of history and the preceding period as a preparation in accordance with the plan of God. The existence of mankind in time has from now on the meaning that we properly call *history* because God is the divine partner of the process that unfolds according to his providence" (*CW,* 19:168–69).

With the realization of the eschatological reality of the kingdom of God in Christ, the eschatological notions that served as the backdrop for the appearance of the Messiah were also transformed. In the Pauline vision

---

20. See *CW,* 19:121–22.
21. Löwith, *Meaning in History,* 185.

of the resurrected Christ, the eschatological idea of the coming Messiah created the possibility for the development of an apocalyptic under-standing of the kingdom of God. "The eschatological expectation of the kingdom implied that the Messiah would appear at a given point of time in the near future and replace the present world order by the kingdom of God." Since, from the perspective of Paul and the Christian community, the Messiah has in fact appeared, a new understanding of the kingdom itself was necessary. "The apocalyptic idea implies that the Messiah has appeared and that his realm is actually established as the community be-tween him, the Resurrected, and his believers." Voegelin maintains that the "eschatological sentiment has not disappeared completely by any means, but the apocalyptic sentiment, the belief in the revealed commu-nity, is growing and finally overshadowing the expectation of the end in the main line of Christian evolution" (*CW,* 19:166).

Contained within the apocalyptic idea is the danger that the reality of the revealed community between Christ and the faithful may not live up to the expectations of those who experience it. This phenomena of frus-trated expectations, combined with the fact that the eschatological un-derstanding of history remains present in the background, would prove extremely problematic—especially since the Christian community had now embarked upon a period of waiting for the second appearance of the Savior to gather his flock to him. The belief in the revealed commu-nity helps make possible the unification of humanity under God, but it also carries with it the potential for difficulties that can be a source of disturbance and disorder into the future. The problem is that "Christian existence is set between an accomplished redemption and an awaited consummation, and it involves dependence on the grace of the Lord who has come, is present and is to come."[22] As Löwith remarks:

> Invisibly, history has fundamentally changed; visibly it is still the same, for the Kingdom of God is already at hand, and yet, as an *es-chaton,* still to come. This ambiguity is essential to all history after Christ: the time is already fulfilled and not yet consummated. The Christian times between Christ's resurrection and his reappearance

22. Beasley-Murray, *Jesus and the Kingdom of God,* 22.

are definitely the last times (1 John 2:18; Matt. 12:28); but, as long as they last, they are penultimate times before the completion of the present, though hidden Kingdom of Christ in the manifest Kingdom of God beyond historical times. On account of this profound ambiguity of the historical fulfillment where everything is "already" what it is "not yet," the Christian believer lives in a radical tension between present and future.[23]

Christ may have "laid open to us both past and present history, and has given us an anticipatory taste of the future as well,"[24] according to Barnabas; but while the end of history may be known for human beings in their immanent lives, the process of history itself is still a mystery.

Closely related to the "compromise with history" is the adoption of "the law of love" into the community of the faithful (Rom. 13:8–10). In accomplishing the compromise with history, Paul had created the historical horizon by the recognition of the civilizational orders with which he was familiar. The laws of Israel and the new law of Christ "were insufficient as an empirical pattern of civilization." To overcome this difficulty, Paul "retains the epochal function of the appearance of the Messiah but he adds to the Israelitic law a natural law, a law of the gentiles. God has revealed himself to the gentiles through his creation (Rom. 1:19–20), to Israel through the written law, and now to mankind through the pneumatic law of Christ that is engraved in the hearts of the believers through their faith" (CW, 19:170).

As for the social rules to govern the new community, Paul was, in Voegelin's words, "strongly traditional," by which he means that Paul imports the written laws of Israel as the social code to be followed (CW, 19:171; Rom. 13:9–10). This importation of a well-established social code was of immense significance in the organization of the first Christian communities. Having the "character of divine law," the social codes of Israel "were received by the Christian community, and Christianity was thereby saved from becoming just one of many similar Hellenistic mystery cults. Possessing the complete Israelitic law was the most important asset of

---

23. Löwith, Meaning in History, 188. See also Collingwood, The Idea of History, 46–49.
24. "The Epistle of Barnabas," 159.

the Church when it had to face the task of ordering social life in the Roman empire" (*CW,* 19:113). Important as well was the content of the law regarding the treatment of the poor and the dispossessed within the society. This was especially true with regard to the creation of the *corpus mysticum.*

The Body of Christ

The second compromise made by Paul is specifically with the weaknesses of human nature brought on by humanity's fallen condition. Voegelin notes that "the renovation of the personality in the Spirit of Christ would in most cases not be so radical that frequent lapses would not occur." The experience of *metanoia,* the turning around by which Paul argues that a human being is made anew, is a fragile thing, given the weaknesses of the flesh. For this reason, "a natural hierarchy" would exist within the Christian community "of higher and lower degrees of perfection that expresses itself in a social stratification into apostles, prophets, evangelists, pastors, and teachers whose function is 'the perfecting of the saints . . . till we all come in the unity of faith, and of the knowledge of the Son of God, unto a perfect man, unto the measure of the stature of the fullness of Christ' (Eph. 4:11–13)" (*CW,* 19:170).

But despite the stratification of the society, there is a unity of the Spirit that transforms individuals into integral parts of the new spiritual body of Christ. Voegelin notes that "Chapter 12 of 1 Corinthians elaborates the idea of the body of Christ in which every personality type has its function, the types complementing each other as the members of the body; the unity between them is constituted by the Spirit by which they have been baptized." Baptism is thus the symbolic representation of the Descent of the Spirit and delivers the baptized individual "into the *corpus mysticum* of which Christ is the head" (*CW,* 19:170).

This organic construction of the whole of the Christian community is important to the expansion of Christianity and its transformation into the political rationale for the imperial order and for the Church as an institution existing in parallel with that order. In *Race and State,* Voegelin argues that "the idea of the kingdom and body of Christ as it was articulated by Paul and his circle expanded in the course of Christian history into the idea of the spiritual-worldly empire." Voegelin goes on to note, "The idea of the *corpus mysticum* did not spring entirely new from the ideas of Paul; the ground had been prepared by the Hellenistic idea of the heavenly person and his embodiment in the cosmos, and especially by the doctrine of the second Adam" (*CW,* 2:132). The Hellenistic idea proceeds from the Stoic perception of the *apospasma,* the piece of the divine logos that pervades the cosmos as the equivalent of the human soul naked before God.

In defining Christ as "the second Adam," Paul was calling upon both the traditions of Israel and the spiritual anthropology that served as the basis for his understanding of the reborn community. In the case of the traditions of Israel, of course, Adam as the first man is the father of humanity. The symbolism of Paul in 1 Corinthians 15:45–49 spiritualizes that condition to make Christ "the spiritual father of the reborn Christian personality" (*CW,* 19:170–71). With regard to the second Adam, since human beings participate in existence with their entire beings, body and soul, the relationship to Adam, the relationship by blood, has an appeal. As Voegelin notes, "The idea of the *corpus mysticum* . . . does not entirely relinquish its grounding in the animal world—without the resonating image of a second Adam, of a second man as the ancestor of a new humanity, it would hardly have attained as strong a response" (*CW,* 2:138).

In addition to the Hellenistic and Adamic elements, the traditions of Israel provided a background for the Christian use of the organic symbol. Although Voegelin himself does not make the linkage between sections of the *History,* in his commentary on Israel he points to the *berith* by which David is installed as the king of Israel and the people of Israel gather together to proclaim that "we are thy bone and thy flesh" (2 Sam. 5:1; 1 Chron. 11:1). Voegelin comments, "The organic symbolism indicates the idea of the mystical body that is created through the choice of a head for the bone and the flesh. The *berith,* instituting a king, is the act that creates the permanent historical personality of the people" (*CW,* 19:111). It creates the idea of the people of God, who compose the community of the Christian faithful, as an organic, interrelated whole through the symbolism of the body.

The compromise with the weaknesses of human beings, in addition to providing the impetus for the creation of a spiritual-worldly empire, also provided something else. In adopting the organic symbolism of the body, Paul had helped to illuminate the perception of the spiritual equality of human beings before God, performing essentially the same function as Plato's Phoenician Tale in *The Republic*. The social stratification is not reflective of greater or lesser worth on the part of the individuals involved but is rather a reflection of the spiritual gifts that are measured out according to the dictates of divine providence. Within the community, these gifts are to be used for the benefit and expansion of the Christian community of the faithful, but before God and Christ each member of the community has value and worth. This is a profound sentiment that, as the community of faith expanded into the imperial sphere, would have profound implications in the development of ethics, politics, and social structures and conventions.[25]

The Powers That Be

The relationship between the Christian community and governmental authority was very simply defined by Paul in Romans 13:1–2: "Let every person be subject to the governing authorities. For there is no authority except from God, and those authorities that exist have been instituted by God. Therefore whoever resists authority resists what God has appointed, and those who resist will incur judgment. For rulers are not a terror to good conduct but to bad." The purpose of government is to maintain the peace and "to wield the power of the sword over evildoers; resistance against the government would be resistance against the will of God." Voegelin argues that this relationship "is . . . determined not by a rule that envisages a permanent establishment, but as a provisional arrangement that is necessitated by the coexistence of the invisible realm with the world until, with the second coming of Christ, the tension between the two is resolved into the visible supernatural glory of the kingdom of God" (*CW,* 19:172).

The provisional nature of this arrangement may have been necessary given the emergence of the Christian community in a Roman province,

---

25. Also see Voegelin's discussion of the symbol of the body in "The Growth of the Race Idea," in *CW,* 10:27–61.

the antipathy of the Jewish communities, and the community's expansion into the pagan world beyond, which included Rome itself. In Acts 19:23–40 the story is told of a riot that is narrowly averted when a silversmith who made icons of the goddess Artemis rallied his workmen and other artisans against the Christians in Ephesus because they might be bad for business. In Rome itself, the destination of the Pauline epistle, the various Jewish communities had already been restricted by the law on congregations from forming any sort of community beyond the individual synagogues. As for Christians, Ernst Bammel argues, "Oriental cults, while permitted with great liberality outside the *urbs,* still came under the critical eye of the city prefect within Rome during the early principate and could only hope to be tolerated if their loyalty and good behavior was beyond question."[26] Thus, the letter of Paul may have been preemptively defensive, intended to make the point that Christianity did not represent a threat to the established order.

The idea that all government is ordained by God is not new either with Paul or within the Christian community. In interpreting the "handwriting on the wall" for King Belshazzar, son of Nebuchadnezzar, the prophet Daniel notes "that the Most High God is sovereign over the kingdoms of men, and sets over them anyone he wishes" (5:21). So Paul's dictum in Romans 13 is a continuation of the prophetic tradition that defined human existence in the world as existence under God. Since God rules all, all that rule must be ordained of God.

It would be a mistake to conflate the existence of the governmental authorities as being ordained of God into the conception that it was representative of the community of the faithful. The Pauline theory of the charismata, of the mystical body of Christ, extended to the community of the faithful as distinct from the political community proper. In a footnote, Voegelin argues, "The *exousia,* the governmental authority, is 'ordained' by God, but it is not permeated by the heavenly dynamis; the magistrate is not a member of the mystical body" (*CW,* 19:172n15). The expansion of the charismata to include the temporal ruler does not occur until the conceptual framework provided by the polis is done away with as a result of the Germanic migrations and the formulation of the

26. Bammel, "Romans 13," 367–68.

Gelasian doctrine regarding the specific functions exercised by the temporal and spiritual authorities and the relationship of those authorities to the person of Christ as "the priest-king" (*CW,* 20:62–63).

Obstacles to *Metanoia* and the Social Order

Closely tied to the compromise with the power of political authorities is what Voegelin calls "Eschatological Indifference to Social Problems." And this, in turn, is related to the primary social teaching associated with Jesus in the great sermons recounted in Luke 6:17–49 and Matthew 5–7: the Sermon on the Plain and the Sermon on the Mount. Voegelin presents the arguments of the respective sermons in terms of the eschatological character of Jesus' ministry overall. Jesus preached that the kingdom of God was at hand and that the believer should repent and turn away from iniquity and believe to enter the kingdom. With this understanding in mind, the sermons are not actually "social" strictures at all, but rather the recognition of the potential obstacles that face the individual in gaining access to the eschatological kingdom heralded by Jesus.

> The question of property and wealth is not considered a social problem at all, but a personal one. The possession of wealth is a personal obstacle for the rich man to achieve complete *metanoia.* The entanglement in the manifold interests of the world that goes with riches makes it more difficult to turn the heart to the point where the insight into what is right, and the desire to do it, determines the conduct of life and directs it toward the impending kingdom of Heaven. The kingdom that is not of this world is more easily accessible to those whose stake in the world is small anyway. (*CW,* 19:156–57)

As Jesus warns those who are gathered to hear him, "where your treasure is, there your heart will be also" (Matt. 6:21). Furthermore, Voegelin asserts, "The rules of the sermon are not a code that can be followed like the Ten Commandments. The radicalism of the demands precludes their use as a system of social ethics" (*CW,* 19:162). As Dietrich Bonhoeffer argues, "Having reached the end of the Beatitudes, we naturally ask if there is any place on this earth for the community which they describe. Clearly, there is one place, and only one, and that is where the Poorest, Meekest, and most sorely Tried of all men is to be found—on the cross at Golgotha."[27]

Neither sermon can be read as the pronouncement of a new social code or an advocacy statement on the desirability of redistributing resources. Voegelin notes with regard to the Sermon on the Mount in particular: "The doctrine of the sermon is an eschatological doctrine. It demands a change of heart and imposes rules of conduct that have their meaning for men who live in the daily expectation of the kingdom of Heaven. It is not a doctrine that can be followed by men who live in a less intense environment, who expect to live out their lives and who wish to make the world livable for their families." And, in a passage reminiscent of Machiavelli's warning to *The Prince* regarding speculation on ideal states, he says, "Following the doctrine of the sermon to the letter would in each individual case inevitably entail social and economic disaster and would probably lead to an early death" (*CW,* 19:161). This is because, while love, in the form advanced by Jesus in Matthew 22:37–40, may be the vine on which "depend all the Law and the prophets," it must be filtered through the imperfect vessel of human nature.[28] A person may repent, but human nature remains what it is.

On the other hand, the sermons do serve a social function to the degree that they provide what may be described as an ideal standard of social behavior that can be used as a rule by which to judge the real social order in which people find themselves. This "regulative function," as Voegelin calls it, is its great strength and potential danger. Because "any set of rules that is accepted by a Christian society as the standard of conduct will inevitably fall far short of the teaching of the sermon," their

27. Dietrich Bonhoeffer, *The Cost of Discipleship,* cited in Kissinger, *The Sermon on the Mount: A History of Interpretation and Bibliography,* 85.

28. Voegelin (*CW,* 19:171) notes that Paul argues, "Love is the comprehensive supplement to the old law"; however, Voegelin seems to neglect the text of Matthew 22:34–40: "Hearing that Jesus had silenced the Sadducees, the Pharisees got together. One of them, an expert in the law, tested him with this question: 'Teacher, which is the greatest commandment in the Law?' Jesus replied: 'Love the Lord your God with all your heart and with all your soul and with all your mind.' This is the first and greatest commandment. And the second is like it: 'Love your neighbor as yourself.' All the Law and the Prophets hang on these two commandments." So, far from merely being a "supplement" to the Law, love is presented in the Gospel account as the spring from which all the Law flows.

very existence as a standard creates an inevitable "tension between the accepted standard and the eschatological sermon." As a consequence, "whenever the standard sinks, it can be pulled up again through a re-orientation toward the radical demands." This lies at the heart of the "wave after wave of *reformations*" that occur throughout the history of Christian civilization in the West. The danger to Christian civilization exists "when the swing toward the eschatological demands goes too far, [imperiling] the civilizational structure, which is based on a compromise with the natural gifts of man" (*CW,* 19:162).

The Sermon on the Mount, in particular, represents a direct challenge to the institutional structures of Israelitic life itself—and by extension, the Christian structures as well. Voegelin's discussion of the sermon is concerned primarily with an exegesis of Matthew 5:1–11, the recounting of those who are blessed. However, Clarence Baumann's analysis of the entire content of the Sermon leads him to observe, "Though the Sermon on the Mount contains no political program . . . and prescribes no sociological lineaments for a new *corpus christianum,* we would miss its social intentions if we assumed . . . that it is inconsequential for the actual structures of life." Baumann argues that the Sermon "takes issue with the fundamentals of institutional life." These include:

(1) the protection of life in accord with the equity of *lex talionis* ("an eye for an eye") and the social binding of the collective ego ("love your neighbor and hate your enemy"), (2) the preservation of the family (by prohibiting adultery) and its social control ("give her a cer-tificate of divorce"), (3) the confirmation of the religious oath ("you shall not swear falsely . . ."), (4) the public scrutiny and social ap-proval of exemplary behavior patterns involving charity, piety and asceticism (alms, prayer, fasting), (5) the social control implicated by reciprocal surveillance, mutual censure, and democratic correction to conform with established custom and convention (you will be judged as you judge and get what you give), (6) the social ownership of public property ("treasures on earth"), and (7) the economic pro-vision of life's necessities (concerning food and clothing).[29]

29. Baumann, *The Sermon on the Mount: The Modern Quest for Its Meaning,* 410–12.

The presentation of the "Antitheses" of Jesus, as Baumann describes them, is thus considered a call for the "reorientation" of the believer "to the Father in heaven rather than to the social approval of the religious establishment." Baumann maintains, "Point by point Jesus confronts the fixed institutional structures with a new understanding of one's place before God and man in a new kind of relationship characterized as the 'Kingdom of God.'" The sermon is a call to recognize the specific condition of the individual human soul in its relationship to God. Baumann writes:

> The institution insures its perpetuation into the future in continu-
> ity with its past while he who seeks the Kingdom of God and his
> righteousness lives in the eternal Now. His is not a disconnected,
> solitary, uncommitted, irresponsible, momentary existence but one
> filled with spontaneously vital meetings with God and other hu-
> man beings. Jesus assumed the essential nature of man to be struc-
> tural openness because any programmed depersonalized fixation
> with his relationships thwarts his spiritual potential and interferes
> with the "way that leads to life" by stifling the life of the spirit.[30]

Voegelin recounts the episode from 1 Timothy 6 in which Paul admonishes slaves in Ephesus to respect their masters as their brethren in Christ, and he equates it to the sixteenth-century revolt of German peasants "who, like the slaves of Ephesus, fell into the misunderstanding that the spiritual freedom of the renovated personality was a charter of social liberties." Voegelin goes on to note that "the transition from the idea of spiritual brotherhood to social revolt is the inevitable result of the tension between the invisible kingdom of Heaven and the all-too-visible order of this world in which it is embedded" (CW, 19:172).

This would seem to ignore the institutional response to very real problems that emerge in the social life of human beings and the unwillingness, or inability of, institutions to confront such problems in a realistic way. The tension between the experience of the individual in a position of immediacy to God and the institutional apparatus that is representative of that relationship is complicated, and the line between reform and

30. Ibid., 412.

revolution is a narrow one. "The goal of the Sermon on the Mount," Baumann argues,

> is not a utopian escape from social existence. Law and the prophets are to be fulfilled not through abolishing all institutions and exploring purely personal ways of conduct that lead directly to life eternal but rather by reifying and reauthenticating the corporate forms of existence so as to fulfill God's covenantal intentions for all his people. . . . The presence of personal openness challenges the institutional fixation from within by creating an intolerable tension which eventually forces it open, relativizes its absolute authority, and qualifies its unconditional validity. In the process of its revitalization, the institution, however, develops an inevitable hostility against the free spirit who surmounts it, resulting in a confrontation which in its crudest form eventuates in crucifixion.[31]

Social revolution is thus more than simply the inevitable result of a new spiritual freedom; it is also reflective of the inability of institutions that are intended to represent the life of the spirit to adapt to the new conditions with which they are presented. The line between reform and revolution is a thin one that requires mediation both individually and institutionally. The problem of Christian political order has been an inability to find the mean between the two.

Saint Augustine and the Construction of Christian History

With that said, however, Christianity made remarkable progress in the world into which it emerged. Already by the early fourth century, Christianity had become prominent enough for the emperor Constantine to legitimately convert to the new faith. This expansion was despite the problems of doctrinal purity and schism, persecutions by and conflicts with the pagans, and the generally unstable atmosphere of both the region and the period.[32]

---

31. Ibid., 412–13.

32. On the expansion of Christianity, see Stark, *The Rise of Christianity: A Sociologist Reconsiders History;* LaTourette, *The First Five Centuries,* vol. 1 of *A History of the Expansion of Christianity;* and Chadwick, *The Early Church.*

This instability was in part what led Saint Augustine to apply himself to the task of explaining the meaning, or lack thereof, of history. Voegelin describes Saint Augustine as "one of the great epochal figures of mankind. His life and work summarize the four centuries of the Roman-Christian age and mark its end; and his work, being the *summa* of the age that has laid the foundation of Western Christian civilization, has remained the foundation of Christian thought to this day" (*CW,* 19:206).

Voegelin notes that by "the time of Augustine [354–430], Christian history had evolved along lines rather different from those envisaged in the imperial idea of Paul. The revealed kingdom of Heaven had progressed stupendously, but by no means to the extent that it could have absorbed paganism" (*CW,* 19:207). This development should come as no great surprise, since the Pauline vision was built around the impending *parousia,* the return of Christ and the gathering of the faithful into the kingdom fully revealed. When this did not occur, the historical existence of the Christian community in the world became somewhat problematic.[33]

The City of God had its origins in the sack of Rome by Alaric in 410. "The conquest of the symbol of Roman eternity by the barbarians had wide repercussions in popular sentiment, the pagans naturally branding the Christianization of the empire as the cause of the disaster, the Christians being deeply perturbed by the fact that even Christianization could not avert it." In response to the attack upon the faith by the pagans and the disquiet among the Christians, Augustine composed his great work. *The City of God,* as Voegelin points out, "began as an *oeuvre de circonstance:* books I–III appeared first as a political pamphlet to deal with the misunderstanding that Christianity was some kind of insurance against disaster" (*CW,* 19:209). In the context of the refutation of the pagans and in his attempt "to repair Christian confidence and to teach Christians what they should expect (and should not expect) of God's sovereignty over history,"[34] Augustine would create a new conception of history and drive the final nail into the coffin of the notion of cyclical recurrence that had been the focal point of Hellenic and Roman historiography.

---

33. A contrary view is expressed by C. K. Barrett in his examination of the Gospel of Luke and the Acts of the Apostles. See Barrett, "Luke-Acts," 84–95.

34. Kaufman, *Redeeming Politics,* 136.

Augustine retains the epochal construction of history. He divides the history of the world into six ages as "the analogue of creation," correlated to "the life of Christ," divided "by the generations of the ancestors of Jesus," and "as an analogue of the phases of human life." With the coming of Christ, the last age had begun. The world is now the "*saeculum senescens* . . . aging and tending toward an inevitable end.*" The inevitable end is, of course, the glorious realization of the Kingdom of God, however, for human beings in the here and now a problem still remains. Voegelin notes:

> The construction has only one weak point, but one of decisive importance: the history of the Christian world has no structure of its own. After the appearance of Christ, history simply goes on having no *internal* aim until at some unknown point of time the aimless course is cut short by the second appearance of Christ, an appearance that, as far as the internal structure of the Christian community life is concerned, might come today as well as tomorrow or in a thousand years. (*CW*, 19:211–12)

This understanding is, in turn, premised on Augustine's conception of parallel histories—of the division of history between the *civitas terrena* and the *civitas Dei*. In the Augustinian formulation, "History runs on a double plan: it is the sacred history of mankind expressed in the six symbolic ages, and it is the history of the good and the souls, beginning with the reign of God in the angel-state, going through the fall of the angels, the split between good and bad human souls, and ending in the reign of the righteous souls with Christ at the end of the world." However, the division between the two cities cannot be understood with reference to human institutions such as "church and state." The church may be "the militant representative" of the City of God on earth, but it is still simply "the kingdom of Christ *qualis nunc est* [as it is now], though not all members of the historical Church . . . will be members of the final Church, *qualis tunc erit* [as it will be then], when the tares are weeded out" (*CW*, 19:214).

Voegelin notes that what is missing from the analysis in the *City of God* is an extended discussion of profane history. For Augustine, the question of profane history was of little consequence because it was merely a time of waiting for the end. As Löwith points out, however, from the "strictly religious viewpoint" of Augustine, "we cannot expect . . . a detailed interest in secular history as such."[35] The rise and fall of empires was a matter of little consequence for a man with his focus on eternity. Christopher Dawson argues that the Christian view of the mystery of history as expressed by Saint Augustine was "essentially the mystery of eternal life. It was not concerned with the life of nature or with culture as a part of the order of nature, but with the redemption and regeneration of humanity by the Incarnation of the Divine Word."[36]

For this reason, the cataloging and examination of profane history was a task that Augustine passed on to his student Orosius to complete. Both Augustine and Orosius, however, worked within the framework imposed by Paul's compromise with history in the formulation of the constitution of the Christian community: that is, their primary focus was upon the world as it was defined by the experience of the pagan, Israelitic, and Christian experience. The dynasties of the Parthian and Sassanid empires in the East were largely irrelevant. Voegelin notes that "the Orient simply dropped out of the Western horizon, though Eastern power did not show any sign of decline" (CW, 19:221)—which would have a profound effect upon the future development of the church when the East was rediscovered.

While Orosius's *Historiiae Adversum Paganos* may be "a systemic part of the Augustinian philosophy of politics and history," it also serves to illustrate the essential difference of Augustine's attitude toward profane history and the direction in which the understanding of profane history was heading. As Ernest L. Fortin observes, "In discharging his mandate, Orosius went well beyond the call of duty. His simpleminded thesis is that, far from boding ill for the Empire, Christianity was responsible for untold favors that had accrued to it in recent times."[37]

Voegelin notices the "symbolic parallel between the closing of the temple of Janus under Augustus and the birth of Jesus with the announcement of peace to all men of good will" (CW, 19:221). However, Voegelin

---

35. Löwith, *Meaning in History*, 171.

36. Dawson, *Religion and the Rise of Western Culture*, 41.

37. Fortin, "Introduction," to *Augustine: Political Writings*, xvii. Fortin's judgment might be a little too harsh. See Löwith, *Meaning in History*, 174–81.

does not point out that Orosius's parallel construction takes place in the context of extolling the virtues of the empire and the triumph of Christianity by linking them. Whereas Augustine argues that the unity of the empire has been forged with "much slaughter and bloodshed" and extols the reader "who thinks with pain on all these great evils, so horrible, so ruthless," to "acknowledge that this is misery,"[38] Orosius sees in the civil wars the creation of the Christian empire. "Behold how under Christians and in these Christian times civil wars, even when they prove unavoidable are brought to a happy issue. The victory has been won, the city stands intact, the tyrant has been laid low."[39]

While Orosius takes joy in the "common fellowship" provided by the order of Rome, Augustine is more sanguine, arguing that "as far as this life of mortals is concerned, which is spent and ended in a few days, what does it matter under whose government a dying man lives, if they who govern do not force him to impiety and iniquity?"[40] Augustine may have broken the linkage between sacred and profane history, but his student saw in the profane the hand of God at work, moving humanity forward into a new age. Like Melito of Sardis, whom Voegelin quotes at the beginning of the section on the emergence of Christianity (CW, 19:149), Orosius sees the future of Christianity in Empire.[41]

The Tyconian Problem

Yet behind the construction of history in both Augustine and Orosius a problem was lurking as demonstrated by the Donatists in Northern Africa and the musings of Tyconius.[42] The issue that led to the schism

---

38. Augustine, The City of God 19.7.683.

39. Orosius, Historia 7.33.

40. Ibid., 5.1; Augustine, City of God 5.17.166.

41. The linkage of Roman success to Christianity was, of course, a position taken by many of the Church fathers. See Dawson, The Making of Europe, 34–35.

42. See Frend, The Donatist Church: A Movement of Protest in North Africa. On the relationship of Saint Augustine to the Donatist movement in particular, see Willis, Saint Augustine and the Donatist Controversy; Heyking, Augustine and Politics as Longing in the World, 224–48; and Kaufman, Redeeming Politics, 139–43. On Donatism and other heretical movements generally, see Clifton, Encyclopedia of Heresies and Heretics, and O'Grady, Heresy: Heretical Truth or Orthodox Error?

between the Donatist church and the universal church concerned the readmission to the community of the faithful of those priests and bishops who had offered sacrifices to pagan gods under threat of persecution. More specifically, the issue that really caused the schism was the relationship of the sacrament to the priest who administered it. The sacraments of baptism and communion by which a person joined and acknowledged his or her membership in the community of the faithful were considered legitimate by the Donatists only if they were administered by one who had not been tainted by apostasy.

Voegelin lays out the essential doctrinal position of the Donatist church as developed by "its theorist" Tyconius:

> The Donatist Church was the true church, according to Tyconian theory, while the main church, which admitted the fallen brethren, stood outside the true church just as did the pagans. Tyconius went even further and admitted that within the true church there were imperfect members who did not actually participate in the spiritual *corpus mysticum* of the saints. Within the visible true church, there was, therefore, an invisible spiritual church of the perfect Christians. . . . This invisible church was the true *civitas Dei,* while the false brethren, the *separati* of the main church and the pagans, belonged to another unit, the *civitas diaboli,* the city of the devil. (*CW,* 19:213)

But even beyond the doctrinal construction of the two cities, the city of God and that of the devil, the Tyconian construction advocated the use of violence in order to maintain doctrinal discipline against the members of the city of the devil who refused to realize the error of their ways. This factor, combined with a rigid interpretation of the forms of Christian observance, marked the Donatists as among the first of many puritanical groups that would emerge throughout Christian history. Ultimately, the success or failure of the distinct Christian civilization would be dependent upon the ability of the church to either absorb such movements through reformist efforts or crush them so completely they would not emerge to terrorize the great body of the faithful. To the degree that the universal church adopted the rigorous doctrinal standards of the Donatists, however, the less representative it would be of the *corpus mixtum* represented by the variety of human types that both Saint Paul and Saint Augustine see in the *civitas Dei*.

Conclusion

Saint Paul's dream of universal Christendom was not realized in the history of Rome, despite Orosius's and Melito's confident expressions of the new epoch linking the fate of Rome to the fate of Christianity. The idea of imperial Christianity would reemerge during the Middle Ages as the evocative underpinning of *sacrum imperium,* which is the subject of the next chapter.

CHAPTER THREE

Imperium

✣

The Political Idea in Voegelin's *History of Political Ideas*

In the introduction to the *History of Political Ideas,* Voegelin writes, "the function proper of order is the creation of a shelter in which man may give to his life a semblance of meaning." As such, the political idea is representative of "a little world of order, a cosmic analogy, a cosmion, leading a precarious life under the pressure of destructive forces from within and without" (*CW,* 19:225). This, in turn, informs Voegelin's discussion of the functional component of the political idea. "The political idea is only to a limited extent descriptive of any reality; its primary function is not a cognitive but a formative one. The political idea is not an instrument of description of a political unit but an instrument of its creation" (*CW,* 19:227–28).

As a practical matter, this explanation is important to an understanding of the sense in which Voegelin examines political ideas as they occur in history; for in its character and in an evocation of meaning, the idea itself may never reach its fruition in an institutional form. Since the idea itself is pure, the realization of the idea may not be fully realizable in the historical existence of human beings in reality. At this point in Voegelin's development there may, in fact, be something of the Platonist within him.

The use of the term *idea* may, in itself, be misleading when it comes to a reading of Voegelin's *History of Political Ideas.* Generally speaking, when Voegelin uses the term *political idea* he is not referring to an "idea" per se, or an idea in the singular. Rather, Voegelin is usually describing matrices of ideas that serve as the basis upon which the Idea is constructed. This approach is indicated by Voegelin's structural analysis of the basis of political ideas. The structure of the Idea is determined by "three sets of ideas: the ideas concerning the constitution of the cosmos as whole; the ideas concerning the internal order; the ideas concerning the status of the cosmion in the simultaneous world and in history" (CW, 19:226).

Paul's evocation of the Christian community had fulfilled the requirements for the evocation of a little world of meaning. In chapter two we noted Voegelin's argument regarding the "greatness of Paul" in the apostle's ability to create a constitution for the community of the faithful that fully took into account both the realities of human beings and human nature and the realities of the world in which Christianity emerged. In his evocation of the Christian community through a series of compromises with the world, Paul had created a complex of ideas that would lead to the expansion of Christianity throughout the known world. With that said, the dream of Paul, in the sense of an overarching community that would extend beyond the boundaries of nations and peoples, failed to materialize in history, but it was transformed into something else: the notion of the *sacrum imperium*. This idea of "imperial Christianity," although never fully realized in history, would become the defining characteristic of the Middle Ages and set the stage for the disorder of the modern period.

The problem with any political idea is that it is dependent upon the historical circumstance in which it happens to be formulated. As such, political ideas are largely contingent upon the moment in time and place in which they emerge. Furthermore, political ideas are also entirely dependent upon the institutionalization of the idea if they are to be translated into concrete human action toward the creation of order or disorder. It is important to remember Voegelin's warning regarding the existence of destructive forces, both "within and without" the political cosmion. An idea can only be effective in history to the degree that it is realized through some form of institutional representation.

In the Christian experience, the representation of the Pauline idea came to be embodied in the institutional church. This was implied both in the idea of the differing spiritual gifts granted to individual human beings in their equality before God and in the necessary requirement that the expansion of the community of the faithful and the realization of imperial Christianity required a corresponding organization by which to undertake the program. Voegelin argues:

> The church has become the great civilizing influence in the Western world because it was able to compromise the strict teachings of the Sermon on the Mount with the weakness of human nature, with the existence of governmental power, and with the historical content of pre-Christian civilization. The compromise with the weakness of man expressed itself in the inclusion of everybody into the mystical body of Christ through the sacraments of baptism and the Lord's Supper; the foundation for membership is laid through the sacramental reception, not through any guarantee that the person is, indeed, a member of the invisible church. The actual status of the soul in salvation or damnation is known to God alone; it cannot be judged by the brethren in the community. The acceptance of governmental power as part of the "world" and willed by God is the second great compromise. It enabled the church to outlast the difficulties of the early centuries and reached its climax in the integration of the royal function into the order of the charismata in the ninth century. The third compromise, equally inaugurated by Saint Paul, was the compromise with history through the recognition that God revealed himself to the pagans through the law of nature and to the Hebrews through the Old Law before he revealed himself to the world at large through the Logos that had become flesh. As a consequence of this third compromise it was possible for the early patres to absorb the Stoic natural law into Christian doctrine, and by virtue of this absorption to create for Christianity a system of ethics that was applicable to relations between men who live in the world. (*CW,* 22:140–41)

Voegelin notes, however, that the importance of these compromises is mitigated by the realization that "they could not have unfolded their full effectiveness unless they had been accompanied by the creation of the sacramental organization" (*CW,* 22:141). In other words, for the compromises to lead to the creation of some form of political order, some corresponding representative institution was required.

Problems arise when the organizational realization of the idea moves through history and faces the pressure of existence in the field of social and institutional forces upon it. In the instance of Christian civilization, the church as an institution was an immanent existential embodiment of a spiritual event. Voegelin observes that in the context of the Christian West, the "public institutions of imperial Christianity (church and empire) have, from their beginning, absorbed the problems of the spiritual soul and its destiny into their pattern" (*CW*, 22:133). The difference between "reform" and "revolution" is thus a reflection of the effectiveness with which the institutional structures are able to absorb those problems or eliminate them.

The experience of Christianity into the Middle Ages had demonstrated that under the surface of the existing institutional order were political, social, and spiritual movements that came into play in the creation of Christian order. For this reason, Voegelin argues, we can distinguish "between two planes of Western civilization, an upper plane and a lower plane." The upper plane consists of "the public institutions; the lower plane as that of the movements that are in permanent revolt against the established institutions." Christian political order was problematic largely because of the inherent tension between the institutional order and the distinctly "Christian idea of the person in immediacy to God" (*CW*, 22:131–33).

This tension was both lessened and, paradoxically, increased by the apparent inclusion of an objective standard by which to measure the success or failure of public institutions in representing the very real demands of the spiritual existence of human beings in society. The social standard created by the sermons of Jesus of Nazareth proved to be the source of order and of disorder. Voegelin argues, "The spiritualism of Christianity, and in particular the spiritualism of the Sermon on the Mount, is a standard that can be invoked against the institution that is supposed to represent it; if the spiritual order of Christianity is grossly violated through the conduct of the ruling groups, the appeal can go to standards that are, on principle, accepted by the ruling groups themselves" (*CW*, 22:134). On the other hand, the dictates of the Sermon on the Mount and the Sermon on the Plain created an impossible standard for institutions to achieve in reality. As a result, there were always elements on the fringe that stood in opposition to the institutional order.

The contingent nature of the idea remained a major problem that, in the course of centuries, would result in the crisis of the Great Reformation. The "general nature of the problem that caused the great religious disruption" of the Great Reformation is characterized by Voegelin as

> the crisis of the accumulated, but intellectually undigested, historical content of Christianity. The Spirit is absolute; but the symbolization of its experience and its institutionalization in the life of human community is historical. In the course of history, symbolizations that express the essence of Christianity adequately at one time may become inadequate in a new age; the essence of Christianity is a matter of permanent readjustment of its historical expression. . . . The flash of eternity that is the church is a flash into history; the doctrinal expressions of the flash—which at the beginnings of the church may have seemed as eternal as the flash itself—reveal their relativity in the light of history that flows on through the ages. (*CW,* 22:223)

The revolution that was the Great Reformation is thus a reflection of the inability of the church itself to adjust to the changing political, social, and religious environment in which it found itself.

In this chapter we shall analyze Voegelin's discussion of the problem of Christian order as it expresses itself in the evocation of the *sacrum imperium* of the Middle Ages. "The political ideas of the Middle Ages are oriented toward the focal evocation of the *sacrum imperium,* of the holy empire, just as Hellenic theory was oriented toward the polis and Christian-Roman theory toward the kingdom of Heaven and the Roman empire"(*CW,* 20:29). However, while the *sacrum imperium* may be understood as an "ideal type," it was, as with most idealized conceptions of what might be, never fully realized in history. As Voegelin observes, "the entelechy of the process failed to reach its stage of perfection; the universal empire as a power organization and the universal spiritual community tended toward each other and finally met, but they did not amalgamate" (*CW,* 20:66).

The very fact that it is not an "ideal type" points to the problem with the realization of the idea in history. Furthermore, it also illustrates the interplay between the calls for reform from the bottom of the social structure and the increasing inability of the institutional order to reflect the reality experienced by the people within the society. Finally, it is in the rise and fall of the idea of the *sacrum imperium* that the compromises with the world that Saint Paul made in his initial contact with the world and the conception of the constitution of the Christian community come undone in the interplay of institutional order and social forces.

In chapter two we discussed the Tyconian problem. The speculations of Tyconius prefigured events within the realm of the *sacrum imperium* and beyond. The Donatist controversy was contained because it took place on the fringes of the empire. But the role of the institutional church as the representative of transcendent order and the conduit by which one entered into the community of the faithful would remain a constant target for those who did not believe that the church was, in fact, truly representative of the spiritual order of the kingdom of God. For the future, the Tyconian problem would reemerge in the middle of Europe, and the conflagration could not be simply brushed aside to the margins of community existence.

The Great Reformation may properly be understood, from the Voegelinian perspective, as the end of a process that has two primary components. The first is the social pressure from the bottom in the form of the reformist impulse, but this only becomes problematic to the degree that the institutions are unable to absorb the demands for reform into themselves or successfully demonstrate that the proposed "reforms" are either unnecessary or unwise. The demands themselves are the result of a narrowing of the ontological perspectives that defined the existence of human beings in history. In other words, the reality in which the reformers worked became increasingly restricted, a situation which in turn limited the range of options available to the institutional order. The other component comprises the institutional order itself, the order of the church specifically, which must bear some of the burden of responsibility in history. The problem with the institutionalization of the spirit is ultimately that it must be representative of the spirit. From the beginning of the experience of the institutional church, however, the field of reality in which it operated began to contract as well into the intramundane reality of the world of statecraft. In fact, it could be argued that the modern state was born out of the experience of the church well before the modern territorial state as we understand it emerged.

The Construction of the *Imperium*

Voegelin argues that the Carolingian empire was the result of a gradual historic evolution that took some 300 years to occur.[1] At the Council of Chalcedon of 451, the Roman church condemned the Monophysite Christology and appealed to Emperor Zeno (d. 491) to enforce the Orthodox doctrine as expressed by Leo I (d. 461). The emperor's response was to propose a compromise that drove the final wedge between Constantinople and Rome. The result of this split was the development of the Gelasian doctrine of the two swords by which temporal and spiritual powers were to be separated between two authorities, with the emperor having primacy in temporal matters and the church having primacy in matters of springing from the spiritual. This, as Voegelin points out, was "incompatible with the practice of Byzantine emperors if not with their theory" (*CW,* 20:53). The solution could not be found in a rapprochement. Instead, relations between Constantinople and Rome stagnated in an uneasy alliance, as the church in Rome remained enamored of the idea of the Roman Empire, to which the Byzantine emperor was ostensibly heir.

The situation had been exacerbated when the power of the Eastern Empire was threatened by pressure brought on by the barbarian invasions and the near-complete breakdown of the empire's administrative apparatus. As a result, the church was thrown back on its own resources; more important, Rome became dependent upon the papal organization and the church for its sustenance. This allowed Gregory I (d. 604) not only to claim papal supremacy over the other churches of the empire and the patriarch in Constantinople, but also to fulfill the functions of a temporal ruler in the West. The final straw consisted of the loss of Byzantine political and military control as a result of the Lombard invasions. The pope "had to look for temporal support elsewhere unless he wanted to become a court bishop in the Lombard kingdom, a position that would have been even less appealing than imperial interference in spiritual matters" (*CW,* 20:55).

1. See Herrin, *The Formation of Christendom,* esp. chap. 11, "The Two Emperors of Christendom," 445–76; LaTourette, *The Thousand Years of Uncertainty: 500 A.D. to 1500 A.D.,* vol. 2 of *A History of the Expansion of Christianity;* and Dawson, *The Making of Europe,* 214–33.

In the long, slow decline of the alliance between Rome and Constantinople, we can see the power of an idea. Voegelin argues that it "is surprising for how long the papacy held the emperor in profound awe, in spite of the humiliations to which a number of popes were exposed." But while the "interference in spiritual matters led to temporary severances of the communion," it did not lead to "a formal breach." Instead, the formal breach only occurred when Constantinople was no longer able to fulfill its temporal functions sufficiently to support the episcopate in Rome (CW, 20:54–55). The break itself was delayed because hovering in the background was the idea of the universal empire—the idea of Rome.

Voegelin argues, "The idea of Rome lay heavily over the historical process, and it required the accumulated force of centuries of events to crystallize the new evocation" (CW, 20:66). The epochal consciousness expressed by Melito of Sardis, and quoted by Voegelin, indicates the perception that the fate of Christianity and the fate of the empire are inextricably linked. Melito writes to the emperor Marcus Aurelius: "Our philosophy first grew up among the barbarians, but its full flower came among your nation in the great reign of your ancestor Augustus, and became an omen of good to your empire, for from that time the power of the Romans became great and splendid. You are now his happy successor, and shall be so along with your son, if you protect the philosophy which grew up with the empire and began with Augustus."[2] Only when the empire proves itself to be inadequate to the maintenance of civil and political order is that linkage broken. The existence of a new evocation for the empire required the destruction of the old one. Christopher Dawson describes the change in terms that Voegelin would undoubtedly understand:

> For centuries a civilization will follow the same path, worshipping the same gods, cherishing the same ideals, acknowledging the same moral and intellectual standards. And then all at once a change will come, the springs of the old life run dry, and men suddenly awaken to a new world, in which the ruling principles of the former age seem to lose their validity and to become inapplicable or meaningless.
>
> This is what occurred in the time of the Roman Empire, when the

2. Eusebius, *Ecclesiastica Historia* 4.26.7, cited by Voegelin at *CW,* 19:149.

ancient world, which had lived for centuries on the inherited capital of the Hellenistic culture, seemed suddenly to come to the end of
its resources and to realize its need of something entirely new. For
four hundred years the civilized world had been reading the same
books, admiring the same works of art, and cultivating the same types
of social and personal expression. Then came the change of the third
and fourth centuries, A.D., when the forms of the Hellenistic culture
lost their vitality and men turned to a new art, a new thought and a
new way of life—from philosophy to theology, from the Greek statue
to the Byzantine mosaic, from the gymnasium to the monastery.[3]

Of course, the new evocation took centuries to fully materialize until it
was realized and institutionalized with the coronation of Charlemagne
(d. 814) in 800—and even then it would never reach the status of com-
pleteness. With the understanding that God was the partner in the destiny
of the church, the "slow ripening" of the "situation that was consummated
in the coronation of Charlemagne" was understood "in the symbolism of
the time" as "decisions of God. For the contemporaries of the coronation,
the transfer of the empire was neither an act of the pope, nor an act of the
Frankish king, nor an act of the people of Rome, but an act of God. Divine
providence had shown its intentions through the course that it let history
take, and the acts of man could do nothing but accept the divine decision"
(*CW,* 20:52). It was within the scope of the new evocation that the entity
properly understood as "Europe" came to be. Dawson observes, "It was
only in so far as the different peoples of the West were incorporated in the
spiritual community of Christendom that they acquired a common culture. It is this, above all, that distinguishes the Western development from
that of the other great world civilizations."[4]

Voegelin notes the irony of the situation: "the papacy and the Frankish
monarchy had developed in directions that, on the surface at least,
seemed to contradict the Gelasian declaration on separation of powers"
(*CW,* 20:59–60). In the case of the Frankish monarchy, even prior to the
coronation of Charlemagne it had "evolved . . . in a theocratic direction
insofar as the church organization was integrated into the administrative

3. Dawson, *Christianity and the New Age,* 1–2.
4. Dawson, *Religion and the Rise of Western Culture,* 23.

hierarchy of the monarchy and the king presided over church assemblies with far-reaching interference in matters of discipline." Voegelin is careful to note that

> it would be rash to assume that the theocratic tendencies in the Western empire duplicated the caesaropapism of the Byzantine empire. While the static relationship is similar, the dynamics are completely different. In the East, the imperial administration represented the old civilizational forces and the Christian Church had to integrate herself into an established system of superior civilizational quality; in the West the church represented the superior civilizational forces, and the temporal power had to grow into political and historical stature by means of ecclesiastical aid. The institutional ascendancy of the temporal power in the Frankish kingdom was balanced, therefore, in practice by the dependence of the Carolingian administration on the church organization and church personnel for the governmental and civilizational penetration of the realm, particularly those sections where the Germanic population was strong in numbers. The compulsory Sunday service with the influence exerted from the pulpit was the main instrument of transmitting temporal power for welding the people into a unit by transmitting the intentions of the central administration to the last village. (*CW*, 20:60–62)

Dawson echoes Voegelin's observation: "The government of the whole Empire was largely ecclesiastical, for the bishop shared equally with the count in the local administration of the 300 counties into which the Empire was divided, while the central government was mainly in the hands of the chancery and of the royal chapel." The church was thus an essential representative of political, as well as spiritual, order.[5] Furthermore, in the cooperation of the imperial administration and the clerical administration, the development of permanent political and legal institutions was made possible.[6]

By the time of the Carolingian empire, the church not only had evolved into a spiritual power but had taken on the trappings of a territorial state.

---

5. Dawson, *The Making of Europe*, 218.
6. See Berman, *Law and Revolution: The Formation of the Western Legal Tradition*, 62–84.

Voegelin notes that the "papacy had grown, already before Gregory I the Great, into a huge domainal administration; since Gregory it had acquired the characteristics of a temporal principality . . . ; the spiritual head of Christianity had become in addition a temporal monarch" (*CW,* 20:60). This evolution of the institutional representative of Christianity into a temporal kingdom would become an increasing source of tension and future problems.

Contributing to the difficulties would be the incorporation of the temporal ruler into the *corpus mysticum.* We have noted that Paul made certain compromises with the world in his creation of the constitution of the Christian community. Among those was the derivation of the gifts of the spirit and the use of the analogy of the body as the representative of the community in the world. By the time of the Carolingian foundation, the temporal ruler has been incorporated into the body of Christ. Voegelin writes: "The Pauline doctrine of the charismata, of the gifts of grace differentiating the functions of the members of the *corpus mysticum,* has been enlarged beyond the early Christian community idea. The body of Christ has absorbed the ruling office into the field of the *dynamis* of Christ. This office had been distinguished as the *exousia* by Saint Paul and been excluded from the *corpus mysticum;* the ruler has become charismatic" (*CW,* 20:63). This development is problematic to some degree as well. With the differentiation of power defined in terms of spiritual and temporal as expressed in the Gelasian doctrine and with the inclusion of the temporal ruler as a member of the *corpus mysticum,* the lines of authority were sometimes confused and confusing to both the church as the recognized spiritual authority and the emperor as the constituted temporal ruler of the community.

The lines of authority, temporal and spiritual, which had never really been clear to begin with, became even more complex and interrelated. There was, in the notion of the *sacrum imperium,* from its foundation with Charlemagne to its destruction following Frederick II, a great degree of what Louis Halphen has termed "systematic confusion" regarding the balance between the spiritual and temporal powers within the empire on the part of the temporal authorities.[7] This, in turn, presents

7. Halphen, *Charlemagne and the Carolingian Empire,* 148.

something of a problem for the relationship of the church to the temporal authority, since the church itself has become a territorial power with interests of its own that may or may not be congruent with the interests of the temporal authority upon which it relies and with which it at the same time competes.

But it would be a mistake to transpose the modern understanding of the division between church and state to the medieval sphere. Dawson maintains that in the Middle Ages, the "conception of Christian society was essentially a unitary one. State and church were not independent organisms but different orders or functions in a single society of which the Pope was the head. Yet at the same time this did not mean that the two orders were confused or identified with one another. The prince had his proper function in Christian society and his own rights within the sphere of its exercise."[8] Voegelin repeatedly stresses this point with regard to the evocation of the *sacrum imperium*. Nevertheless, the potential existed for conflict between the two orders of power within the Holy Empire, and this potential would become increasingly apparent with the subsequent development of the church into the first "Renaissance monarchy."

Monasteries as Repositories of Reform: The Question of Community

Of significant importance in the creation of the new Christian community, the new Christian "people," was the monastery. Voegelin maintains, "The institutions gained their function as the uniformly civilizing factor of the countryside with the introduction of the Rule of Saint Benedict in the ninth century." In the adoption of the Rule of Saint Benedict (c. 530), the monasteries transferred "the Hellenic ideal of the self-sufficient community from the polis to a select Christian community." However, unlike in the Hellenic case, the select Christian community had a function outside of itself. Whereas "the Platonic polis was a self-sufficient politico-religious unit . . . the Benedictine polis had its meaning in the larger Christian community as a form of life supplemented by, and supplementing the functions of, the secular clergy and the tempo-

---

8. Dawson, "Church and State in the Middle Ages," in *Medieval Essays,* 86.

ral power." As such, the monastery becomes "the symbol of the changes that occurred in the transition from ancient Mediterranean civilization to Western Civilization: from the polis to the territorial empire (and later the territorial state), from urban civilization to agricultural feudal civilization, . . . from pagan myth to the spirit of Christ" (*CW,* 20:64).

In addition to its role in the foundation of the new evocation, the monasteries also functioned as a regulative force upon the spiritual-temporal community of the church. We have noted that the line between reform and revolution is a thin one, and the monasteries were an important source of the impetus toward the first and the avoidance of the second. Voegelin notes that in the context of the *sacrum imperium,*

> reform was concerned in principle with a reassertion of the evangelical demands against the evils that had encroached on the life of the Christian community in the centuries after Charlemagne. The demands of poverty, celibacy, and Christian discipline were directed against the main evils of lay investiture, simony, and clerical marriage in particular, and they were directed in general against the engrossment of the representatives of Christian life, of the secular clergy, and of the monasteries, in the interests of the world. The reform began where the contrast between the spiritual idea of Christianity and reality was felt most keenly, and where at the same time the resistance of vested interests could be overcome most easily: in the monasteries. (*CW,* 20:68)

It is an irony of history that the reform movements themselves, while intended to supplement and revivify the connection between the spiritual existence of human beings as members of an overarching community in the church, would also serve to undermine the existing foundations of the representative institutions of the church itself.[9]

The Cluniac reform (910) consisted of the creation of an "order" as distinct from a "house." In the Benedictine model, each monastery was an independent organization. The establishment of the Cluniac orders created a hierarchical system in which authority flowed downward from the abbot of the original house to all houses that composed the order.

9. See Dawson, *Religion and the Rise of Western Culture,* 243–64.

This provided a model for the church as a whole, and, paradoxically, for the temporal authorities. As Voegelin notes,

> The strict observance of the rule and the centralizing constitution recommended the order to the papacy as the model of a hierarchical spiritual organization with ultimate concentration of authority in the head of the church; it was precisely the type of organization that could serve as a pattern for the organizational independence of the church herself from secular power. In a most unworldly corner of the Christian community, in the midst of a diffuse field of regional feudal powers, the type of a well-integrated sovereign organization emerged that could be put to use in the organization of the church as well as later of secular political authority. (*CW,* 20:69)

Contrary to the Cluniac concern with its organization in the world and the relationship between the monastery and the world, the Anchorite reforms concerned the spiritual development of the individual person. But the Anchorite movement (c. 1000), with its emphasis upon the withdrawal from the world and contemplative life, had little influence beyond itself. "Individual hermits . . . could exert an influence as models of extreme Christian unworldliness and thus become a regenerative force, but as soon as the anchoritic principles were transferred to a larger group a shading off into Benedictine cenobitism ensued" (*CW,* 20:70). The asceticism of the hermit is largely incompatible with life in society.

The importance of the Anchorite movement only emerges with the creation of the Cistercian orders (1098), which sought to combine "the organizational element of Cluny with the anchoritic element of asceticism on a new spiritual level" (*CW,* 20:71). It is in the combination of the two that Voegelin sees the maximal differentiation of the spiritual consciousness. The Cistercian establishment took place largely as a reform of the Cluniac system established some two hundred years previously and as a result of the effective failure of the Anchorite movement.

> The achievements of Cluny were discipline, obedience, and organization; the achievements of the anchorite foundations were poverty, asceticism, and the contemplative life in solitude. Two hundred years of success had brought to Cluny a wealth and ex-

ternal splendor that cast a shadow on the Christian spirituality that it was supposed to represent. The hermit movement, on the other hand, was inevitably asocial; the attempt at recapturing Christian primitive simplicity implied the withdrawal from effectiveness in Christian community life. (*CW*, 20:70–71)

It is in the amalgamation of the two approaches that a compromise is reached between the demands of Christian spirituality and the concern for community existence. Voegelin writes:

> Organizationally, the Charter of Charity provided for relative independence of the monasteries. . . . The influence of the abbot of Cîteaux was purely spiritual and could not extend to temporal exactions. The new foundations were, furthermore, not directly under Cîteaux, but formed a hierarchy so that only the immediate foundations of Cîteaux were under the spiritual supervision of the founding house, while the houses founded by the filial establishments were spiritually dependent on their own founding houses, etc. This organizational feature reflected the basic principle of spiritual father- and sonship. The element of spiritual fatherhood, of spiritual formation from man to man, defines the new level of Christianity. . . . The relationship resembles in some respects the Platonic eros, though in substance it is worlds apart from it: for the soul of the spiritual father does not create a new cosmion, but father and son are members of the pneumatic community in Christ. (*CW*, 20:71)

The construction of the pneumatic community of Christ is thus based on the spiritual equality of persons. As Voegelin reflects on the correspondence between Saint Bernard (d. 1153) and Eugenius III (d. 1151), the spiritual equality of the individual person is the focus. The pope's power derives from his office, not from any quality of spiritual superiority. Bernard's thesis, in Voegelin's view, represents the spiritual maturation of the Christian West.

Concomitant with the internal reforms of the monastic movement that led to the development of the spiritual self-consciousness of Saint Bernard, the "second strain in the Western process was the defense against Islam" (*CW*, 20:72). Voegelin sees three stages

> in the concentration of the physical and spiritual substance that gives its peculiar dynamic expansiveness to our Western civilization. As a first stage we may count the migration events up to the eighth century, by which time the area of the West was set off, as a new ethnic and civilizational unit, against the ancient Mediterranean. A second stage was marked by the migratory disturbances of the ninth and tenth centuries, ending in the check of the Slavic and Magyar advances in the east and the stemming of the Islamic tide in the south. The third stage was reached with the Crusades proper, in which the external relations of the West evolved from the semi-consciousness of natural growth and defensive reaction into a fully conscious attitude of self-assertion and offensive action, paralleling the internal process in which the logic of ideas asserting itself against the infidels is followed by peaceful missionary activity. (*CW,* 20:72)

The rise of the military and mendicant orders is a part of, and reflective of, this growing imperial self-consciousness on the part of the West. Perhaps even more important was the planting of the spiritual seeds of destruction to the unity of the distinctly Western civilization that was inadvertently brought on by the establishment of the mendicant orders.

Voegelin notes that the "activist order of the military type was supplemented a century later by a movement for the spiritualization and intellectualization of self-conscious expansiveness" (*CW,* 20:77). Once the "point was reached where the absolutism of the Christian drive was bent, in principle, into a consciousness of its relativity through contact with a world of superior force that followed its own laws" (*CW,* 20:79), the danger began to grow that such movements might turn inward. Voegelin argues that the mendicant orders became "the great instrument of orthodox mass Christianization, positively as well as in the negative form of the papal Inquisition," and in carrying out this function they provided a tremendous service—in their time and ours—in maintaining the learning of the past and in adding to it as "their schools became . . . the great centers of intellectual, theological, and philosophical activity" (*CW,* 20:78).

Voegelin observes the problems that accrue to the mendicant spirit, especially as it became manifest in the Franciscans (1209). First, there is the understanding that developed concerning Saint Francis (d. 1226) "as the symbol of a new Christian dispensation." Second, the "movement of Saint Francis and his *poverelli* is distinguished, in its original form, by the personality of the saint, but it does not differ otherwise in essence from similar movements of the time. . . . It is typical . . . of the popular religious movements spreading over the towns of Europe in the great heretical undercurrent that broke finally through into the institutional sphere of the *sacrum imperium* in the Great Reformation." The "second form" of the Franciscan Order, "the conventual with permanent houses, and the Dominican Order may best be characterized . . . as successful attempts at integrating the activist spirit of popular sectarianism into acceptable, nonheretical institutions" (*CW,* 20:77–78). But the spirit of popular sectarianism could not be contained in the absence of an ongoing process of institutional reform in the church hierarchy.

In order for the symbol of Saint Francis as the symbol of a new Christian dispensation to come to the fore, the meaning of history had to be revealed—or rather, changed—in a way that Saint Augustine, the original expositor of Christian history, could not have expected. J. G. A. Pocock defines the problem to be confronted in terms of Saint Augustine's construction of history. The "separation of salvation and society, redemption and history, soul and body, sundered but did not abolish the problem of the eschatological present. . . . Within the *saeculum,* there remained the problem of assigning meaning to the social and historical events experienced by individuals throughout the remembered past and henceforth to the end of time."[10]

The Investiture Controversy and the Contraction of Reality

The dispute that began in the conflict between Gregory VII (d. 1085) and Henry IV (d. 1108) known as the Investiture Controversy (1000–1122) is notable for Voegelin because it illustrates some of the inherent tensions in the West and pointed in the direction that events would take. Voegelin's interpretation of the Investiture Controversy is based on the perception that all too often in history, "the spectacular tends to obscure the essential." The underlying question that needed to be resolved was,

10. Pocock, *The Machiavellian Moment,* 35.

Who was responsible for the consecration of bishops? However, as Voegelin argues,

> The question of lay investiture was no "question" at all. Under the accepted canonical law the papacy had control over the bishops, and this control could not be exerted if the ecclesiastical appointments were due to lay influence; a reform, asserting the church investiture, was clearly indicated. The reform became a practical problem because the bishops had become heads of temporal administrative bodies and an assertion of papal control would destroy the system of government by which medieval feudal society existed. The canonical answer to the question was clear as soon as it was put; and the political solution, the compromise that was reached in the Concordat of Worms in 1122, was a foregone conclusion. (*CW*, 20:67–68)

Although it held no real question to be resolved, the Investiture Controversy would serve to raise several questions that would require answers.

Here was a pivotal moment. Within the context of the debate concerning investiture, "political theory came at last to grips with the compromises implied in the Pauline decision to establish the realm of God as a realm in this world for the duration." To fully examine the implications of this "coming to grips," Voegelin focuses on "the great intellectual radicals who, as far as the central evocation of the empire is concerned, were marginal to the controversy" (*CW*, 20:91–92). The reason Voegelin focuses on the extremes of the debate is twofold. On the one hand, the fundamental area of agreement between the extreme partisans in the debate indicates an evolution of sentiments with regard to the meaning of intramundane history. On the other hand, the extreme examples give a better indication of the shape of things to come.

The real issue that underlay the question of simony was the objectivity of the sacrament by which a member joined the body of Christ. In 1052, Peter Damian (d. 1072) advanced the argument that the worthiness of the priest was irrelevant to the relevance of the spiritual gift granted by the sacrament. "The spiritual life of the church emanates directly from Christ, the head of the mystical body. Hence the sacramental charisma is always pure, however unworthy may be the hand that administers it. The sacrament is only *administered* by the priest; its *substance* remains unaffected by his personal qualities" (*CW*, 20:83). What really mattered was the spiritual condition of the person receiving the sacrament. Voegelin sees in this construction a fundamental "precondition for the function of the church as the unifying spiritual organization of the *sacrum imperium*. When the accents lie too heavily on the personal worthiness of the members, the danger of revolutionary disruption of the church unit arises if sufficient social forces are available for a violent reform" (*CW*, 20:84). In other words, simony may be abusive, but it does not strike at the heart of the spiritual community of Christ.

By the time of the Investiture Controversy proper, the issue was still not resolved. For the papacy, Cardinal Humbert (d. 1054) argued that simony was more than simply abuse; it constituted heresy. Humbert's argument was based on the notion that the proper mediation of the sacraments required both the giver and the receiver to be participants "in free actuality in the spirit of Christ. . . . Here we meet with a precise formula for the opposition between sacramental objectivity as the principle of a mystical body mixed of good and bad (which for that very reason can become the human corpus of a Christian civilization), and the radical postulate of spiritual freedom that of necessity has to distinguish between a pure body of Christ and a mystical counterbody of the devil" (*CW*, 20:92). That this is the tack that Humbert means to take is clarified by his construction of history in which "the Tyconian problem breaks through with full force. The spiritually free church is the body of Christ; the simonically infected body is the *corpus diaboli*." Furthermore, the *corpus diaboli* can be reformed through action in history. More important, regarding the investiture of bishops, Voegelin argues that

> Humbert decides that sacerdotal dignity is inseparable from the administration of church property, that the property is just as sacred as the spiritual structure of the church, and that it is, therefore, impermissible to have the worldly power precede the spiritual in the investiture. The reversal of the procedure, what was actually practiced, would pervert the true order and function of the members of the mystical body. The sphere of material goods, thus, becomes integrated into the realm of the spirit; the realm of God is not a realm

of persons only but comprises the physical dimension of this world. . . . The world in its full historico-political reality, with its material equipment, has become so firm a part of the Christian order of thought that the early eschatological tension between a realm of God that is not of this world and the world itself has practically disappeared. (*CW,* 20:93–94)

But also of importance, and largely ignored by Voegelin, is the sense of antagonism that Cardinal Humbert has toward the laity generally and the temporal power in particular. The responsibility for simoniac practices rests, in Humbert's view, not with the church, but rather with the temporal authorities. Uta-Renate Blumenthal describes the problem:

Unlike Abbot Abbo of Fleury . . . who had branded simony as an evil within the church and particularly blamed the bishops, Humbert relates simony primarily to lay influence in the church. From top to bottom, from the highest to the lowest order, he sees trade in ecclesiastical goods flourishing. Primarily, however, it was emperors, kings, princes, judges, and just about anyone with some kind of secular power, who engaged in this shameful trade. Never mind that they had been entrusted with the defense of the church. All of them therefore carried the sword in vain. They neglected their proper tasks, only to devote themselves body and soul to the acquisition of ecclesiastical property.[11]

This interpretation contains a sense of the particularity of the sacerdotal offices that is missing in Voegelin's analysis, although it will appear later in his discussion of the hardening of the institutional church. The clear antagonism between the contracted *ecclesia* of Saint Francis is prefigured in the attack on the temporal powers based on the perception of interference by Humbert.

The evidence for the assertion that the world has become part of the Christian order of thought is found in the construction of the Norman Anonymous.[12] Whereas Humbert supported the papacy, the Norman

11. Blumenthal, *The Investiture Controversy,* 89.
12. The identity of the Norman Anonymous is a matter of some academic controversy, so I have avoided the appellation "The Anonymous of York." Apparently, the Norman

Anonymous supports the authority of the emperor, though there is a fundamental issue upon which Humbert and the Norman Anonymous agree. Both parties in the dispute tend to acknowledge the fundamental importance of the world itself in the divine plan of human salvation. Voegelin notes, "On the level of the controversy Humbert and the author of the *York Tracts* are opponents, the one enhancing the dignity of the *sacerdotium,* the other that of the *regnum;* but in their fundamental attitudes they are brothers under the skin, the Anonymous being the more radical since the world is for him sufficiently imbued with the spirit to make the priest as its special custodian a secondary if not a superfluous figure; the world of the Anonymous can spiritually take care of itself" (*CW,* 20:96). In order to support his argument, the Anonymous constructs a theory of the present *saeculum* that is contrary to the original Pauline and Augustinian constructions. The result of this radical reconstruction is a conception of history as one of three ages, each of which is "distinguished by the degree to which the full participation of mankind in the realm of God is realized." By means of this construction, the "spiritual history of mankind receives a new teleological orderliness; the redemption is not an inordinate act of divine grace but a step leading to the ultimate general kingship of man" (*CW,* 20:97–98).

The great danger posed by the Anonymous is not his argument per se but rather the fact that he is representative of a growing threat to the order of the *imperium.* Voegelin argues, "The *York Tracts* revealed what had happened and what was going to happen." More than simply an argument in favor of the temporal order as such, "they implied a fact: the fact of the free personality of the author who could live in the age of Christ under the guidance of the sacred writings without assistance from the Church of Rome" (*CW,* 20:105). This is problematic, since the order posited by the idea of the *sacrum imperium* is premised upon the structure of authority being divided between the spiritual authority of the church and the temporal

---

Anonymous may actually be the Anonymous of Rouen. See Nineham, "The So-Called Anonymous of York." On the other hand, Norman F. Cantor vigorously maintains that the Anonymous was Gerard of York. See Cantor, *Church, Kingship, and Lay Investiture in England,* 174–97. On the Norman Anonymous's theory of kingship, see Kantorowicz, *The Kings' Two Bodies: A Study in Mediaeval Political Theology,* 42–61, in addition to the previously cited section of Cantor.

authority of the government. From the point of view of the Anonymous, however, the church as such is largely irrelevant.

> The general priesthood of the Christian is not a mere theoretical proposition but is living reality in the opinion of the Anonymous. With frank brutality he denies that the Roman Church has any teaching function with regard to the Christian people; we possess the prophetic, evangelical, and apostolic Scriptures, and we know them better than the pope . . . ; if the papacy wants to assume the function of a teacher of mankind it has the pagan world for a field of operation; in Western Christianity it is superfluous. The forces can be felt that will disrupt the ecclesiastical unit of the *sacrum imperium*, as the national will disrupt the precarious temporal in the upheaval of the Great Reformation. (*CW,* 20:101)

At the core of the arguments advanced in the Investiture Controversy, Voegelin sees the specter of the age of religious wars—the attack upon the order of the world and the complete breakdown of the Pauline compromises with the world. In Voegelin's analysis the historical period between the Concordat of Worms (1122) and the *Summa Theologicae* of Saint Thomas Aquinas (d. 1274) is a time of profound confusion in terms of the evocative idea that lay at the heart of the *sacrum imperium.* Voegelin notes,

> The "compromise with the world" and its institutionalization in the *sacrum imperium* have had the effect of gradually weakening the sentiment of distinction between the world and the realm that is not of this world; the eschatological component in the Christian sentiment was receding rapidly and, correspondingly, the sentiment that the structure of the world was part of the Christian realm was growing; the world had entered the realm of God. . . .
> . . . The transcendental order of God was supplemented by an intramundane order of forces filling the realm. (*CW,* 20:108–9)

It was only a matter of time before the "intramundane order of forces filling the realm" would begin to take precedence in the life of the community of the faithful.

Joachim and the New Age

The movement reached its peak in the speculation of Joachim of Flora (d. 1202) and his new construction of immanent Christian history. Prefigured by the ideas advanced by the Norman Anonymous, Joachim of Flora's influential history of the three realms would result in the appearance of the symbolic "Third Realm" that "has remained ever since a basic category of Western speculation, reappearing when a rising force wished to express its claim to dominance of the age" (*CW,* 20:111). Joachim, according to Voegelin, represents "the end of an evolution" away from the understanding of the Augustinian construction of history (*CW,* 20:127). The impetus for the evolutionary change was the existence of the religious orders that began to infuse European life with a new religious sentiment and a "feeling that the rise of the orders was symptomatic of progressive spirituality inaugurating a new phase of Christian life." This, in turn, created the conditions by which the "revelational experience of Joachim" was able "to touch off the potentialities of this field of sentiments and to create the new pattern of Christian history. The decisive step is the conception of the Third Realm, not as the eternal Sabbath, but as an age that is to follow the dispensation of the Son as the last age of human history" (*CW,* 20:128–29). As Nicholas Campion wryly observes, "There is almost nothing original in Joachim's ideas, and his importance lies in the simple fact that he was the right person in the right place at the right time."[13]

Joachim of Flora was a Cistercian monk who had experienced the call to enter the order during a pilgrimage to the Holy Land. Like the Norman Anonymous, Joachim found the essential pessimism regarding human existence in history he saw in the *civitas Dei* of Saint Augustine to be less desirable than the search for a meaning of and direction to history as it was experienced by human beings in their worldly existence.

According to Joachim's speculation, "The history of mankind is a progress of spiritual evolution from the natural, pre-Mosaic law, through the Mosaic and evangelical laws, to the fullness of spiritual freedom" (*CW,*

---

13. Campion, *The Great Year: Astrology, Millenarianism, and History in the Western Tradition,* 372.

20:129). This evolutionary passage is marked by human existence in the ages of history, each of which corresponds to one of the persons of the Holy Trinity. And the beginning of each realm is preceded by a period of preparation. Joachim was to be the prophet of the third age, the age of the Holy Spirit, in which the spiritual freedom of the individual human person will be realized under the guidance of a new leader, the *dux*.

The Trinitarian structure of history was nothing new. In the Gospel of Matthew, the generations to Christ were reckoned in three groups, each encompassing fourteen generations (1:1–17). The logic of the identities of the Holy Trinity lent itself to divisions of three. Thus, Irenaeus was the first patristic leader to divide history into three ages and natural phenomena into three types.[14] In the Manichean heresy, the struggle between the opposing forces of light and darkness passed through three stages.[15] Even Saint Augustine had appropriated the use of the number three for the divisions of human affairs and the human qualities necessary for their study. But while "the trinitarian scheme of history was taken for granted by Christian of the first millennium," the mystical revelation of Joachim would give the symbol a resonance that would move through history.[16]

Voegelin maintains that Joachim's construction of history and its entering into "the main stock of Western political speculation" has had a profound effect upon the understanding of history generally. Joachim's periodization of a progressive history resulting in the appearance of the Third Realm has created the impression that "history has to have an intelligible structure. The present age must not be a time of meaningless transition; it has to be a meaningful step toward a definite goal. The Augustinian pessimistic waiting for the end of a structureless *saeculum* has disappeared" (*CW,* 20:130). Accordingly, the "third age would be to its predecessors as broad daylight compared with starlight and dawn, as high summer compared with winter and spring. . . . The Empire would be no more and the Church of Rome would give place to a free community of perfected beings who would have no need of clergy or sacraments or Bible."[17]

14. Ibid., 321–22.
15. Jonas, *The Gnostic Religion,* 206–37.
16. Campion, *The Great Year,* 322.
17. Cohn, *The Pursuit of the Millennium,* 100.

Joachim's construction of history is premised upon "the sentiments engendered by the Cistercian environment. The three realms are characterized by the predominance of the law, of grace, and of the spirit" (*CW,* 20:133). As such, the third age, the age of the Spirit, was supposed to be realized in the community in "the perfect contemplative life of the monk," and "the perfection of life . . . in the three elements of contemplation, liberty, and spirit" (*CW,* 20:133). There is something almost tragic about the uses to which his symbolic construction would be put. Löwith writes:

> Joachim . . . could not foresee that his religious intention—that of desecularizing the church and restoring its spiritual fervor—would, in the hands of others, turn into its opposite: the secularization of the world which became increasingly worldly by the very fact that eschatological thinking about last things was introduced into penultimate matters, a fact which intensified the power of the secular drive toward a final solution of problems which cannot be solved by their own means and on their own level. . . . The revolution which had been proclaimed within the framework of an eschatological faith and with reference to the perfect monastic life was taken over, five centuries later, by a philosophical priesthood, which interpreted the process of secularization in terms of a "spiritual" realization of the Kingdom of God on earth. As an attempt at realization the spiritual pattern of Lessing, Ficht, Schelling, and Hegel could be transposed into the positivistic and materialistic schemes of Comte and Marx. The third dispensation of the Joachites reappeared as a third International and a third *Reich* inaugurated by a *dux* or a *Führer* who was acclaimed as a savior and greeted by millions with *Heil!*[18]

In summary, it may be that the Pauline compromise with history was based on the idea that the kingdom of God is both present and future. Saint Augustine had conceived of the division between sacred and profane history with the realization of the destiny of human beings beyond history. However, the consciousness of epoch seen in Melito and Orosius had planted the seed of an idea regarding a progressive history of human beings in the world under the hand of Providence that was tempered

18. Löwith, *Meaning in History,* 158–59.

through the Norman Anonymous to reach its fruition in the visionary revelation of Joachim of Flora. The imperial ruler of Joachitic speculation would be transposed from a spiritual to a political figure in Dante (*CW*, 21:79–80), and although Dante would seek to offset his temporal Dux with a new spiritual head of the empire, it would be the transfigured temporal ruler that would rule the march of history from Dante forward. Thomas Aquinas attempted to stem the tide released by the Joachitic speculation, but the genie was out of the bottle.

Symbols of the Epoch

The influence of Joachim is most clearly seen in the program of Saint Francis of Assisi. As Voegelin notes, "As symbolic figures of their age, the persons of Saint Francis of Assisi and Joachim of Fiore are intimately connected. Saint Francis could not have been seen by the Spirituals as the decisive figure inaugurating a new epoch of Christian history unless the prophecies of Joachim had furnished the symbolic pattern for their interpretation" (*CW*, 20:135).

Voegelin argues that with Saint Francis and the Franciscan movement,

> The penetration of the spirit into the realm of nature has now reached its full development. Saint Francis uses the formulas of eschatological hardness, and he can act hard, but the sentiment that moves him does not deny the world; on the contrary, it adds to the world a dimension of which it had been hitherto deprived in the Christian dispensation. The joy of creaturely existence and the joyful expansion of his soul, reaching out in brotherly love to that section of the world that glorifies God by nothing but the humbleness of being created, this simple joy in the newly discovered fellowship of God's creation, makes Saint Francis the great saint.
>
> Through his discovery and acceptance of the lowest stratum of creation as a meaningful part of the world, he became one of the momentous figures of Western history. He took the humble by the hand and led them to their dignity, not in an otherworldly realm of God, but in a realm of God that is not of this world. And he gave nature its Christian soul and with it the dignity that made it the object of observation. (*CW*, 20:141)

The new realm that Francis opened up was "distinctly intramundane" and stood "in opposition to the *imperium* with its Gelasian principles" (*CW,* 20:140). Saint Francis attempted to construct the third age of Joachim's historical speculation. Instead of opening up the realm of the spirit, Saint Francis created the complex of ideas concerning the construction of community that stood in opposition to the evocation of the *sacrum imperium.*

Furthermore, there is a certain militancy to Saint Francis and the Franciscans generally that would become increasingly problematic and, in fact, is reminiscent of the Tyconian problem to which we have repeatedly referred. In the case of the Franciscan Spirituals, the puritanical struggle against vice echoes the puritanical struggle of the Donatists against the established institution of the church. Voegelin points to the Franciscan tract *Praise of Virtues* and argues that it indicates the "tragic necessity that the creation of an order, even of love, requires demonic ruthlessness of action, offensive to the environment." To struggle against vice, however, is a collective struggle against the world itself. Voegelin notes:

> It is impossible to understand the Franciscan attitude if the ethical categories of virtues and vices are supposed to refer to the character of the individual person alone. In the context of the *Praise,* virtues and vices are forces emanating from the supreme powers of good and evil, from God and Satan, and taking possession of men. The struggle of virtues against vices becomes a collective undertaking; the virtues of the one group have the function of "confounding" the vices of the other. . . . The possession of the virtues thus serves the attack on the world with its institutions of family, property, inheritance, governmental authority, and intellectual civilization. (*CW,* 20:135–37)

In the case of Saint Francis personally, this struggle against the vices and the world takes the form of simple preaching and a general call to repentance for the faithful. However, to paraphrase "Publius," wise men will not always rule. Voegelin observes that what "distinguished Saint Francis from other sectarian leaders, and made him a saint instead of a heresiarch, was his convincing sincerity, his exemplary personal realization of the ideals he taught, his charm, his humility, and his unworldly naïveté" (*CW,* 20:138–39). It was perhaps this odd combination that made him so effective and also so myopic regarding the forces he was inadvertently unleashing on the world.

The Franciscan formulation was not simply a matter of recognizing the human dignity of the poor, but rather it was an elevation of "the poor" to the status of agents of change. Voegelin argues, "The spirit of revolt against the established powers was spreading all over the Western world, ranging from the intellectuals to the townspeople and the peasants. The movement was increasingly directed against the feudal organization of society" (*CW,* 20:138). Saint Francis transformed the image of Christ and in so doing provided a symbol of opposition to the established order of the society generally. Voegelin argues that in his conformance to the life of Christ, "Saint Francis had conformed the image of Christ to the human possibilities," but the grandeur of "Christ the king in his glory" was lost.

> In the sequence of intramundane forces using Christian symbols for their self-interpretation, Saint Francis had created the symbol of the intramundane Christ, but this symbol can absorb only that aspect of the person of the Savior that conforms with the humble and the suffering of this world. The function of Christ as the priestly-royal hierarch had to be neglected; the Christ of Saint Francis is an inner-worldly Christ of the poor; he is no longer the head of the whole *corpus mysticum* of mankind. The great evocative achievement of the compromise with the world, particularly in the Western imperial period, was the understanding of the natural differentiation of men and of the spiritual and temporal hierarchies as functions in the mystical body. In this preference for the Christ of the poor and his neglect for the hierarchical Christ, this great civilizational work was, in principle, undone by Saint Francis. The world had to break asunder when Christ was no longer the head of the differentiated body of Christianity but only the symbol of particular forces who claimed for themselves a privileged status in conformance with him. (*CW,* 20:142)

This is not to say that the imperial image of imperial Christ had simply vanished. Indeed, nearly contemporaneously with the new reality proposed by the Franciscans emerged Frederick II (d. 1250). Voegelin asserts: "We have seen how Saint Francis transformed the image of Christ into that of the suffering Jesus with the consequence that Christ became an intramundane symbol to which the poor and humble could conform while the hierarchies were left without the messianic head. The ideas of Frederick II represent the opposite attempt at creating an image of ruler-ship in conformance with Christ as the cosmocrator, with the Messiah in his glory" (*CW,* 20:157). Voegelin notes with some irony that the "last medieval emperor was the founder of the first modern state. In him the crisis of the age met with the man who became its perfect symbol through the circumstances of his descent and through his personal ge-nius" (*CW,* 20:144). Frederick II came to power as the *sacrum imperium* was being battered by political and spiritual powers on the "'fringe' that, by their sheer weight, shifted the center of politics to the west and the south. The rise of these powers had the consequence of dissolving the imperial idea and of supplanting it with new evocative ideas adapted to a world of rival powers; the Gelasian principle as the dominating evoca-tive idea of the West was on the wane, and the problems of power pol-itics in the modern sense emerged" (*CW,* 20:148). In his capacity to recognize and adapt to the changing situation Frederick II's greatness and weakness may be observed.

In the *Prooemium* to the *Constitutions of Melfi,* Frederick II advanced an idea of rulership that Voegelin describes as a "naturalistic theory of gov-ernment, deriving the function of rulership from the structure of intra-mundane human reality" (*CW,* 20:153). But it does so by the use of "Christian language." The theory advanced in the *Prooemium* is that gov-ernment was instituted among human beings after the Fall, which had resulted in the loss of immortality as a punishment. "With the death of man, however, creation would have lost its meaning, and in order not to destroy creation with the first man, God made him fertile. The inclina-tion to transgression being inherited, men fell out among themselves, and God provided rulers of the people to preserve the order of human soci-ety." Through this construction, the grace of God as represented by the Incarnation of Christ is removed from the calculation. Furthermore, "the substitution of the community of mortal man for immortal man re-forms the hierarchical structure of the world; the creation reaches its climax in the ruler who has to preserve the order of the people" (*CW,* 20:153). There was nothing at all remarkable in the idea that political life was made necessary by the transgression of human nature—after all, Saint Augustine had argued essentially the same thing. What Frederick II did, however, was transfer the hierarchy of creation that reaches its pinnacle in God, to the realm of politics with himself as the apex of creation.

The third, and perhaps most important, element of the construction is what Voegelin describes as its "Averroist" element. "The place in the hierarchy of the paradisiacal immortal couple has been taken, after the Fall, by the succession of generations of mortal man. The collective immortality of mankind has succeeded the individual immortality of Paradise." The importance of this sentiment lies in the fact that by adopting a position that substitutes the immortality of the species for the immortality of the individual, Frederick II struck at the heart of the Pauline conception of the body of Christ.

> The collectivist interpretation of mankind is, by principle, opposed to the Christian idea of the *corpus mysticum.* The idea of the mystical body achieves an understanding of the spiritual unity of mankind while leaving the natural gifts as well as the human personality and the immortality of the soul intact. The collectivist idea, in its logically elaborated form, absorbs the human personality into the spirit of the group. Man is the individuation of a generic intellect, and death means depersonalization through dissolution into the world-mind (or the group-mind). . . . In the field of ethics and politics this anthropological assumption may have the consequence of supporting the ideal of conformance to a type, a group discipline, and of governmental measures for the enforcement of such conformance and discipline. The Averroist anthropology may become, in brief, the philosophical basis for a collectivist, totalitarian organization of society. (*CW,* 20:154)

In place of the *corpus mysticum,* in which the spiritual equality of individual human beings is taken as the origin of community, Frederick II would substitute a system in which the ruler is elevated in order to maintain order in God's creation. Thus, the evocation of the *Constitutions* tends to reserve the dignity of full humanity to one person in the community only, the ruler. This severe irruption of the intramundane force of rulership into the realm of Christian ideas, the transformation of the mystical body of the immortal faithful under the leadership of Christ into a mystical body of mortals under the leadership of the ruler, had to precipitate a crisis when it went beyond the stage of implications, as it actually did in the deeds and pronouncements of the emperor and his associates. (*CW,* 20:156–57)

In the case of Frederick II, his conflicts with the papacy destroyed the existential representation of the idea of the *sacrum imperium* and plunged the papacy into a slow death spiral that would not reach final fruition until Boniface VIII issued the *Unam Sanctum.*

The idea of the *sacrum imperium* does not die with Frederick, but the personality and institutions that have any hope of achieving the realization of the idea are swept from the stage of history. Instead of the grandeur of a communal empire bound together by the spirit of Christ, a system of competing powers would be rationalized and justified by new, emerging ideas. The idea of the sacred empire began to give way to the demands of *realpolitik.*

In the dichotomy between Saint Francis and Frederick II is the symbolic representation of what had occurred within the *sacrum imperium.* The elements of the Christian personality, indeed of the personality of Christ himself, had been split into two images. Neither one was complete in itself, yet both were clung to by their adherents with a ferocity that only extreme faith could give. The broken body of the *corpus mysticum* would move into the future and be given another opportunity at life through the philosophical and theological explorations of Saint Thomas Aquinas. Unfortunately, like Plato trying to salvage the polis from the depths of his own soul, Saint Thomas's vision would likewise be frustrated.

Conclusion

For all practical purposes, the break in the idea of the *imperium* had occurred when Frederick II died, but the potential for renewal remained in the willingness of the church to adapt to the changes brought on by the shifting political situation. Saint Thomas Aquinas would offer a way out of the mess that the wreck of the *imperium* had created. But because the church lacked the ability to recognize what had happened, it failed to adjust itself to the dramatically altered circumstances with which it would be confronted.

CHAPTER FOUR

The Age of Confusion

c‽

Saint Thomas Aquinas at the Edge of the Abyss

In *The New Science of Politics,* Voegelin would remark that the substance of history consisted of the differentiation of reality through experience and that "the maximum of differentiation was achieved through Greek philosophy and Christianity." Furthermore, Voegelin argued that to "recede from the maximum of differentiation is theoretical retrogression" (*CW,* 5:152). The meaning of the phrase "maximum differentiation" that occurs with Christianity, however, cannot be understood without reference to the work of Saint Thomas Aquinas (d. 1274). It is through Saint Thomas that the maximum differentiation of which Voegelin speaks actually occurs. This fact is illustrated by Voegelin's analysis of Saint Thomas in the *History of Political Ideas.* Indeed, the problem of Christian political order may be defined in terms of "Before Aquinas" and "After Aquinas" in much the same way that history is conventionally designated in terms of the Incarnation.

As part of the analysis in the *History,* Voegelin writes: "Since the time of Dante the spiritual realist has been faced with the problem that the surrounding political reality of the Western world no longer can adequately absorb the spirit into its public institutions" (*CW,* 21:68). The *sacrum imperium,* the organizing principle of the Middle Ages, had been broken. The nearly contemporaneous lives of Frederick II and Saint Francis of Assisi are a fitting symbol of what had occurred. The *sacrum imperium* had been constructed with the central idea of the Pauline *corpus mysticum,* the body of Christ that consisted of the believers in a unified whole with Christ as the head. With Saint Francis and Frederick II, the perception of a unified whole was irreparably broken. The ties that bound the imperial order together were broken.

Saint Thomas had witnessed what had happened, and perhaps he perceived what was going to happen. In Voegelin's estimation, Aquinas offers a compromise that, had it been adopted, could have salvaged order from impending chaos. Unfortunately, as Voegelin observes, Aquinas is a representative of "the spiritually and intellectually mature Western man" (CW, 20:232)—and as such, is not necessarily representative of human beings generally. Rather, the intellectual, personal, and spiritual qualities of Aquinas must be accepted as the exception rather than the rule. More precisely, Aquinas is representative of the maximum human potential realized.

The problem with the contraction of the reality given to human beings that began with Orosius's conception of the linkage between Christianity and Rome and continued through Cardinal Humbert, the Norman Anonymous, and the speculations of Joachim of Flora was that in each instance the contraction of the overall reality of existence was also a contraction of the meaning of human being itself. Frederick II and Saint Francis are symbolic of the age because each represents different aspects of the complete human existence under God. After Joachim, however, the full reality of human existence was no longer a primary concern. Hence, with Siger de Brabant (d. ca. 1284) and Boetheius of Dacia (fl. 1270), a contraction of human existence under God occurs within their interpretations of the Aristotle of Averroës. As Voegelin writes, "The idea of mankind as the mystical body of Christ is replaced by the idea of the human species as a collective unit existing through the process of generation from eternity. No individual soul, furthermore, gives form to the body, but the Intellect *uno in numero*, one in number, operates on the human beings" (CW, 20:190–92). This, in turn, results in a hierarchical structure of the human collective based on the degree of participation in the collective mind and "the ideal of intellectual life is coupled with the idea that the man of substance is morally superior to the poor man" (CW, 20:192–93). Voegelin argues that this "strict immanentist construction of the world permits the idea neither of a creative divine act as the beginning nor of divine intervention at a later point. The world exists from eternity, and its existence in time is governed by nothing but by the laws of its fixed internal structure" (*CW*, 20:194).

In Saint Thomas, we see the shape of rebellion against this construction and, as it happens, against things to come. Aquinas's great insight, cited by Voegelin—"The order of things in Truth, is the order of things in Being"—is nothing less than "the experience of identity between the truth of God and the reality of the world" (*CW*, 20:207). And in Thomas, the intellectual life is indeed elevated. This insight is informed by Thomas's reading of Aristotle, but while the intellectual "is still superior in understanding to the common man . . . the common man is not a *vilis homo*," as in the construction of Siger. "What the philosopher knows through the activity of his intellect, the layman knows through the revelation of God in Christ. The supernatural manifestation of the Truth in Christ and its natural manifestation in the intellectual as the mature man stand side by side" (*CW*, 20:208–9). In other words, the hierarchy of human order is not conditioned upon an understanding of an intrinsic moral superiority on the part of the intellectual; all share equally in the capacity to experience reason and revelation. Part of the genius of Saint Thomas's construction is the understanding of the essential equality of human beings before God.

Indeed, it is the parallel construction of reason and revelation that Voegelin sees as the greatest element of Saint Thomas's thought. "Faith and reason," Voegelin writes

> cannot be in conflict because the human intellect carries the impression of the divine intellect; it is impossible that God should be guilty of deceiving man by leading him through his intellect to results conflicting with the revealed faith. It follows that the human intellect, though capable of errors, will arrive at the truth wherever it goes. The revealed faith, however, contains besides the truths that are accessible to the natural intellect, such as the existence of God, other truths, such as the Trinitarian character of the divinity, that are inaccessible to reason.

Through this construction, Saint Thomas "faces the intramundane forces that threaten to wreck the Christian world and he successfully attempts a synthesis. . . . The authority of the intellect is preserved, but through its transcendental orientation it is transformed from an intramundane rival of the faith into a legitimate expression of natural man" (*CW,* 20:209–10).

In terms of its implications for politics, the best regime is that which is constituted to allow the mutual cooperation of spiritually free individuals. As Voegelin notes, "Thomas makes freedom or servitude the criterion of good or bad government. If the members of the community cooperate freely in the enterprise of common existence, the government is good, be it a monarchy, aristocracy, or polity. If one or many are free and conduct the government in their [own] interest by exploiting the others, the government is bad" (*CW,* 20:218–19). As for the relationship between the powers of the *imperium,* temporal and spiritual, Voegelin argues,

> The order of the multitude of Christian men has to be under the ruler who is the spiritual king of mankind—that is, under Christ. The ministry of this spiritual reign is entrusted to the priesthood, in order to keep it distinct from the natural earthly affairs, and in particular to the Roman pontiff, "to whom all kings of the Christian people are subordinate as to the Lord Jesus himself." Under the hands of Thomas the term *political* begins to assume its modern meaning; the Gelasian dichotomy of spiritual and temporal powers began to be replaced by the modern dichotomy of religion and politics. With Thomas, the political sphere, in the modern sense, was still completely oriented toward the spiritual, but the beginning of the momentous evolution that led, through the Lockean privatization of religion and the assignment of a public monopoly to politics, to the totalitarian integration of an intramundane spirituality into the public sphere of politics can be discerned. (*CW,* 20:220)

Perhaps the reason for this shift is illuminated by the fact that the

> *sacrum imperium* with the Gelasian powers is no longer topical; we are in the time of the Interregnum. The temporal power, which at the time of the Investiture Struggle was still implicitly understood as the imperial power, is now replaced by the plurality of political units with their immanent natural structure, and the spiritual power recedes from its place as an order within the unit of the Christian empire into the position of a spiritual superstructure over the multitude of *civitates.* (*CW,* 20:212)

This reality made it easy for Aquinas to import the political categories established by Aristotle as the criteria by which types of regimes may be defined, with this caveat: Aquinas argues that even Aristotle's "good regimes" could be bad because of the theory of "natural slavery" contained therein. "For Thomas there are no natural slaves. His anthropology operates with the idea of the mature, free Christian, and in his magnanimous idea of freedom we can even feel a touch of the aristocratic egalitarianism of Saint Francis" (*CW,* 20:219).

Saint Thomas is at his most profound in his description of the "free Christian." As part of the development of the theory of law, Saint Thomas confronts the question of the New Law of Christ. In a discussion that Voegelin describes as "revolutionary," Saint Thomas skirts the edges of the theological position of the institutional church. Voegelin writes: "The *lex nova* is written by the grace of the spirit into the hearts of the faithful; only secondarily is it a written law. With a radical sweep, not eliminating but at least not mentioning the church, the essence of Christianity is put directly in the faith, in the *pistis* in the Pauline sense. . . . The principle of justification by faith is made the essence of the *lex nova*" (*CW,* 20:230). In a footnote, Voegelin warns against understanding that one can find hints of "Lutheranism in the theology of Thomas Aquinas," however, he also notes that "within the disquisition of the *lex nova,* taken for itself, the spiritualism of Aquinas becomes, indeed, somewhat forgetful of the institutions" (*CW,* 20:230n).

In seeking to categorize Saint Thomas for the purpose of the *History of Political Ideas,* Voegelin argues that his place

> has to be fixed with regard to the irruption of the intramundane forces since the Investiture Struggle. The new age, announcing itself in the stirring of these forces, could be characterized by the entrance of the "world" into the orbit of the otherworldly spiritualism of Christianity. Thomas stands on the dividing line of the ages in the sense that his harmonizing powers were able to create a Christian spiritual system that absorbed the contents of the stirring world in all its aspects: of the revolutionary people, of the natural prince, and of the independent intellectual. His system is medieval as a manifestation of Christian spiritualism with its claim to universal validity. It is modern because it expresses the forces that were to

determine the political history of the West to this time: the consti-
tutionally organized people, the bourgeois commercial society, the
spiritualism of the Reformation, and the intellectualism of science.
(*CW,* 20:231)

The greatness of Saint Thomas cannot obscure the fact that ultimately
his sentiments did not prevail. Voegelin argues, "The work of Saint
Thomas was a triumph of the spirit and the intellect over the forces of
the age, but it did not change their course" (*CW,* 21:37).

The course of history was not represented in the creation of Saint
Thomas, but rather was more closely related to the symbols of Saint Francis
and Frederick II, the broken body of the *sacrum imperium,* and the inci-
sion placed between the realm of the spirit and the realm of politics. Instead
of following the path of compromise opened by Saint Thomas, the church
and the nations would follow divergent courses through the later Middle
Ages to the Great Reformation. It was the epoch in which the spiritual
orientation of the comprehensive community of the West was transformed
and transferred to other carriers of spiritual authority outside of the universal church. It was the age of increasing national consciousness and
conflict between newly emerging nation-states. It was the age in which
"the people" became the determinants of political systems. More important, perhaps, is the fact that it was also the period in which the church
abandoned its proper position as the institutional representative of spiritual truth. And finally, to paraphrase Leo Strauss, it was the epoch in
which the orientation toward what was highest in human beings no longer
became the fundamental principle of order.

After the work of Aquinas, Voegelin argues, "the complexes of sentiments and ideas" that emerged can be placed into two broad categories.
"On the one side, the spiritualism of the church has developed into the
ecclesiasticism of Boniface VIII and Giles of Rome, and on the other side
we can observe the national sentiments reaching the stage where they
inject problems of national institutions into general political theory" (*CW,*
21:104). The first category may be further subdivided in that the influx
of the intramundane forces is most clearly seen in the ecclesiasticism of
the church.

The problem of Christian political order in the period between Aquinas
and the Great Reformation should not be misunderstood as a problem of

church and state, or as church and states, or even as church under state, although each of these aspects does enter into the picture. The real difficulty of Christian political order consisted of the doctrinal hardening that occurred as a result of the church *as* state. This particular problem is the great underlying factor that allowed the increasing tensions that ultimately broke in the final schism of the church known as the Great Reformation. It also represents the final destruction of the Pauline compromises with the world that had made Christian political order possible in the first place.

The Church as State: *Unam Sanctum*

In a previous chapter, we noted that even prior to the emergence of the idea of the *sacrum imperium* as an evocation of the post-Roman order, when Gregory I was pope, "the papacy had grown . . . into a huge domainal administration" and "since Gregory it had acquired the characteristics of a temporal principality . . . the spiritual head of Christianity had become in addition a temporal monarch" (*CW,* 20:60). This process had continued throughout the Middle Ages. Indeed, Voegelin argues that an understanding of the devolution of temporal authority as a distinct order within the universal empire of the *imperium* into what we today would define in terms of the purely political, as distinct from the spiritual, must be understood in light of the changing nature of the spiritual authority as represented in the offices of the universal church with the papacy at its head.[1] "The great transformation of the charismatic temporal power within the *imperium* into political power in the modern sense was paralleled in the church by the transformation of the papal spiritual power within the imperial order into the ecclesiastical organization as a distinct power unit side by side with the secular political units. . . . By the end of the thirteenth century the church herself had become a power unit organized as an absolute monarchy" (*CW,* 21:41). Indeed, by 1310 at the latest, "the church became the first absolute Renaissance monarchy with a competent central bureaucracy and a ruthlessly efficient financial system. Similar standards of efficiency were reached in the national realms only toward the end of the fifteenth century, in Tudor

---

1. For background on the development of the papal theory, see Watt, "Spiritual and Temporal Powers."

England and in the France of Louis XI" (*CW,* 21:167). Thus, Voegelin maintains that the "history of the church in the period after Saint Thomas is the history of the clash with the political powers and of the attempts at finding working relations between the church and the national political forces" (*CW,* 21:41).

The most important papal pronouncement, for our purposes, by which we can discern the changing nature of the church was prompted by the dispute between Philip the Fair of France (d. 1314) and Boniface VIII (d. 1303). The origin of the conflict was a financial dispute in which Philip attempted to levy the clergy in France. This, of course, upset the financial system that the papacy had established to keep itself "on a lavish scale" (*CW,* 21:41). The conflict was resolved with the death of Boniface VIII shortly after the affair of Anagni in 1303 in which mercenaries, hired by the French king, were unable to arrest the pontiff.[2] In part, however, it was the issuance of the papal bull, the *Unam Sanctum* (1302), that prompted Philip to act.[3]

A charitable interpretation of the *Unam Sanctum* is that it represents the changing circumstances in which the church and the papacy found themselves at the beginning of the fourteenth century. The old order of the *sacrum imperium* was gone, and in its place nothing had yet emerged. Implicit in the pronouncement is the understanding that the old order has passed, or is passing, away. In fact, the papal decree may be understood as the explicit recognition of that change. Voegelin argues, "The clash between the pope and France was the very occasion on which the problem of secular national politics, without relation to the interests of the papacy, was discovered. Up to this time the political interests of the spiritual and temporal powers had been, on the whole, parallel" (*CW,* 21:44). These parallel interests had occurred only within the context of the mythical structure of the Sacred Empire, however. Once that link has been severed, the interests of the temporal and spiritual authorities began to move in different directions.

---

2. For an interesting account of the affair at Anagni, see "William of Hundlehy's Account of the Anagni Outrage."

3. On the history of the conflict between Philip and the papacy, see Strayer, *The Reign of Philip the Fair,* 237–300; and Curry, *The Conflict between Pope Boniface VIII and King Philip IV, the Fair.* The complete text of *Unam Sanctum* is available at www.fordham.edu/halsall/source/b8-unam.html.

Again, a charitable interpretation would note that from the perspective of Boniface VIII, the relevance of the church as the spiritual authority for a universal community was under attack. Furthermore, such an attack required a vigorous response to reclaim the sanctity of the institutional representative of eternity. In other words, it could be argued that Boniface VIII was attempting to salvage the dream of universal Christendom from the wreck of the *sacrum imperium*. Voegelin hints at as much in his analysis: "The theory of the charismata and of the Gelasian balance of powers was applicable only as long as the temporal power was represented by the more or less uncontested single imperial head. When the unity of Christian mankind split up into national bodies politic, the absolutist construction of the power hierarchy was one possible means of saving the spiritual unit of Western mankind." The alternative, what actually happened, was "a disintegration of the spiritual power paralleling and following the disintegration of the imperial power. The several temporal political units would tend to acquire the status of separate spiritual units, as they actually did with the rise of nationalism as the spiritual determinant of Western political communities" (*CW,* 21:46).

But as the issuance of the bull itself made clear, the spiritual authority, rather than moving in a direction that would clarify its position as the institutional realization of a universal spiritual movement, was instead demonstrating that its perceived interests were really quite different.

Voegelin argues that the "critical statement" made in the *Unam Sanctum* is this declaration: "That every human creature is under the Roman pontiff we declare, say and define, and pronounce it necessary for salvation" (*CW,* 21:43). Furthermore, in the Gelasian language of the two swords, the logical extension of the idea is taken to mean that the two swords, spiritual and temporal, are to be administered, in the first instance, "in the hands of the priest," and in the second, "at the sufferance of the priest." The papal bull, quoted by Voegelin, gives this explanation: "For according to the order of the universe things cannot be equal or immediate but the lowest will be brought into order by the intermediate, and the lower by the higher" (*CW,* 21:45). In other words, there is a hierarchy of powers that exists, and the spiritual power, as represented by the administrative bodies of the church, is a higher power. All powers are organized, according to the logic of the bull, in a hierarchical structure, and the papacy sits at the apex of all powers, temporal and spiritual.

Voegelin detects the influence of Giles of Rome (Aegidius Romanus, d. 1316) lurking under the papal pronouncement. In Giles, who was papal counselor and author of *De ecclesiastica potestate,* Voegelin sees "the will to power of the intellectual" personified (*CW,* 21:48). Coupled with this is the observation "that Giles was less interested in spiritual or temporal power than in power as such. He was willing to advocate any power as absolute as long as he was associated with it. If Giles were placed in a modern environment we would have to say that he was a Fascist by temperament. His fundamental position is perhaps best revealed in this remark: 'it is natural that those who are superior in intellect and excel in industry should rule.' This is the confession of an intellectual activist" (*CW,* 21:49). As a result of Giles's indulgence in the *libido dominandi,* he developed a theory of power that is distinctly modern, "the first Western treatise on power as such" (*CW,* 21:50).

Giles elaborates a theory of power through an explanation of the power of the papacy. "The plenitude of the spiritual and material powers belongs to the pope. Both swords are in the hands of the church, but they are not held in the same manner." In an argument that was advanced in the bull itself, Voegelin notes that according to Giles's theory, "the church has the spiritual sword to use herself, and she has the material sword to be used at her command . . . by the secular princes. The princely power is completely subordinate to the papal. . . . Secular power has the function of 'ordering matter at the disposition of the ecclesiastical power.'" In order to realize this goal,

> All organs and instruments of government, the arms, the earthly goods, and the laws have to be administered in obedience to, and at the will of, the church. . . . All laws specifically, imperial as well as those of other princes, are invalid if they are in conflict with ecclesiastical laws; and confirmation by the spiritual power is required for their validity. . . . These technical rules make Christian mankind a closed governmental system with respect to legislation, administration, and the use of the instruments of coercion. (*CW,* 21:51)

Furthermore, this "closed system" extends to the practice of philosophy and theology. Voegelin argues, "A generation after Saint Thomas, who could establish the freedom and independence of the intellect because he was a great spiritualist, there appeared in Giles the first modern political intellectual to use the intellect as a subservient instrument for the support of a dogmatic position in much the same manner as do our contemporary leftist and rightist intellectuals." Indeed, according to Voegelin, in Giles's "tendency toward a rigidly controlled and closed political system" we can observe the first stirrings of a system "that today we should call ideological" (*CW,* 21:52).

Indeed, within the closed system of power advocated by both *Unam Sanctum* and the theoretical justification of Giles, the role of the individual human person outside of the ecclesiastical hierarchy is that of a "subject" as opposed to the "free citizen" of the realm. And this is, in fact, the reason for Voegelin's opprobrium toward both the papal bull and Giles's formulation. Unlike Aquinas, who sought to ground the "good" regime in terms of the maximum spiritual freedom of the human person before God, Giles's theoretical construction requires the contraction of individual freedom under a powerful ruler. According to Giles's argument, the spiritual power, with its representation in the hierarchical order of the papacy, is the supreme power on earth.

> Corresponding to the powerful ruler appears, at the other end of the scale, the powerless subject, obedient and completely subservient, having no natural rights, but only such rights as are derived from his status in the power organization and granted by the absolute holder of all power. The subjects are *servi ascripticii, servi empticii, censuarii, tributarii;* they are in a state of servitude *(servitus);* and they have no total dominion over earthly goods, but only a *dominium particulare* with obligation of tribute to the power. . . . This harsh doctrine is aggravated by the theory that God, who might have exerted the dominion of the world without earthly rulers, has given power to the princes because he wanted the creatures to participate in his dignity; the creatures should not be idle but have a sphere of power and action of their own. . . . This human dignity in the image of omnipotent divinity is given to the rulers only. It does not become clear whether the subjects share in this dignity; the creation of man in the image of God becomes dangerously close to being a privilege of those who hold power. (*CW,* 21:50–51)

In one fell swoop, Giles has redefined human nature and the community of the faithful and has destroyed the Pauline compromise with the natural gifts of humanity.

Voegelin clarifies this point with a discussion of the relationship between the argument advanced in *Unam Sanctum* regarding the "judging" of the pontiff, or spiritual authority, and the biblical justification offered within the bull itself, which cites 1 Corinthians 2:15. In the papal pronouncement, Boniface VIII offers the argument that "when a temporal power deviates, it will be judged by the spiritual power; and when a minor spiritual power deviates it can be judged only by God, not by man. For this the Apostle is witness when he says: 'The spiritual man judges all things; but he himself is not judged by anybody' (1 Cor. 2:15)." The use of the scriptural passage, however, indicates a severe case of selective interpretation, as Voegelin is quick to point out. In the context from which the pope pulled his quotation, Saint Paul is in fact clarifying the distinction between the *pneumatikos* and the *psychikos*. The *pneumatikos* is the mature Christian who has been touched by the spirit of God. Because of this experience, he or she is capable of discussing the wisdom of God. The *psychikos*, the person who is concerned only with the wisdom of human beings, cannot know the wisdom of God until such time as he or she responds to the call and is transformed into the *pneumatikos*. Thus, the use to which Boniface VIII attempts to put this particular scriptural passage is somewhat diabolical in both interpretation and intent. Voegelin clarifies the issue:

> The meaning of the sentence from 1 Corinthians thus can be summarized: the *pneumatikos* cannot be judged by the mere *psychikos*. Obviously, this is not the meaning the sentence has in the argument of the *Unam Sanctum*. The bull uses the term *spiritual* equivocally so that it refers to the spiritual power as distinguished from the temporal power in the Christian mystical body. For Saint Paul every Christian is on principle a *pneumatikos*, whether cleric or layman, while the bull arrogates the spirituality of man to the clerical order, and within this order in a highest degree to the Supreme Pontiff. (*CW*, 22:206)

The issuance of the *Unam Sanctum* cannot be dismissed as "a mere matter of equivocation, perhaps for the purpose of gaining a momentary political advantage" (*CW,* 22:207). J. A. Watt notes, "The argument that *Unam sanctum* was atypical and to be set aside as a serious misinterpretation of conventional papal theory before and after the pontificate of Boniface VIII cannot be taken seriously."[4] T. S. R. Boase, in his sympathetic biography of Boniface VIII and charitable reading of the *Unam Sanctum,* maintains, "The whole form of it is as a general statement detached from any particular circumstance"[5]—and that is indeed the problem. Instead of not being taken seriously, the bull has to be understood as a general statement, as the expression of a new doctrine in which "sectarian spirituality and an imperial will to power" are made manifest.

> The sectarian element is revealed in the distinction between *pneumatici* and *psychici.* In 1 Corinthians the distinction simply means Christians and non-Christians; the bull, however, does not imply that the *psychici* are not Christians; they are Christians, but of a lower spiritual rank. Neither does the bull identify the two types with the distinction between elect and condemned souls; the *pneumatici* are not the invisible church, nor do the *psychici* belong to the *civitas diaboli.* On the contrary, the *homines spirituales* are very visible insofar as they constitute the hierarchy of the church. The bull, indeed, transfers the spiritual ranks, as we should find them in a Gnostic sect, to the whole body of Christianity. (*CW,* 22:207)

Whereas the Pauline theory of the charismata had conceived of the gifts of the spirit meted out equally to human beings according to their nature and enhancing their natural gifts, Boniface VIII would transfer those gifts into a signification of the elect as represented in the hierarchy of the church. Voegelin notes, "In the theory of the *sacrum imperium* the charismata are given by God directly; the functions within the *corpus mysticum* are exercised freely; the members are held together by mutual love in the Pauline sense (1 Cor. 13). The hierarchical theory of power is a new element, incompatible with the Pauline doctrine as well as the Gelasian. It rationalizes the older Christian evocation in the direction of a hierarchical system with an absolute power at the top of the pyramid" (*CW,* 21:46).

4. Watt, "Spiritual and Temporal Powers," 367.
5. Boase, *Boniface VIII,* 318.

The *Unam Sanctum* was in many ways a logical outcome of the contraction of reality that had been occurring since the Investiture Controversy within the hierarchy of the church itself. The evidence for this is seen in the contraction of the meaning of the term *ecclesia*. The increasing ecclesiasticism of the church is more than simply a "political" problem proper but rather is indicative of a general trend toward the closure of the universal religion to the experience of transcendent being. In the early church, the *ecclesia* was a reference to the individual church communities that "formed the island organizations of the *populus Christianus* in a sea of paganism." With the linkage of temporal and spiritual authority in the *corpus mysticum* through the Gelasian formula, the *ecclesiae* were joined in the body of Christ under the twin hierarchies of the spiritual and the temporal authorities. However, "in the twelfth century, a process of dissociation began. In the language of Saint Francis the *ecclesia* is on the point of contracting into a sacerdotal organization while the laymen, the *idiotae,* form a community of their own that tries, however, to live in peace with the traditional hierarchy" (*CW,* 20:140).

By the time Boniface VIII issued the *Unam Sanctum* in 1302, this process of contraction was complete. It is fine to maintain, as R. W. Carlyle and A. J. Carlyle have done, that the extremism of the church died with Boniface VIII,[6] but the fact remains that for all practical purposes the institutional order of Christianity was understood by the church hierarchy to consist of the administrative apparatus of the church. The new princes and the laity constituted a different community that was joined to the church hierarchy and upon whom it depended for material support. As Voegelin notes, with "the contraction of the term *ecclesia* to the meaning of the hierarchy with Saint Francis, and the withdrawal of the spiritual power into an organization ranking over the multitude of political units with Saint Thomas . . . the formulation of the claims of the church had shifted slowly but irresistibly from claims of a spiritual order to legal jurisdictional claims" (*CW,* 21:41). Thus, the *Unam Sanctum* is representative of the new situation of the church with regard to the temporal powers, but it is also representative of the church's understanding of itself as a

6. Carlyle and Carlyle, *A History of Medieval Political Theory in the West,* vol. 5, *The Political Theory of the Thirteenth Century,* 438.

temporal power. But even beyond that, through the issuance of the bull, the papacy had redefined human nature so that it would have been unrecognizable to the experience of Saint Paul.

In his analysis of the *Defensor Pacis* of Marsilius of Padua (d. ca. 1342), Voegelin maintains that, in the chapter that contains the discussion of Christianity,[7] Marsilius writes "as if the treatise were written for readers who had never heard of Christianity before" and "could have been written only by a man to whom Christianity had become a cultural curiosity and did not appeal to any more profound sentiments" (*CW*, 21:98). This is largely true because of the actions of the church itself and the development of a doctrinal position that was, in many ways, contrary to the experience of faith. The church had been coopted by the slow encroachment of intramundane forces that would begin to define the meaning of life for the people who lived it, and the church itself would become increasingly incapable of dealing with the problems that confronted it. It is a great irony that in seeking to establish both the relevance and the necessity of the papacy, Boniface VIII set in motion the end of universal Christendom—at least as it was constituted in the Catholic Church. As Mandell Creighton observes,

> With Boniface VIII fell the medieval Papacy. He had striven to develop the idea of the Papal monarchy into a definite system. He had claimed for it the noble position of arbiter amongst the nations of Europe. Had he succeeded, the power which, according to the mediaeval theory of Christendom, was vested in the Empire, would have passed over to the Papacy no longer as a theoretical right, but as an actual possession; and the Papacy would have asserted its supremacy over the rising state system in Europe. His failure showed that with the destruction of the Empire the Papacy had fallen likewise. Both continued to exist in name, and set forth their old pretensions; but the Empire, in its old aspect of head of Christendom, had become a name of the past or a dream of the future since the failure of Frederick II. The failure of Boniface VIII showed that a like fate had overtaken the Papacy.[8]

---

7. *Defensor Pacis* 1.6.
8. Creighton, *A History of the Papacy from the Great Schism to the Sack of Rome,* 32.

Authoritarian Faith

Voegelin saw the end as well, but not necessarily in the pronounce-ment of Boniface VIII. According to Voegelin, "a great cycle of Western Christianity comes to its end" (*CW,* 21:109) in the nominalism of William of Ockham (d. 1374). Through the nominalism of Ockham the division reemerges between faith and reason, first posited in the reception of the Averroist Aristotle and then demolished by Saint Thomas. Voegelin ar-gues, "There is nothing in William of the sublime certainty of Saint Thomas that the order of the world is a manifestation of the divine intellect and that it is to be re-created by man in the order of truth." Thus the "order of nature does not have a structure of real universals; we cannot know, therefore, any substance in itself but can know it only by its accidentals." The effect of this construction is to restrict reality to prevent any inter-ference with the adherence to faith.

> The establishment of a critical theory of knowledge is undertaken not . . . primarily in order to secure the progress of science but in order to restrict science critically to its field of possibilities. The sub-stance of the world, including man . . . and God, cannot be reached by science. The critical confinement of science to the accidentals has the purpose of saving faith from its encroachments. In the realm of revealed faith and of theology reigns the *potestas absoluta* of God; it is the field of the completely irrational, defying attempts at a ra-tional theology. The revealed religion is a miracle of God, not to be caught in the categories of science; its content cannot be penetrated by natural reason and, hence, its acceptance is possible only through the miracle of faith operated by God in man. The irrational content of the dogma is believable because God has, through his *potestas absoluta,* infused faith in man, compelling the sacrifice of intellect. William gives the first construction of a strictly fideistic religious position, accepting the rationally impenetrable dogma by an act of faith that is worked in man by a miracle of God. (*CW,* 21:106–7)

The experience of faith as the loving response to the call of God is done away with, and in its place is "the idea of an absolute authoritarian God who posits the content of faith at his will" (*CW,* 21:111).

In Voegelin's account, William of Ockham is representative of the forces that were first unleashed in the twelfth century and that have finally found a home. Voegelin argues that "the cycle that began with the realism of the *York Tracts* . . . now peters out in the nominalism of the late scholastics. The world has been integrated into the realm of God spiritually, but its structure could not be integrated into the rational system of faith intellectually. The harmonization of the spirit and the intellect had failed" (*CW*, 21:109). Instead of the compromise of Aquinas, something dramatically different had occurred—a situation that still comprises a fundamental element in the understanding of what constitutes "modernity."

William of Ockham stands at the center of the formal division between the notions of religious and secular that have been the prominent feature of Western polities to the present. Voegelin writes:

> The attitude adopted by William is symptomatic of the momentous situation that the Christian penetration of the "world," progressing since the foundation of the Western empire, has now to be stopped. Factors have grown in the world that have to remain in the world; the period of imperial Christianity with its, at least attempted, complete integration of the life of man in the life of the *corpus mysticum* had come to an end. An intramundane civilizational process would now run parallel with the Christian civilizational process as organized in the church. . . .
>
> The tension between the independent intellect and the authority of faith changes fundamentally the relations between the church and the temporal sphere because from this point on the temporal sphere becomes increasingly identified with secularism and laicism, in the precise meaning of a realm of human existence that is organized under the authority of the critical intellect. The coordination of the two powers as orders within the one body of Christian mankind gives way to a new order in which the church is on the defensive as an enclave within the process of secular civilization. The result for the church is a hardening and drying up of its intellectual life, for any movement that might touch the dogmatic sphere involves the risk of shaking the system on principle and opening it to the destructive invasion of the secular intellect and, therefore, has to be shunned. (*CW*, 21:110–11)

This hardening and drying up is the source of much of the difficulties that led to the Great Reformation. The institutional church became increasingly unable to cope with its changing situation in light of the burgeoning national movements.

Indeed, the great attempt at compromise, the Conciliar Movement that began as a result of the Great Schism (1378–1417), must be counted as a failure insofar as it did not revitalize the church sufficiently to stem the growing tide of sectarianism. Instead, the most notable thing about the Conciliar Movement is that it demonstrated how far into the world the church itself had penetrated. As Voegelin points out, "the reforming zeal of the council was less absorbed by a reform of the spirit than by a jockeying for institutional positions. The nominalism of the Ockhamist type had now, indeed, become institutional practice. The spiritual reality of the *corpus mysticum* was dissolving into the positions and rights of the factions—that is, of the popes, the cardinals, the general councils, the 'nations' within the council, and the national councils—and it was dissolving into ordinary jurisdictions and emergency measures" (*CW,* 21:250).

The Conciliar Movement did result in the realization of what was, at the time, an accomplished fact. As a result of the Gallican movement toward institutional autonomy of the French church, the Council of Constance promulgated the notion of "national concordats," agreements between the papacy and the national churches controlled by their respective sovereigns. "The concordats were . . . a revolutionary innovation. The idea of the *sacrum imperium,* which contains the spiritual and temporal powers as *ordines* within its mystical body, was now definitely destroyed. The church appears as an autonomous society that can enter into contractual relations with the secular realms." And while Voegelin is correct in saying that the "recognition of this new relationship between the church and the secular powers . . . was the most important permanent result of the conciliar period," it must be understood also as, essentially and simply, the overdue acknowledgment of a situation that had already been in existence for some time prior to the convention of the first council (*CW,* 21:255).

The Church and the Nations in History

In chapter three we had occasion to note the twin planes upon which the course of Western civilization has moved from the emergence of the Christian order to the present. The upper plane consists of the established institutions; the lower plane, that of those social groups and forces that exist in opposition to those institutions. In the later Middle Ages, the conflict between these two institutions and their opponents would become increasingly problematic for the maintenance of public order. In many ways, the situation of the church from the early fourteenth century through the Great Reformation was similar to that which confronted Saint Paul in the propagation of the faith.

Through the vessel of the compromises with the world Paul had created the conditions for the expansion of the Christian community throughout the Roman world. However, Paul's "imperial idea of Christianity" and its creation in the Roman world was never "realized in history." The major impediment to its realization was "the national and civilizational diversification of mankind." Voegelin notes that while the "nations of the Mediterranean and the Near Eastern world had succumbed to the conquests of Alexander and Rome politically . . . their individualities were strong enough to reassert themselves in the contact with Christianity and to split the unity of the kingdom of God into several Christian churches" (*CW,* 19:174).

This understanding points to two areas of consideration. The first is the changing nature of political order in light of the experience of conquest and empire. Second, there is the confrontation of the early church with the natural diversity of humanity.

With regard to the first, it is interesting that Voegelin begins his study of "political" ideas with and exploration of the "Problem of Apolitism" (*CW,* 19:70–74). In the context of the overall study, Voegelin's concern in the introductory chapter is to explain the rise of the Hellenic "schools" as the receptors of the drive for a meaningful community life for those who have experienced the implosion of the *polis.* The issue of apolitism is critical also to understanding the changing perception of politics that created the world within which Christianity emerged.

Examining the conquests of Alexander the Great (d. 323 B.C.), Voegelin observes that "the technical performance of the conquest was not backed by an idea, and . . . the unit of conquest, which could hardly be called an empire, dissolved into smaller units after the exhilaration of the conquering drive was exhausted. The conquered peoples, widely divergent in their civilizations, had not been welded into a new political unit, and nothing indicated that this aim could be achieved at the time" (*CW,* 19:90–91). With the drive to empire and the expansion of the imperial order, the orientation of social and political life was transformed. No longer was political order dependent upon a conception of "the people," understood in relation to other groups of people external to the social community. Rather, political life was determined by relations of power. What had occurred with the institution of imperial order was, as Voegelin puts it, "the dissociation of the power structure from the people." In the new dispensation of the imperial orders, Voegelin writes,

> Politics was no longer seen as the internal affair of an unquestioned community, but as a movement of power structures on a world scale expressed by the new categories of the vicissitudes of history and of fortune. The imperial organizations and the men dominating them had lost what roots they had in the life of a people; power became a game in the abstract to be played by professionals, while millions of people could do nothing but bow and dodge in order to escape the worst blows of the storm raging over them. (*CW,* 19:120–21)

Despite the bowing and dodging, conquered peoples were quite capable of maintaining a sense of themselves as a "people" separate and distinct from those who had conquered them and from others similarly situated in a condition of subservience to the imperial order. As a particular political organization, the "empire was primarily a power apparatus, not the manifestation of the political will of a people" (*CW,* 19:178). Particular peoples, therefore, did not simply cease to be.

This problem was one of which Alexander himself was acutely aware. Voegelin recounts Alexander's prayer at Opis for *homonoia* between the Macedonians and the Persians as an attempt to create "a spiritual substance" for the empire he was seeking to create. Voegelin maintains, "The idea of Alexander may not have gone beyond a desire to fuse the Macedonian and Persian aristocracies into one. Nevertheless it marks the beginning of a great development. Homonoia became the basic community concept of the Hellenistic and later of the Roman world . . . and through the Epistles of Saint Paul the idea became one of the founding elements of democracy." However, while "Alexander was strong enough to shatter the old world materially . . . it took more than Alexander to create a new one spiritually" (*CW,* 19:91–95).

More important, perhaps, is that the prayer of Alexander at Opis is an illustration of what had changed in the field of sentiments by the time of the consolidation of Rome. The Stoics had conceived of the idea of the "cosmopolis," the world community that exists between wise individuals who see the divine spark of the *koinos nomos,* the logos of the universe in one another (*CW,* 19:97–98). As such, the cosmopolis is incapable of being realized as a political order in the world, since it exists solely for the wise person capable of recognizing the attributes of the divine in other wise people.

In Cicero (d. 43 B.C.) we see the transformation of the idea of the cosmopolis into the idea of Roman order itself. Cicero observes a "generic equality of men as a consequence of their equal participation in the divine logos; the universe is a community of God and men." But the cosmopolis of the Stoics is not solely the province of the wise; it exists, and its name is Rome.

> Cicero was able to merge the idea of Rome into the idea of the cosmopolis, and thus to bridge with sublime complacency the problems that had been the torment of Greek political theory. The ideal state is no problem for Cicero; he does not have to create it out of his soul; he just has to look around him: Rome is the ideal state; all he has to do is to describe the constitution and the civil and religious law of Rome. . . . Rome is the ideal materialized; the Stoic problem of making the cosmopolis compatible with the coexistence of a multitude of finite states is solved through the actuality of the ideal Rome. . . . The *imperium Romanum* has grown into the cosmopolis; the Stoic idea that man has two fatherlands, that of his birth and the city of the world, has evolved into the formula that man has two fatherlands, the countryside of his birth and Rome. (*CW,* 19:134–35)

The Ciceronian equation of the cosmopolis with Rome itself makes the question of the spiritual substance of the community irrelevant.

"Through the myth of Cicero, Rome has become more than Rome; it has become the political order in the absolute, accepted as it is, as a part of the universe, not to be questioned in its right to existence as a whole, nor in its mode of existence. The people exist, and the government exists; no inquiry into the material or spiritual conditions of the existence of a political community is either desirable or necessary" (*CW,* 19:136). For this reason, Cicero is the exemplar of the change in attitude that confronted Paul. Voegelin notes that the "profound difference between the Greek and the Roman spirit can find no symbol more eloquent than the difference between the attitude of Alexander, who prayed at Opis to the Gods for homonoia between the Greeks and barbarians, and the attitude of Cicero, who believed that the legions would do the job" (*CW,* 19:197).

However, the problem of the maintenance of order in the absence of some degree of spiritual cohesion is a problem that cannot be whisked away by rhetorical fiat. Rome may exist, but it exists as a system of power only: it lacked an internal justification for its existence. Thus "the public appearance of Jesus" occurred when, in Voegelin's words,

> the time was certainly "ripe" for something to happen—within Judaea in the atmosphere of eschatological tension, and within the Hellenic world with its epochal consciousness that neither the decaying local cults nor the machinery of the Roman administration could satisfy as to its spiritual substance. A world empire had come into existence as a power organization, but there was no spiritually coherent people corresponding to the vast organizational range; to be exact: the Roman empire had only a population, it did not have a people. (*CW,* 19:150)

The Pauline vision of the Christian community infusing Rome with the vitality of its new life as the kingdom of God would seem to satisfy the requirement—provided, of course, that Paul and the early Church could find a way to overcome the national and civilizational diversity of humanity that had frustrated Alexander. Paul himself was frustrated in the attempt, but the idea had been reborn with the infusion of Stoic theory into Christianity and its transformation into the core element in the evocation of the *sacrum imperium.*

Paul, of course, had firsthand experience with the problem posed by the diversity of humanity. Voegelin cites Paul's complaint in 1 Corinthians 1:22–24: "The Jews want signs and the Greeks seek wisdom, but we preach the crucified Christ; that is a scandal to the Jews and a folly to the nations; to those, however, who are called, be they Jews or Greeks, Christ is the power of God and the wisdom of God" (*CW,* 19:174). The particular issue that prompted the outburst, the practice of Hellenistic pneumatics of "speaking in tongues," is emblematic of the problems faced by Paul. In spreading the news of the new kingdom he was dealing with a conglomeration of ethnic and national groups, each with some degree of cultural distinctiveness that they brought to the table. As the Christian message was taken out of Judea and into the larger world, the problem became more apparent. As Voegelin points out, "Wherever Christianity penetrated, the regional and national traditions produced variations of the Christian experience that became the seeds of schisms" (*CW,* 19:176).

Sectarian Movements

By the later Middle Ages, this problem would reemerge through the increasing sectarianism of population groups throughout Europe. Sectarian movements were problematic because they were legitimate expressions of the need for spiritual order beyond that represented by the existing institution of the church. As Voegelin notes,

> The objectification of the spirit in the sacerdotal and sacramental institution, the adaptation to the exigencies of the world, the gradualism of spiritual realization—all this is certainly an authentic unfolding of the potentialities of Christianity. Nevertheless, developments in an entirely different direction are possible. It is equally possible to develop Christianity in the direction of an uncompromising realization of the evangelical counsels, of renouncing the universalism of the institution, and of concentrating on the realization of the spirit in small communities with high standards of personal religiousness and moral conduct. Within the history of Christianity, there is always possible the return from the apocalyptic to the eschatological mood, from the objective sacramental institution to the intense personal religiousness of the small group, from the compromises with the world to an

uncompromising evangelical Christianity, from the universal church to the small sect. We must recognize church and sect as equally authentic manifestations of Christianity, if we wish to understand the dynamic force for the sectarian movements in their struggle with the church; only because they are authentic Christian movements can they demand a reform of the church and can they threaten the very institution of the church by the demand for a more perfect realization of Christianity. (*CW,* 22:142)

This potential became more realizable because of the reemergence of the national core as an identifiable point of focus. It is not merely a matter of the cupidity of Henry VIII that the Church of England became, for all intents and purposes, the first church to break away from the universal church. The rupture had more to do with the peculiar geography of England that gave its people a greater sense of national consciousness. Even in this, however, the Catholic Church contributed to the break through its own intransigence in the face of royal opposition (see *CW,* 21:166–68).

However, the "organizational resistance of the realms against the centralized church administration, which is known as Anglicanism and Gallicanism, would not have been possible unless a profound restructuring of religious sentiment had taken place in the direction of . . . parochial Christianity" (*CW,* 21:168). In other words, the organized resistance of the emerging realms in opposition to the dictates of the universal church takes place against the backdrop of a preexisting sectarianism within the general population.

We have noted the capacity of the church in the early days of the *imperium* to absorb reformist and sectarian impulses into it through the monastic reforms. And it was the breakdown in this ability that helped bring about an end to the dream of universal Christendom. As Dawson observes, "the breach between the papacy and the spiritual reformers is the vital cause of the decline of the medieval Church and is one of the main factors in the dissolution of the medieval unity and the transformation that passed over Europe in the later Middle Ages."[9]

9. Dawson, "Medieval Theology," in *Medieval Essays,* 113.

Yet in many ways, the monastic reforms become a contributing factor in the disorder apparent in universal Christendom as we move into the fourteenth and fifteenth centuries. The mendicant orders had successfully spiritualized the population, but those same orders were becoming increasingly incapable of controlling the spiritual movements they unleashed.

> The Franciscans could absorb in their ranks . . . a proportion of the religiously moved people of the towns. And both orders, the Franciscans and the Dominicans, could, through their missionary work spreading over Europe, control an appreciable part of the people and attach their sentiments through their orders to the church. But a not inconsiderable part of the movement escaped such control and developed into the heretical sects. As far as these sects remained small and localized, they do not concern us in this context. But parallel with the foundation of the mendicant order a social form of the movement began to appear in outlines that prognosticate the later events of the pre-Reformation and the Reformation. (*CW,* 21:171–72)

Yet the Franciscans themselves demonstrated the dangerous storm that was gathering against the established order of the church. Dawson notes that the "decline in the unity of the church can be identified in its earliest manifestation. . . . [I]n the extreme wing of the Franciscan order, the followers of John Peter Olivi [d. 1298] and Angelo Clareno [d. 1337], and the disruption of the Franciscan movement is the first sign of the approaching disruption of medieval Christendom."[10] Regarding the Franciscans specifically, Voegelin argues, "The very success" of the order in the "channeling of the movement" led to

> a revival of the movement character within the order. With the institutionalizaton, the inevitable degenerative symptoms of routinization and abuse began to appear, and a radical spiritual wing within the order attempted to restore the pristine character of the movement. This wing of the Franciscan Spirituals was finally forced out of the order by the Conventuals; the Spirituals outside the order split

10. Ibid., 114.

into smaller groups, were persecuted as heretics, and disappeared in the fourteenth century, while the order itself degenerated to the point that, for a while, it became an outstanding scandal in the life of the church. (*CW,* 22:149–50)[11]

Thus, the very success of the reformist impulse could serve as an impetus to crush it, both within the order and under the rubric of the larger community of the church. Or, to put it another way, the institutionalization of the idea brings with it a complex of problems, not least of which is the degree to which the idea can be realized in light of changing circumstances and determined opposition.

Voegelin observes that the struggle among the Franciscans is a microcosmic glimpse of what was occurring generally within the European world. The proximate cause of the conflict of the papacy with the Franciscan community concerned the ideal of poverty. Put in its simplest terms, it revolved around whether or not extreme poverty was a requirement for living a life in conformance with Christ. By the middle of the fourteenth century, the argument had devolved into a "legal dispute." Voegelin sees in this an indication that the "Christian substance was getting thinner and thinner; in the great process of despiritualization of Christianity we have seen the hand of God in the translation of empire change into a legal transaction, we have seen the spiritual reform of the church hardening into ecclesiastical legalism, and we see now the life of Christ and the apostles discussed in terms of private and communal property." Ultimately, of course, those involved in the conflicts were unable to see what Voegelin sees as the essential problem. "Both partners to the struggle were wrong; neither is the kingdom of Christ a temporal principality bristling with regalia as the papal legalist wanted it, nor is the eschatological indifference toward property of the early Christians a form of communism as the general of the Franciscans would have it in the interest of the intramundane poverty ideal of his order" (*CW,* 21:114). The kingdom of God remains "not of this world," although the faithful must endure this world in communion with the unseen yet present kingdom.

---

11. On the history of the Franciscan Spirituals, see Burr, *The Spiritual Franciscans: From Protest to Persecution in the Century after Saint Francis.*

With the hardening of the church, the capacity to absorb the movements was in decline. Furthermore, the accretion of dogmatic positions by the church presented a problem insofar as its capacity to reform itself in response to exigent circumstances became increasingly more difficult. Voegelin notes "that the degree of absorptiveness was very high until 1300 and declined decisively after this date. Up to 1300 the church was still capable of grappling with its problems, on the whole. The most notable feat was the absorption of popular religious movements of the early thirteenth century into the church by means of the new mendicant orders" (CW, 22:136).

Even before 1300 the direction of the church had been telescoped through the suppression of the Albigensians in the thirteenth century and the subsequent creation of the Inquisition.[12] Voegelin argues, "we should . . . note that the Albigensian Crusade shows a grave weakness with regard to absorptiveness, precisely because it was conducted with complete military success to the destruction of the Albigensian movement" (CW, 22:136). The Albigensian movement, however, had features that were absent from most heretical movements prior to 1300.

> In the case of the Albigensians, a heretical movement spread through the towns of a large region, the Provence, and found favor with the regional nobility. This is the first instance in which a new religious movement, outside the church, penetrated a cultural area and rose above the level of its origin in the towns into the ruling nobility. The Provence had a culture, but it was not a realm; if it had remained undisturbed it might have developed into a realm and a Provençal nation might have grown.

Thus while the "Albigensian movement does not have the characteristics of a national struggle that are typical of the later regional movements in England, Bohemia, and Germany . . . we have to classify it, nevertheless, as the first in the series of upheavals that resulted in the parochialization of Christianity" (CW, 21:172). This parochialization would gain increased impetus by the emerging nation states and the growing sense

12. See Clifton, *Encyclopedia of Heresies and Heretics*, 6–12; O'Grady, *Heresy*, 64–72; Joseph R. Strayer, *The Albigensian Crusades*.

of national consciousness held by members of the various communities. Indeed, the Hussite rebellion was a nationalist movement hidden behind the veil of a religious heresy, and some have argued that the Albigensian Crusades were in fact a political maneuver on the part of the Capets to gain control of southern France.[13] Be that as it may, Voegelin maintains:

> We may say . . . that the organization of the realm and nationalism were the factors, still missing in the Abigensian case, that provided the ethical, civilizational, and political foundation for the continuous evolution toward parochial Christianity, although the religious movement was not yet strong enough to accomplish the ecclesiastical schism. More precisely, the weakness of the movement can be defined as the inability of the pre-Reformation leaders to unify the forces of sectarianism and to direct them into the foundation of parochial counterchurches to the church of Rome. (*CW*, 21:174)

The movement to the towns and the changing social structure of the feudal world brought on by the town movement helped to provide the organizational infrastructure that had been lacking in the sectarian movements against the established church. The reliance of the population upon the newly established centers of the rural economy provided a fertile ground for religious and social movements to coalesce. Voegelin notes that most sectarian movements are rooted in towns and are intimately connected to them. This is because the town became the enclave of feudal society in which the great leveling of corporate existence occurred. For this reason, the spread of social and sectarian movements tended to follow the regional emergence of towns themselves. Furthermore, in the process of the movement—a process that would go beyond the purely religious and into the secular world of modernity—it is the intellectually sophisticated member of the bourgeois class that would be essential to the movement. As Voegelin argues, "The middle class in the towns is the nourishing center of the movements. In critical periods, however, this center can radiate its unrest into other sectors of society and the movement can find support from almost any group with momentary grievances against the established institutions" (*CW*, 22:150).

13. Madaule, *The Albigensian Crusade: An Historical Essay.*

The fact that the town should become the center of revolutionary fervor should be of no surprise, given the revolutionary nature of the institution itself. "The town," Voegelin argues,

> obviously was more than just another form of government; it was rather a new mode of life determining a type of political man who differed radically from the ruling as well as from the subject types of the feudal order—that is, from the noble, the ecclesiastic, and the peasant. The town was, furthermore, not a mere addition to the feudal world, but rather the representative of a new phase of Western civilization. Historical dynamics were on the side of the economic services, the rationality of business and politics, the amenities of luxury, the superior intellectual aliveness, the advancement of literacy, the arts and the sciences, and the active religiousness of the towns. It is this civilizational style of the towns that entered into rivalry with the style of the primary estates and was ultimately to dominate our civilization. (*CW,* 21:218–19)

The town was a revolutionary system of social order; but it would be more remarkable if the town had not realized itself as the source of revolutionary disorder. It would be from the archetypal town of Voegelin's presentation, the Italian city-state, that speculation concerning a new order of power would emerge through the work of a man whose name "still lies in the shadow of moralistic condemnation," Niccolò Machiavelli (*CW,* 22:31).

Machiavelli as the New Man

What Voegelin sees in Machiavelli (d. 1527) as "historically unique" is the convergence of "the peculiar constellation of circumstances" and "the genius of Machiavelli" that was "bent . . . toward crystallizing the ideas of the age in the symbol of the prince who, through *fortuna* and *virtù,* will be the savior and restorer of Italy" (*CW,* 22:32). As for the characterization of Machiavelli that stems solely from the posthumous publication of *The Prince,* it is an obstacle that must be overcome in order to understand Machiavelli in light of the circumstances in which he found himself. Voegelin does recognize that, with qualifications: "All we can retain from the caricature is the consciousness that something extraordinary had

occurred, a severe break with the traditions for treating political questions—that with the author of the *Prince* we have passed the threshold
into a new, 'modern' era" (*CW,* 22:31). As Frederick Vaughan observes
with regard to Machiavelli, "The key word which permeates Machiavelli's
writings is 'new'; whether it be a 'wholly new Prince,' or a 'wholly new
regime,' or 'new modes and orders,' there can be no doubt that Machiavelli
understood himself to be involved in the great task of a new founding, a
new beginning."[14]

What makes Machiavelli seem so new, so modern, are the circumstances in which he grappled with the problems of order. As Voegelin
points out,

> The medieval *Christianitas* was falling apart into the church and the
> national states. . . . The disintegration of the *Christianitas* affected
> both the spiritual and the temporal order insofar as in both spheres
> the common spirit that induces effective cooperation between per-
> sons in spite of divergence of interests, as well as the sense of an
> obligation to compromise in the spirit of the whole, was seeping
> out. The "falling apart" means literally the breaking up of a spiri-
> tually animated whole into legal jurisdictions; it means the inflex-
> ible insistence on rights, and the pursuit of personal and institutional
> interests without regard to the destruction of the total order. (*CW,*
> 22:34–35)

The new existential representative of spiritual cohesion had assumed the
form of a monarchy and was increasingly impervious to internal reform
in light of changing circumstances. The temporal orders were reforming
in the nation states as the old "field of personal, feudal associations was
disentangled and the old political units were consolidated in the national,
territorial realms" (*CW,* 22:35) of England, France and Spain. However,
the warring states of the Italian peninsula were unable to reach a similar situation with their European neighbors and were thus an easy target for the ambitions of the new European monarchs. Some four hundred
years later, Abraham Lincoln would consider the disorder of his historical circumstance and assert, "As our case is new, so we must think anew,

14. Vaughan, *The Tradition of Political Hedonism,* 21.

and act anew."[15] It was in that same spirit that Machiavelli undertook to address the problem of order.

In shaping his new approach to the problems of politics, Machiavelli was aided by a revolution in historiography brought on by the redis- covery of Asia. The main import of the new historiography was to call into question the validity of the universal historical model of Christianized Europe. Voegelin argues, "Roman Christian universalism with its linear construction of history is now seriously disturbed by the emergence of Asiatic powers and of an Asiatic 'parallel' history" (*CW,* 22:51). This re- discovery of the East in turn reinforced the move toward the increasing secularization of the political world by making Christian history itself relative to the history of other powers. Voegelin notes that the

> rise of Ottoman power, and the episode of Timur, had traumatic consequences for the Western idea of politics. Even before the shock of 1494[16] the Italians had formed the idea of nihilistic, ra- tional power as an absolute force cutting its swath blindly across meaningful existence. Moreover, through the Near Eastern events, Asiatic history had become a fact that no longer could be overlooked; the imperial finality of the West lost its magic of absoluteness when the Turks were *ante portas*. . . . The structure of this new historical situation was understood in classical images . . . the reactivation of the Homeric and Herodotean mythical conflict in Europe, as well as the use of classic formulas in describing the new Xerxes. The

---

15. Abraham Lincoln, 2nd Annual Address to Congress, Dec. 1, 1862, in *Speeches and Writings, 1859–1865.*

16. The reduction of the Italian city states to complete political impotence was a re- sult of French, Spanish, and German invaders, which Voegelin describes as making no sense "in terms of a reduction of a poor, backward colonial region by economically pro- gressive countries; neither did it make sense in terms of a social revolution, perhaps the rise of a third estate, or a populist uprising; neither were any issues of moral or political principles involved; neither was there any question of a religious movement, as later in the wars of the Reformation. In brief: economics, morals, principles of social justice, ideas concerning political organization, spiritual movements, or religious factions had nothing to do with the event; it was a clear case of a stronger power and better military organization in ruthless victory over a weaker and militarily less-well-equipped power" (*CW,* 22:36–37).

search for the typical, furthermore, determined the twisting and se-
lecting of historical materials in such a manner that it would fit the
established system of classification. And behind the use of history
for understanding the typical in the events, we could . . . discern
the attempt at penetrating into the mystery of power and destruction through the creation of the mythical image of the *terror gen-
tium* beyond good and evil. (*CW,* 22:54–55)

This is the source of the "myth of order through intramundane power"
that Voegelin argues lies at the heart of Machiavelli's examinations of politics and the problems of political order (*CW,* 22:59). "The experience of
crushing power has sharpened the awareness of the fact that the order
of a polity ultimately is the manifestation of an existential force beyond
good and evil," writes Voegelin.

The stronger force will break the weaker existence, however high
its rank may be in the realm of civilizational values. The response
to this experience, however, is not a naturalistic nihilism that would
deny the meaning of power and order. The weaker order, while physically crushed, still is a meaningful human order and not a natural
phenomenon; and the stronger order, while physically crushing, is
not a natural catastrophe, but the force of organized human existence. The stronger existence, while crushing the weaker order, establishes itself as the power that maintains the new human order.
Hence, the response to the experience is a heightening of the human existence that destroys and creates order into a mythical image. . . . The *virtù* of the conquering prince becomes the source of
order; and since the Christian, transcendental order of existence
had become a dead letter for the Italian thinkers of the fifteenth
century, the *virtù ordinata* of the prince, as the principle of the only
order that is experienced as real, acquires human-divine, heroic pro-
portions. (*CW,* 22:55–56)

Furthermore, the opening of the historical horizon, the breaking of
the Pauline compromise with history, had the added effect of bringing
into focus anew the problem of history. Voegelin argues that the emergence of the problem of Asia created a situation in which a "world scene
of politics had opened, with a structure of its own, and the idea of the

Christian *imperium* had become irrelevant. When the meaning of history in the sense of Saint Augustine's *civitas Dei* disappears, the 'natural' structure of history, in the ancient sense, becomes visible again" (*CW,* 22:85). Hence Machiavelli's recourse to the ancient perception of cyclical history and natural recurrence, as they appeared in Polybius, in which *virtù* and *fortuna* are the primary agents of historical change.

For Machiavelli, borrowing again from Polybius, the existence of human beings in society is part of the cosmic cycles governed by *virtù* and *fortuna.* "The nature of man is for Machiavelli part of the nature of political society in history. Hence, the constancy of the passions determines recurrences in the gestalt of history" (*CW,* 22:61). And while the "great Christian orienting experience of morality, the *amor Dei,* has disappeared . . . that does not mean that now the *amor sui* has become the determinant of action. The *virtù* of the hero is the substantive force that drives toward expression in the order of the republic; it is not a self-centered lust for power" (*CW,* 22:64).

Indeed, it is the task of the prince to orient the *virtù* of the citizens toward the society and the common good, which is exactly where religion, and Christianity in particular, comes into conflict with the society. Machiavelli subordinates the church not only because it has been an obstacle to the achievement of Italian unity, which it was, but also, in the words of J. G. A. Pocock, "on the grounds that it gives men other than civic values."[17] In Machiavelli's view, Voegelin writes, "the misery of Italy is caused by the decay of Christianity; this in its turn is caused by the degenerate papacy. . . . Not only is the corruption of religion through the papacy a problem, but the value of Christianity itself is in doubt" (*CW,* 22:68).

Voegelin notes Machiavelli's famous disquisition regarding why the ancients loved freedom more than do the moderns.[18] Whereas the pagans had valued honor most highly, "Christianity values humility, renunciation, and contempt of human affairs; the ancients valued greatness of soul, strength of body, and everything else that makes a man strong. Christianity wants a man to show his strength in suffering rather than in

17. Pocock, *The Machiavellian Moment,* 192.
18. Machiavelli, *The Discourses.* The standard study of Machiavelli's political thought remains Strauss, *Thoughts on Machiavelli.* Strauss's discussion of Machiavelli and religion may be found at 225–32.

doing strong deeds. This way of life has made the world weak and a prey to the rascals" (*CW,* 22:68). However, Machiavelli is perceptive enough to know that the problem lies, not with the faith itself, but rather with the expositors of it who have, according to his account, weakened it. "Hence the false interpretation rather than Christianity itself is the cause of the diminished love of freedom" (*CW,* 22:69). This diagnosis of the problem of Christian action may be what lies at the heart of Voegelin's generally positive analysis of Machiavelli's political thought in conjunction with Machiavelli's realization that the "community needs a sacramental bond" in order to exist (*CW,* 22:70).

The fundamental problem with Machiavelli's political program, however, is an ontological one. In trying to create his new republic, Machiavelli called upon the wisdom of the ancients regarding history and, more important, the myth of nature contained therein. Of course, the

> only flaw in this system—of which Machiavelli himself was very much aware—is the fact that we do not live in Hellenic Roman antiquity but in Western Christian civilization. The metaphysic of cosmic force and the myth of *virtù* make sense only under the condition that the *onore del mondo* is religiously accepted as the *summum bonum.* When the *summum bonum* is placed in the beatific vision of God, then the honor of the world sinks to second rank in the hierarchy of values, and not the heroic, ordering manifestation of cosmic force but the *amor Dei* will become the orienting principle of conduct. On this point, Machiavelli is insecure. He recognizes the fact of Christianity; but his own soul is closed against it; the fact is dead. (*CW,* 22:70)

The fact that Machiavelli was not "a solitary figure, something like a moral freak" (*CW,* 22:31) is what makes him a compelling representative of what had happened to the notion of universal Christian order. The attempt by Machiavelli to reestablish the order of society on the basis of a new paganism was doomed to failure because its time had passed. Voegelin argues: "Once Christianity is in the world and has formed a civilization, one cannot simply turn around and be a pagan—and a pre-Platonic one at that. The call has gone to all; and Machiavelli cannot be excepted. In its historical place, the paganism of Machiavelli is not the 'people's myth' that Plato strove to overcome; it is a lack of faith in the Christian sense, a demonic closure of the soul against transcendental reality" (*CW*, 22:86). In this respect, Machiavelli may in fact be the first representative of "modern man."[19]

Conclusion

Machiavelli may have been the first modern man, but the world itself was still clinging to the dream of the *imperium*. Some great event would have to occur to bring modern man to the stage of history. In this instance, that "event" would be a confluence of events called the Great Reformation.

19. This is not to say, however, that Machiavelli had not correctly seen the shape of the future. See, for example, Gay, *The Enlightenment: An Interpretation,* in which he argues that the Enlightenment of the eighteenth century represents the triumph of a new paganism.

CHAPTER FIVE

Crisis

Existence in Tension

Machiavelli had clearly seen that something was wrong, yet he lacked the spiritual and intellectual resources required to create a new evocation commensurate with the crisis of order in which he found himself. Indeed, in large measure, Machiavelli had failed to fully comprehend the meaning of the crisis engendered by the collapse of the *imperium*. However, while Machiavelli himself was impervious to the pull of the golden cord, he did have one profound insight that must have been somewhat redemptive for him in Voegelin's perception. Machiavelli, Voegelin asserts, "understood quite clearly that Christianity is living by reformation" (*CW*, 22:86). Voegelin's phrasing needs explication in two important senses that are critical to an understanding of his approach to the problems of Christian political order.

In the first instance, the life lived by reformation is an understanding that is couched in terms of the individual existence of the human being under God. It is an oblique reference to the experience of faith and the resulting *metanoia,* or turning, that occurs in the believer as a result of the call of the spirit. It is the understanding of Saint Paul as expressed in 2 Corinthians, "Therefore, if anyone is in Christ, he is a new creation; the old has gone, the new has come!" (2 Cor. 5:17). The experience of the reformed human being, the reformed personality in its contact with the transcendent spirit of Christ, is what makes Christian *homonoia* possible and establishes the ground of cooperation between individuals toward the realization of the spiritual kingdom announced by Christ and instituted by Saint Paul.

The second sense of living by reformation is a reference to the political and social life of Christian civilization generally. As a result of Saint Paul's judicious compromises with the world and the sacramental objectification of grace through the administration of the sacraments in the church, Christianity had become one of the most powerful social forces in history. It had succeeded in expanding the "little world of order," which Voegelin maintains is the essential function of the political idea, to encompass most of Europe and, with the discovery of the New World, beyond. This expansion had been made possible, in large measure, as a result of the fleshing out of the compromises through successive reformations that were internalized within the institutional structures of the church. When the church began to close itself off to the possibility of reformation through the absorption of reform movements, the tension between the kingdom of God as a spiritual condition of the community of the faithful and the institutional representation of that kingdom in the church itself became unbearable.

In the introduction to the *History of Political Ideas,* Voegelin observes that in "any system of political ideas" there exists a "basic conflict between the finite character of the cosmion and the absoluteness at which it aims" (*CW,* 19:227). The proclamation of the kingdom of God presented just such a conflict for the existence of human beings in the world. Since the kingdom of God was not of this earth, the cosmion created by the Pauline compromises and the objectification of grace through the institution of the church was problematic to the extent that the immanent representative of the transcendent kingdom conformed to the spiritual understanding of the kingdom. It was this understanding of the tension between the two realms that prompted Saint Augustine to argue that the *civitas Dei* was not the church itself.

Instead, the institutional order of the church was itself the result of the initial compromises Saint Paul made with the world in the constitution of the Christian community. First, Paul had welcomed the people of Israel, the pagans, and the followers of Jesus of Nazareth into the community through the compromise with history that recognized the law of nature as it was revealed to the pagans and the law of the prophets as it was revealed to Israel. Second, Paul had incorporated the members of the community into the organic construction of the *corpus mysticum* by which the charisma of Christ could be shared among the members of the community, each according to his or her gifts. And to make the new community adaptable to any society in which it might find itself, Paul compromised with governmental authority, recognizing that authority was ordained by God to wield the sword against evildoers and those who would disturb the peace of the community. Saint Augustine had contributed to the constitution of the community with the construction of the two cities and the bifurcation of history into sacred and profane. It was through these compromises that Christianity was institutionalized and civilized the European continent.

The crisis of the Great Reformation was always a possibility that existed as a result of that tension. Indeed, the Great Reformation itself, as Voegelin asserts, is really only a "phase" in a "much more comprehensive process" (*CW,* 22:131). Thus far we have examined the process from the perspective of the emergence of the Christian community around the person of Jesus himself, and the reaction of his followers to his death and resurrection. In addition, we have noted the partial realization of the Christian idea of the universal empire through the evocation of the *sacrum imperium* as the organizing principle of order throughout the Middle Ages. With regard to the *imperium,* we have noticed the problems created by the irruption of intramundane forces upon the structure of the idea and the institutions intended to represent it. More particularly, we have examined the changing perception of immanent history with regard to the drama of salvation and the capacity of the institutional church to grow through reform. Finally, we have discussed the actual destruction of the *sacrum imperium* as a force for order. In large measure this was the result of changing political and social circumstances on the part of temporal authority, but this does not absolve the institutional church for its role in the debacle. The destruction of the *sacrum imperium* was precipitated not only by the hubris of Frederick II but also by the decreasing permeability of the church as the immanent representative of the Christian dispensation into an arbiter of dogmatic truth that increasingly lacked the capacity to absorb spiritual movements.

In this chapter, we will examine the great political, religious, and social upheaval of the Great Reformation from the perspective of Voegelin's

History of Political Ideas. First we will examine Voegelin's treatment of Martin Luther and John Calvin as they sought to usher in a new age of the spirit with disastrous results for the institutional order of the spirit and order generally. Essentially, the ultimate problem with the Great Reformation from Voegelin's perspective is not simply that the great reformers stood in opposition to the universal church—there is little pity for the church itself in Voegelin's presentation—but rather that in Luther and Calvin there exists the propensity to burn the village in order to save it. However, Luther and Calvin are reflective of the social and spiritual pressures that were building in opposition to the institutional church and the order of civilization that it represented.

The Tyconian problem has not disappeared. Indeed, if anything, the Tyconian problem is the root of the general problem of modernity. This is especially true when the puritanical drive of the Tyconian program is transferred to the new secular carriers of the spirit that will emerge as a result of the Great Reformation. The rise of sectarian movements in opposition to the established institutionalization of the spirit is the great problem of Christian political order. And to the degree that this religious sectarianism is made manifest in a political program, it can result in the wholesale destruction of order itself and represents an assault upon the very idea of civilization. In the rise of the ideological religions of modernity, however, Western Christian civilization would find itself disarmed because of the privatization of the spirit through the idea of toleration expressed by John Locke.

In light of the examination of people and events up to the actualization of the political, religious, and social movement that comes to us under the rubric of the Great Reformation, the event itself is something of an anticlimax. As we have seen from the study thus far, the Great Reformation is in many ways reflective of an event that had already occurred but had yet to crystallize into new institutions. To use the language of Voegelin's early works, the ideas for new evocations were there, but the institutional representation of those ideas had yet to emerge. In the institutionalization of the spirit in history, the church had failed. Luther and Calvin, as well as the generation of "reformers" who immediately followed them, thought that a new institutionalization of the spirit was needed. What most often occurred, however, was not the elevation of the spiritual life of human beings through a new evocation of order, but rather evocations that would seek to eliminate the life of the spirit from political and social existence.

Machiavelli is important in understanding what was going to happen because, as we have argued, he was the first modern man. As the first modern man, he was still the man alone, despite being representative of the tenor of sentiment at the time. For the modern man to be the determinant of history would require a reformulation of human existence in general and the relationship of human beings to the comprehensive order of reality in particular. Unfortunately, in making this reformulation, Luther and Calvin would abandon the Christian idea of human being as it was initially understood by Saint Paul and then later elaborated upon and expanded by Saint Augustine and Saint Thomas Aquinas.

This understanding of the problem is what underscores Voegelin's rather vitriolic reflections upon Luther and Calvin. It is important to note that the fourth volume of the *History of Political Ideas* is the only book of the series that comes with the equivalent of a "Surgeon General's Warning" from the editors. The purpose of "A Note on Voegelin's Reading of Luther and Calvin," written by David L. Morse and William M. Thompson, seems to be an attempt to mitigate against the potential indignation of the reader that might accrue from Voegelin's interpretation of two of the founders of modern Protestantism.[1]

Such a warning was thought to be required because of Voegelin's near brutal assault upon Luther and Calvin. Voegelin traces most of the social and political disorder from modernity and places it squarely on the doorstep of Luther and Calvin. In large measure, Voegelin's analysis is correct. However, in many ways the very tenor of Voegelin's argument obscures a clear understanding of the legitimate issues raised in the context of the analysis. Ultimately, the reason Voegelin seemingly loathes Luther and Calvin stems from their success in feeding the sectarian impulses that led to their own work. In other words, Luther and Calvin were reflective of their time and the social forces that were at work.[2]

---

1. Morse and Thompson, "Editors' Introduction," in *CW,* 22:15–20.

2. It is important to note in this context that Voegelin himself had been baptized a Lutheran and buried a Lutheran. In other words, his argument with Luther cannot be read as a polemic in favor of Roman Catholicism.

The Folly of Martin Luther

In the case of Luther, Voegelin's presentation is of a man who should have known better—and might have known but we cannot really be sure—the implications of what he was trying to accomplish.[3] Luther does not rise to the level of an "intellectual swindler," which would be the epithet that Voegelin would apply later to Karl Marx in the analysis of Marx's ideological program.[4] The first problem with Luther, from Voegelin's perspective, is his willingness to throw the baby out with the bathwater in terms of his anti-scholasticism. Luther's animus toward the theological and philosophical history that preceded him restricted the horizon of his own work and had severe consequences for the general tenor and implications of what he accomplished. Luther had correctly diagnosed the spiritual crisis of his time; however, he was either unwilling or unable to use the tools at his disposal to address it.

The proximate issue that thrust Luther into a position of prominence was the sale of indulgences by the church. Indulgences were viewed by the church as a source of revenue and as the repudiation of temporal punishment imposed by the church against those who had sinned. The real problem emerged from the popular misunderstanding that not only did an indulgence stave off temporal punishment for sinful acts, it also absolved the sinner generally of the guilt associated with them. The failure of the church to address this popular misunderstanding and its dependence upon the sale of indulgences as a revenue source made the situation ripe for scandal. Luther's Ninety-Five Theses "On the Power and Efficacy of Indulgences," nailed to the door of the Castle Church in Wittenberg on October 31, 1517, catapulted this "star of the lowest magnitude" to international prominence.[5] But the posting of the theses was also the hammering of the final nail in the coffin of the old order as understood by the idea of the *imperium*. In the firestorm that followed the posting of the Ninety-Five Theses, a new world would be made.

---

3. For biographical information, see Bainton, *Here I Stand: A Life of Martin Luther;* Brendler, *Martin Luther: Theology and Revolution;* and Marius, *Martin Luther: The Christian between God and Death.*

4. Voegelin, *Science, Politics, and Gnosticism,* 28.

5. Aland, "Introduction," in *Martin Luther's 95 Theses,* ed. Aland, 4.

The most complete overtly political document produced by Luther was published in 1520. "To the Christian Nobility of the German Nation Concerning the Reform of the Christian Estate" is, in Voegelin's view, "the most comprehensive statement of Luther's social doctrine and program of reform" (*CW,* 22:232).[6] It is also, according to Voegelin, "probably the biggest piece of political mischief concocted by a man" (*CW,* 22:245).

Three fundamental principles emerge from the address. The first is the general priesthood of the individual Christian. The second is that of the equality of the charismata of all functions within the body of the faithful. The third principle secures the rank of office within the clerical office. However, by clerical office, Luther clearly means to exclude the hierarchy of the church as it was constituted under the papacy. This is indicated by the fact that Luther repeatedly attacks "the Romanists" as violating the ordinances of God and acting contrary to scripture. As Voegelin observes, the consequences of the general priesthood of every Christian were seemingly never fully considered. Voegelin writes, "it seems almost unbelievable that a man of considerable intellectual training could be unaware that, in order to escape the procedural concentration of the infallibility of the church in its monarchical head, he dispersed it among the individual Christians, that in fact he made every Christian his own infallible pope—with the inevitable consequence of opening the anarchy of conflicting interpretations" (*CW,* 22:235).

But this is not the end of it. Voegelin sees in Luther's address the ideological opposite of what Boniface VIII tried to accomplish in *Unam Sanctum* with regard to the charismata. In particular, Luther argues from the same Biblical passage as Boniface VIII, 1 Corinthians 2:15, in order to strip the charismatic authority of the papacy away from the pope because he "has neither faith nor the Spirit."[7] Voegelin maintains,

> While the fronts have changed, the structure of the attack inevitably must be the same; the appeal to the *homo spiritualis* has a point only when somebody else is thereby deprived of his spiritual status. . . . The appeal was dangerous enough when the ruling head of the

6. Luther, "To the Christian Nobility of the German Nation Concerning the Reform of the Christian Estate," 123–217.

7. Ibid., 135.

church arrogated the rank to himself; with the transfer of the appeal from the head of an established institution to the man in the street, the situation inexorably tended toward a Gnostic sectarianism, disrupting the organization of the church. (*CW,* 22:235–36)

Disrupting the organization of the church is more than simply a relatively minor annoyance. In doing so to the church as it was then constituted, Luther was striking at the very heart of the institutionalization of the spirit that had been accomplished through the Pauline compromises and the objectification of grace through the sacraments. By denying the charismatic authority of the papacy, Luther was in fact undoing Christian order itself.

But what seems to amaze Voegelin is that Luther never seemed to have considered or understood the consequences of his own theoretical discourse. In Luther, Voegelin argues, we see "the first major instance of a political thinker who wants to create a new social order through the partial destruction of the existing civilizational order and then is appalled when more radical men carry the work of destruction far beyond the limits that he had set himself" (*CW,* 22:238). Ultimately, the danger that Voegelin sees in the attack on the institutional order would be reflected in the psychology of the passions and the state of nature conceived by Hobbes as the basis for his *Leviathan.* "When the order of tradition and institutions is destroyed, when order is put at the decisionist mercy of the individual conscience, we have descended to the level of the war of all against all" (*CW,* 22:265).

More problematic from Voegelin's perspective is the primary area of disagreement he has with Luther concerning the spiritual anthropology of human being itself. For a political theorist of Voegelin's persuasion, this is a matter of fundamental importance because the "problem of politics has to be considered in the larger setting of an interpretation of human nature" (*CW,* 19:231). This is because virtually all political theory or philosophy contains within it an understanding of what constitutes "human nature," either explicit or implied. Luther's spiritual anthropology as explicated in his conception of "justification through faith alone" is, in Voegelin's view, at the very least an extreme exercise in spiritual reductionism, at the very worse an abomination.

In Luther's promulgation of the doctrine of *sola fide,* Voegelin sees the "first deliberate attack on the doctrine of *amicitia*" (*CW,* 22:251) as it had been developed by Saint Thomas in the *Summa contra Gentiles. Amicitia,* the friendship between God and human beings, is the central element in Saint Thomas's doctrine of *fides caritate formata,* which Voegelin describes as "one of the most subtle achievements in the scholastic culture of spiritual life" (*CW,* 22:249).[8] The idea of *fides caritate formata* represents, from Voegelin's perspective, "the medieval climax of the interpenetration of Christianity with the body of a historical civilization. Here perhaps we touch the historical raison d'être of the West, and certainly we touch the empirical standard by which the further course of Western intellectual history must be measured" (*CW,* 22:251).

In the Thomistic construction, the essence of faith lies in the reciprocal relationship between God and human beings. As Voegelin describes the phenomenon:

> Saint Thomas puts the essence of faith in the *amicitia,* the friendship between God and man. True faith has an intellectual component insofar as loving, voluntary adherence to God is impossible without intellectual apprehension of the beatific vision as the *summum bonum,* as the end toward which the life of man is oriented; intellectual apprehension, however, needs completion through the volitional adherence of love "for by means of his will man, as it were, rests in what he has apprehended by intellect." The relationship of *amicitia* is mutual; it cannot be forced through an élan of human passion but presupposes the love of God toward man, an act of grace through which the nature of man is heightened by a supernatural *forma.* The loving orientation of man toward God is possible only when the faith of man is formed through the prior love of God toward man. . . . Saint Thomas has created a linguistic instrument for designating the component of supernatural formation in the experience of faith—that is, the penetration of the person, through infusion of grace, with the love of God as the spiritually orienting center of existence (*CW,* 22:249–50).[9]

8. Aquinas, *Summa contra gentiles,* chap. 116.

9. This, of course, is a parallel to the experience of Aristotelian *noesis* as explained by the later Voegelin in "Reason: The Classic Experience," in *CW,* 12:265–91.

It is this reciprocal relationship between the call of God and the response of the spirit that Voegelin sees as the characteristic that is most intimately human. It is closely related to the core of human existence in the "in-between" and a tacit recognition of the capacity of the human spirit to partake of something beyond itself for which it longs. For Saint Thomas, the clearest indication of *amicitia* was 1 John 4:7, 10: "Beloved, let us love one another; for love is of God, and he who loves is born of God and knows God. . . . We love because He first loved us." In chapter two we commented upon the fact that the experience of *metanoia* among the followers of Jesus was never forced. The call was given and it was up to each individual to determine whether or not to answer. In Saint Thomas's formulation of *amicitia* this principle is extended, although the substance is essentially the same.

Luther's attack upon the Thomistic conception of *amicitia* is, at its root, an assertion of the power of the human will alone to compel salvation. It is in essence the recognition of the *libido dominandi* as the ordering force of the human spirit. Voegelin's line of attack follows the logic advanced in Luther's treatise on Christian liberty, *The Freedom of a Christian*.[10] Luther argues that the corruption of human nature may be overcome by an act of will, defined in terms of faith, alone. To make the case, Luther cites Saint Paul in Romans 1:17. This, in turn, is a quotation from the Old Testament book of Habakkuk (2:4): "the righteous shall live by faith." Voegelin observes that in Luther's citation of the relevant scripture, one term is added, "alone." So that the entire passage is rendered, "the righteous shall live by faith alone." Human beings, according to Luther's argument, cannot, by their sinful natures, conform to the dictates of the law as established in the Old Testament.[11] As a result, they begin to despair of their condition. However, it is in that moment of despair that they then reach out and "receive the promise . . . the revealed word of God. . . . He who adheres to it with truth faith will thereby unite his soul

10. Luther, "The Freedom of a Christian."

11. Voegelin may be being more charitable here than Morse and Thompson give him credit for in that Luther's description of the Old Testament law is rather cavalier. "That which is impossible for you to accomplish by trying to fulfill all the works of the law—many and useless as they all are—you will accomplish quickly and easily through faith" (ibid., 349).

with the word. In this act of faith, the 'virtue of the word' . . . becomes the property of the soul. . . . All the Christian needs is his faith" (*CW*, 22:251–53).

The spiritual anthropology that emerges from Luther's discourse on Christian freedom is remarkably similar to that offered by Boniface VIII and Giles of Rome. In *Unam Sanctum* Boniface VIII had delivered the proposition that the charismata of Christ was the property of the ecclesiastical hierarchy. The gifts of the spirit available to all human beings by nature of their spiritual existence before God as conceived of by Saint Paul were transformed into a justification for the apparatus of the church. In the construction of Luther, the charismata is not received and experienced in the loving response of the soul to the call of Christ but is rather the property of the individual to assert against God when and where he or she wills it to happen.

We opened this chapter with an examination of the meaning of "living by reformation" as it applied to the individual through an exegesis of Paul's second letter to the church at Corinth. Paul asserts that in the call of the spirit of Christ and the soul's response to it a person is made anew. Luther will have none of that. As Voegelin asserts with regard to Luther's justification by faith alone: "The optimistical sounding exposition covers a spiritual tragedy; for the exchange of properties in the mystical marriage of the soul with Christ means exactly what it says. The unburdening of sin through faith is no more than a vivid conviction of salvation, assuaging the despair of the soul; it does not redeem the fallen nature itself and raise man through the imprint of grace into the *amicitia* with God" (*CW*, 22:253).[12] Instead of a transformation of the indi-

---

12. The text to which Voegelin is referring reads: "The . . . incomparable benefit of faith is that it unites the soul with Christ as a bride is united with her bridegroom. By this mystery, as the Apostle teaches, Christ and the soul become one flesh (Eph. 5:31–32). And if they are one flesh and there is between them a true marriage—indeed the most perfect of all marriages . . . it follows that everything they have they hold in common, the good as well as the evil. Accordingly the believing soul can boast of and glory in whatever Christ has as though it were its own, and whatever the soul has Christ claims as his own. . . . Christ is full of grace, life, and salvation. The soul is full of sins, death, and damnation. Now let faith come between them and sins, death, and damnation will be Christ's, while grace, life, and salvation will be the soul's" (ibid., 351).

vidual human soul in its contact with the divine being, the relationship between God and the individual is presented as "something that comes dangerously close to mutual trust between respectable burghers" (*CW,* 22:254n14). The sublime relationship between God and the individual person, in a specifically Christian sense as understood by Saint Paul and Saint Thomas, is transformed into a practical business arrangement. "We are not," in Luther's words, "recreated."[13]

Of course Luther was aware the justification by faith alone contained a potential pitfall with regard to human action. If the soul is justified by faith alone, then it would seem to naturally follow that any action undertaken by the human being who has sufficient faith would, by definition, be good. After all, as Luther points out, good works do not contribute one bit to the achievement of grace, and "the believing soul by means of the pledge of its faith is free in Christ . . . free from all sins, secure against death and hell, and is endowed with the eternal righteousness."[14] In order to prevent a descent into licentiousness, Luther is forced to integrate something that approaches the *amicitia* of the Thomistic construction through the incorporation of good works done for the love of God.

The realization of the new Christian community in which the good works are realized as truly good is only possible if one adopts what Voegelin calls the "respectable eschatology" of Luther (*CW,* 22:259). The love between God and human beings that results in the reformation of the personality of human beings may be missing from Luther's construction, but love itself is not absent. In Luther's vision of the Christian estate in which all functions are equal in charismatic gifts, the community itself is held together by a "love that has become world immanent." No longer is the love of the community secured by the knowledge of the beatific vision; after all, faith, not love, is the justification of the human soul. But

13. Ibid., 360. Jacques Maritain notes that in Luther's description of justification by faith alone, "faith can exist with sin . . . in the sense that our nature *as such* remains essentially bad and accursed beneath faith and mercy, which nevertheless, save it without making us just from within"; and "in the sense that actual sins, which of themselves are excluded by faith (but which through weakness, we commit in spite of faith) do not, however, make us lose the faith which saves us. Fantasies of an incurably nominalist philosophy which places opposites side by side" (*Three Reformers,* 176n2).

14. Ibid., 352. See also Marius, *Luther,* 268.

in order for there to be good works, there must be a community built upon love for one's neighbors that is fortified by the faith in God. The problem, of course, is that in history, as the tenuous bonds of faith are loosened, the consequences are revealed. Voegelin maintains, "With the atrophy of faith, the idea will degenerate in practice into the aggressive, utilitarian welfare society without culture of intellect and spirit that we know all too well. And theoretically, the tenuous connection with Christian tradition may be dropped altogether, and Luther's world-immanent love will become the altruism of Comte and his positivist successors" (*CW,* 22:259).

The final area of attack Voegelin pursues upon the doctrines of Luther concerns the corruption of Augustinian symbolism for the purposes of Luther's assault upon the civilizational order of Christianity. In 1523, Luther published *On Secular Authority: How Far Does the Obedience Owed to It Extend?*[15] According to Voegelin, that year marks the formal end of the Middle Ages, because within the short pamphlet Luther, with the "hubris of a private individual," would destroy "the symbols of Western Christian public order" (*CW,* 22:263).

In carrying out the destruction of the remaining vestiges of Christian public order in Western civilization, Luther would use the tools provided by Saint Augustine and the construction of the two cities.[16] Voegelin notes that with the destruction already wrought by Luther's writings, Luther's position was in fact similar to that faced by the earliest Christian communities. In 1520, Luther had addressed the members of the Christian estate. By 1523, there was no Christian estate as represented by the governmental authorities. The evidence for this proposition is the fact that the proximate issue that prompted Luther to evaluate the authority of the temporal magistrate was the banning of his translation of the New Testament by the governmental authorities in at least three German territories. If these particular magistrates were truly Christian, how could they object to the issuance and promulgation of the doctrine of Christ as set down by Luther? The fact was that between 1520 and 1523, "the

15. Luther, "On Secular Authority: How Far Does Obedience to It Extend?" 1–43.

16. On the development of Luther's doctrine regarding the two cities, see Cranz, *An Essay on the Development of Luther's Thought on Justice, Law, and Society,* 159–73.

individualization and privatization of religious existence had destroyed both the spiritual and the charismatic temporal powers of the medieval Gelasian balance. The faithful already had to rely on the Bible against the authority of the church and its councils, and now Luther had to admonish them to rely on it against the princes as well" (*CW,* 22:262).

According to Luther's construction, all human beings belong either to the *civitas Dei* or the *civitas terrena.* Those who have been justified by faith live in the realm of God, while those who have not belong to the world. The power of the sword exists in the hand of the unrighteous ruler, though, because it provides the stability necessary to get on with living the Christian life. This stability is required because although a Christian society would have no need of the sword, the two realms, the realm of God and the realm of the world, are intermingled in their immanent existence.

The problem, of course, is that the Augustinian construction does not lend itself to a description of the immanent world of human existence. Through the construction of the cities as offered by Luther, he is reverting "to something like their Tyconian meaning. The Augustinian idea of the church is destroyed through the doctrine of *sola fide;* Christianity becomes a matter of purchasing a book and using it according to Luther's interpretation; if you follow the directions and trust in God you are saved, otherwise you are not" (*CW,* 22:264–65). Ultimately, the determination as to who is saved and who is not is determined not by God but rests in the self-assurance of the believer who has been justified by faith alone.

In the writings of Luther, Voegelin sees the strength of the man as a "vital force that irresistibly cuts its swath across the historical scene" (*CW,* 22:245). Unfortunately, the strength of the individual man was sufficient only to destroy the civilization he believed that he was called upon to reform. In part, however, this was because of technological innovation. The printing press had allowed the conflict on the question of indulgences to spread and grow with a rapidity that no one could have anticipated, and by the time anyone realized what was happening it was too late. It was clear, however, in the aftermath of the revolution that Luther helped bring into the world the new symbols of order that needed to be found. It was against this backdrop that John Calvin would undertake to create a new universal church to take the place of the old one that had fallen.

Calvin and the Spiritual Elite

If Voegelin's treatment of Luther was harsh, his examination of Calvin borders on the scandalous.[17] While Voegelin describes Calvin's *Institutes of the Christian Religion*[18] as an "overwhelmingly impressive . . . achievement of a precocious genius," and Calvin himself is described as a "man of unusual qualities" with regard to his "intenseness of religious experience, by industry and erudition, by clearness of exposition and literary achievement, and by intellectual clearness with regard to the problems about which" he "wished to be clear" (*CW*, 22:271). Voegelin also notes that Calvin was a person with "a will to power without intellectual conscience" (*CW*, 22:276).

In terms of a political program per se, the Great Reformation would lead to the institution of Calvin's Geneva—or, as Voegelin calls the construction, "the Calvin of Geneva" (*CW*, 23:49)—in 1541. Calvin saw the purpose of civil government as the protection of the faith and the preservation of the pure doctrine of religion. Thus, the only government that would be adequate would be one that was under the control of the religious authorities. Through "Calvin's unrivaled gift for unscrupulous interpretation" (*CW*, 23:47) of scripture he was able to find what had been hidden for 1500 years in the Epistles of Paul—the charismatic function of the temporal ruler. Although there can be little doubt that the function of rulership only extends as far as the authorities of the faith will allow, there is no confusion in Calvin's construction regarding the status of authority within the polity. Calvin was intent on creating a religious polity in which the magistrate would answer to the authority of the spiritual divines. It is Boniface VIII's *Unam Sanctum* taken to its logical conclusion. Voegelin sees in this development the potential realization of the "autonomous polity" that will emerge "when the voice of the people replaces the word of God," leading to "a secular polity with a government that is strictly subordinated to the law as understood by the people" (*CW*, 23:49)—a secular polity that is devoid of any institutional representation of the longing of the spirit.

17. For biographical information, see Parker, *John Calvin: A Biography*.
18. Calvin, *Institutes of the Christian Religion*.

In Voegelin's treatment of Calvin, the realization of the political program is secondary to the problem that Calvin poses for the future through
the promulgation of his new Christian doctrine and his attempt to create a new universal Christianity. Calvin's primary mission was to seek to
create a new universal church that would supplant the church of Rome—
the detour to Geneva was only reluctantly taken. In this endeavor, Calvin
would seek to gather up the "remnant" of the *civitas Dei* of Luther and
through them create a new institutionalization of the spirit through his
interpretation of the scriptural basis for a new Christian community. But
in the "foundation of a new universal church" Calvin would play the "role"
not simply "of a successor to Saint Peter, but of a new Saint Peter himself" (*CW,* 22:277). In a footnote, Voegelin illustrates his argument with
a passage from the *Institutes* in which Calvin recounts how Saint Paul
created the government of the church through the creation of offices. In
building a new foundation, Calvin writes, "I deny not, that afterward
God occasionally raised up Apostles, or at least Evangelists, in their stead,
as has been done in our time. For such were needed to bring back the
Church from the revolt of the Antichrist. The office I nevertheless call
extraordinary, because it has no place in churches duly constituted."[19]
Voegelin is rather impressed with the construction, if not with the intent
of the author. "The apostolic function is secured for him; at the same
time it is barred for others once he has constituted the true church" (*CW,*
22:277n31).

There are several things that the founder of a new institutional order
for Christianity must have in order to make a go of it. First, Calvin needed
some sacraments. In order to secure the viability of the institutional framework, the new church cannot rely upon the doctrine of *sola fide* as it was
expressed by Luther and adopted by Calvin. With this in mind, salvation has to be related to membership in the church and the willing sub-
mission to its authority. The mediation of the sacraments justifies the
existence of the structural church with its offices and orders. However,
the idea of objectification of grace through the sacraments is, in fact, in
direct opposition to the notion of *sola fide*. It is a problem that Calvin
cannot adequately resolve. In regard to the chapters of the *Institutes* that

19. Ibid., 4.3.4 (2:319; refers to volume and page number in the edition cited).

deal with the question of sacraments, Voegelin notes that Calvin "accomplishes the feat of proving, first, that sacraments do not mediate grace and in no way touch the exclusiveness of justification through faith, and second, that nobody at least who has an opportunity of church membership can be justified by faith unless he joins" (*CW,* 22:278).[20] It is a remarkable achievement in literary legerdemain.

Having established that sacraments secure the unity of the spiritual body, Calvin now must demonstrate why the "Romanist" church is corrupt to the core. At most, Calvin can demonstrate that the church of Rome is really no church at all. More important, however—and this is a point upon which Voegelin does not dwell—such an argument has to be made in the context of leaving nothing on the table that might come back to haunt the new institution. Throughout the first chapter of book IV, Calvin extols the "true" church,[21] but not until the second chapter does he bring the hammer of righteousness down on the church of Rome. Calvin argues that "in place of the Lord's Supper, the foulest sacrilege has entered, the worship of God is deformed by a varied mass of intolerable superstitions; doctrine (without which Christianity would exist not) is wholly buried and exploded, the public assemblies are schools of idolatry and impiety. Wherefore, in declining fatal participation in such wickedness, we run no risk of being dissevered from the Church of Christ."[22] As Voegelin observes, "When the reader has reached the end of this part of the argument, he wonders how anybody ever could be so misguided as to belong to this foul institution" (*CW,* 22:279).

This program, however, will successfully gather the remnant. The expansion of the church requires a mission to the reprobates, but there is an obstacle to the achievement of universality in the doctrine of *sola fide.* Confronted with this seemingly intractable problem, Calvin focuses upon the doctrine of predestination as the cure for the evils that beset him. The problem of predestination had existed at least since the develop-

---

20. The chapters in the *Institutes* dealing with the sacraments are 4.14–19.

21. Voegelin notes that by the "end of the exhortation" the reader is forced to wonder "how anybody could be so mean as to separate from the church and especially how Calvin himself could separate from the Catholic Church" (*CW,* 22:279).

22. Calvin, *Institutes,* 4.2.2 (2:305).

ment of the two cities by Saint Augustine and the idea that no one knew whom God would choose to be the elect to achieve salvation. Calvin would use the ambiguity to good purpose. Since no one knew whom God was going to take, the reprobate who had not been justified by faith could coexist in the church with those whose justification by faith had been assured. Although this point raises difficulties that Calvin refused to confront directly, it was an effective device in establishing the universality of Calvin's new church.

It is in the doctrine of predestination that Voegelin sees the greatest problems in Calvin's new theology. Calvin, Voegelin writes,

> lets God grow into the formidable proportions of the despot who, at his pleasure, shows mercy to a few while he metes out the just punishment of damnation to the mass in order to show the majesty of his omnipotence and justice. . . . Taken at its face value, this doctrinal construction is usually called Calvin's "theocentrism"; experientially, however, his dogmatic theocentrism is something that we may perhaps call Calvin's "electocentrism," the attempt at an immanentization of a transcendental God through nailing him down on his promises in the experience of the "call." (*CW*, 22:283–84)

In language reminiscent of his later work, Voegelin notes that in the creation of his doctrine of predestination, Calvin has taken the symbols of the theological problem of predestination out of their proper context and misapplied them to his doctrinal construction. The essence of the doctrine of predestination is related to the timelessness of God, for whom all time is the eternal present. For human beings it is a speculative problem: Because human beings do not exist in a state of timelessness, there is no ground by which the question of predestination can be resolved satisfactorily. Predestination exists as a theological and philosophical problem, but it cannot be reified into a doctrinal statement without stripping it of its meaning.

As a practical matter, Voegelin maintains, "Calvin's immanentization of predestination in the consciousness of the elect is what today we would call the theory of a new elite. . . . Calvin's struggle for a new universal church is no more than the struggle for the new elite and its authority" (*CW*, 22:289). Injected into Calvin's new universal church is the eschatological vision of the Old Testament and the notion of a Chosen People under God marching forward to victory. What we are left with in Voegelin's presentation of Calvin is an image that will be a familiar one to students of Voegelin's thought:

> Western civilization itself is now torn asunder into the elite of the Lord whose march is the meaning of history, while the rest must submit, if necessary, under force. This new conception of the spiritual elite, which will prove itself in historical immanence, has left its indelible imprint on the later course of Western political history. In the age of Calvin the elite was a group of predestinarian elect; with the exhaustion of the Protestant struggle and the discrediting of the religious elites, the group became secularized into the enlightened intellectuals of the eighteenth century; after the French revolution began the systematic attempts at creating new intramundane elites, with the prototypical attempt of Comte, who has many traits in common with Calvin; and by the middle of the nineteenth century, arose new elitarian movements that issued into the totalitarian churches of our time. (*CW,* 22:291)

We should bear in mind that the revolutionary fervor of the Great Reformation would not have been possible had not the ground already been seeded. As Voegelin points out, "A revolution . . . is not made by the revolutionaries; it flares up from a society that is pregnant with it; the guilt rests primarily with the dominant classes of the established institutions, not with the revolutionaries who are the product of a situation that has been mismanaged by the responsible authorities" (*CW,* 22:285). With this in mind, we turn to the seeds of revolution that created the conditions by which the order of the world could be turned upside down.

Sectarianism and the Failure of Reform

The tension that exists between institutions as representatives of order and the movement of people in opposition to those institutions is not a trait that is peculiar to Western Christian civilization. Voegelin maintains that it is "a general trait of the civilizational process." In Western Christian civilization, though, the situation is made even more problematic "because the Christian idea of the person in immediacy to God would prove a permanent irritant against the institutions. The idea of the Christian person would function doubly as an agent of revolt against the institutionalization of relations between the soul and God and as an agent of regeneration of the institutions" (*CW*, 22:132–33). It is this notion of the person as an agent of regeneration that makes the idea of "reformation" as it applies to public institutions a trait that is peculiar to Western Christian civilization.

The idea that institutions representing the spiritual order of human beings can be reformed to meet the exigencies of circumstances is made possible by the existence of an objective standard to which the agents of revolt against the institutions of Christian order can refer in order to make their case. Through the recourse to the spiritualism of the Sermon on the Mount and the standards set therein, both the agents of revolt and the institutions that represent the spiritual order have a common frame of reference. This admixture makes the idea of reform distinct to Western Christian civilization. As Voegelin asserts,

> It would seem impossible, on principle, that situations like the popular dissatisfaction with the empire religion of Ikhnaton, or the apolitism of the Hellenic schools, or the Chinese "associationism" in conflict with the Confucian public order could arise in a Christian civilization. As a matter of fact, situations of this particular kind do not arise; the tensions assume specifically different forms. For the designation of this specific difference we may appropriately use the term *reformation*. The movement of the spirit has become institutionalized in the church; hence, the spiritual movements from the bottom of society cannot be in generic opposition to the institutions. The oppositional movement is intimately related to the spirit of the institution itself and must express itself in a call for reform.

Because of this peculiar interrelationship between the movement of the spirit from the bottom of society and the institutional representation of the spirit in the church, "the answer to a spiritual movement from the bottom need not be a collapse; it can be the reformation of the institution. The category of reformation, thus, becomes an idea that distinguishes medieval and modern Western civilization from the Hellenic" (*CW*, 22:133–34). And this idea of "reform" is, in turn, made possible by the recourse to the standards set forth in the Sermon.

According to Voegelin's analysis, Western Christian civilization had been created upon the basis of the compromises of Saint Paul, the theological understanding of Saint Augustine, and the resulting realization of an institutional order for the spiritual community through the church. Paul's compromises had created the primary conditions by which individuals could become part of the community and the community could expand into the world in which it emerged in accommodation with the human condition itself. However, the compromises by themselves would have been an inadequate foundation upon which to build a civilization. The creation of a sacramental organization in the church had important consequences and stood as a necessary precondition for the realization of Western Christian civilization. Voegelin maintains,

> The mediation of grace through the sacraments makes grace objective. The state of grace cannot be obtained through religious enthusiasm or through the efforts of heroic saintliness; it must be obtained through sacramental incorporation into the mystical body of Christ. The development of the sacerdotal office with its administration of grace through the sacraments and the objectivity of the priest's administration that makes the sacrament effective independently of his personal worthiness are the decisive organizational steps without which the compromises with the natural and historical order of society could not have fully unfolded their potentialities. The church as divine-human organism is the social body of the God-man; and the sacramental Christ renews the union of God and Man when the priest celebrates the sacrament. Through the administration of the sacrament, the Incarnation is continued objectively in the historical medium. (*CW*, 22:141)

The very objectification of grace through the creation of the sacramental organization is problematic, however. In many ways, the success of Christian civilization is also the reason for its decline. As Voegelin notes, "The civilizationally magnificent merger with the 'world' is the cause of the sectarian reaction" (*CW*, 22:142).

This merger had been made possible by the compromises of Paul and the sacramental objectification of grace. Indeed, by Voegelin's account, Western Christian civilization itself is the result of these two factors taken together.

> The compromises, together with the sacramental objectification of grace, are the basis for the civilizing function of the church. Through its compromises the church is enabled to accept the social structure of a people as a whole, with its occupations, habits, and legal and economic institutions, and to inject into the social body the spiritual and ethical values of Christianity with such gradations as are bearable for the average human being at the time. No revolution is required, no eschatological upheaval that would establish the realm of Christ within the generation of the living. The tension of eschatological expectation is toned down to the atmosphere of a civilizing process that may take its good time; in slow and patient work it may extend over centuries. By virtue of its compromises the church can operate on the masses; it can utilize the wealth of natural gifts and slowly ennoble them by giving them direction toward supernatural aims. Moreover, the grace that is objectively with the whole body of the community allows a very important socialization of the individual gifts for the Christian life. (*CW,* 22:141–42)

But the problem remained: How would the individual experience of faith in the soul of the believer be incorporated into the institution of the church? The fact that a sacerdotal institution existed did not mean that of necessity all were going to conform to its dictates or even that the institution itself would be truly representative of the experience it was intended to represent. We noted in chapter three that church and sect are both legitimate expressions of the spiritual impulse, a fact that presented a quandary for the institutional authorities. If there could only be one true faith, then the sectarian impulses had to either be absorbed or put down. With the passage of time, the latter increasingly became the recourse of first resort.

There is a *prima facie* case to be made whenever a sectarian movement arises against a given institution that something has gone wrong in the interplay between the evocative idea and the institutionalization of it.

Thus Voegelin asserts, "When a popular movement of mass relevance is forming in opposition to an institution, this formation is the definite proof that the institution has somehow failed in handling the problems entrusted to its care; to this extent, the idea of *vox populi, vox Dei* is golden wisdom." Yet while the emergence of a movement may be evidence that something is wrong, it does not necessarily follow that the movement, or movements, in question offer real solutions to the problems that led to the initial demands against the institutional order. "The formation of such a movement," Voegelin writes,

> is never a proof that the direction in which it is moving is endowed with any intrinsic value. The movement may represent a drive toward the social realization of spiritual values; but this drive may be no more than a nucleus that is surrounded by wide fringes of destructive hatred against the institution that has failed with regard to a specific task. From this possibility arise peculiar dangers of the tensions between institutions and movements. (*CW* 22:134)

In large measure, prior to 1300, the church had been able to absorb sectarian movements into the larger body of the church. Voegelin observes, "It was clear to the thinkers of the high Middle Ages that the church preserved its spiritual effectiveness through a series of renovations. It was, furthermore, clear that the social carriers of the successive renovations were the orders. The Benedictine reform and the Cluniac reform were the main events in this series; and a new lease on life was given to the church through the absorption of sectarian tendencies into the mendicant orders" (*CW,* 22:149). The reforms reinvigorated the church and reduced the need for competitors to arise in order to challenge the virtual spiritual monopoly of the universal church.

The absorptiveness of the church declined precipitously after 1300. The doctrinal hardening of the church had led to the unenviable circumstance that even legitimate questions of reform had to be classified as heretical, since the church had lost permeability. The institutional capacity of the church to absorb the movements was lost. Thus, "the movements of the so-called pre-Reformation were fought down by violence. . . . The same inability of coping with the new problems is revealed in the increasing national influences on the schismatic papacy, in the failure in creating an international parliamentary constitution for the church, in the withdrawal into an absolute form of church government, and in the creation of the new legal form of the concordat for dealing with national governments." Voegelin puts his finger on the real difficulty at the heart of the increasing pressure upon the institution of the church: "the problem of developing Christian doctrine further through a differentiation of mystical culture from the symbolism of the dogma as well as the problem of reinterpreting the meaning of dogmatic symbols in the light of active religious experience" (CW, 22:137). In other words, the church was finding it increasingly difficult to "keep up" with the differentiations within the spiritual community of which it was supposed to be representative.

This potential problem is further exacerbated by the cycle of the call for reform and the institutional reaction to the expressed desire for reform, especially in light of reformist demands that extend beyond the strictly spiritual reforms of the institution and touch upon the values of the civilization itself. Voegelin notes that in many cases, the

> legitimate grievances of a spiritual movement, its call for reform in the Christian sense, may be accompanied by a hostile attitude toward civilizational values. This admixture of civilizational hostility is a practically inevitable feature of movements from the bottom of the social scale; the resentment against the intellectual and aesthetic values realized by the upper class will supply a good deal of motive power in the call for reform. The cry for spiritual reform is typically coupled with demands for a "burning of the books," for the suppression of literary and artistic culture, and for the abolition of the prevalent property order. (CW, 22:134–35)

The extent to which a sectarian movement is focused upon hostility toward the civilizational values themselves creates a justification on the part of the institution to seek to simply crush the movement. Voegelin asserts that the assault on civilizational values generally "lends legitimacy to the institutional resistance against movements: the anticivilizational elements in movements become the excuse for the ruling groups not to satisfy legitimate grievances, and the momentary victory of the institution may become, as a consequence, the cause of even worse outbreaks in the future" (CW, 22:135). The ease with which an institution is able to repel even legitimate demands for reform may serve to make the institution more intractable in the future.

In Voegelin's account, this is a matter of profound import for Western civilization generally because it creates a spiral of reform and reaction that inevitably ends in disaster. The "cumulative effect of resistance against legitimate calls for reform," Voegelin writes,

> has especially grave consequences in a civilization of the Western Christian type. If the reforms are not forthcoming, the resentment that always is easily directed against the civilizational values embodied in institutions may turn against the spiritual values themselves. The process that has started with movements for spiritual reform may end with movements against the spirit. This has, in fact, been the course of the movements in Western civilization: the course begins with movements of the Albigensian type; it ends with movements of the Communist and National Socialist type. The development is without parallel in history. Western Christian civilization has a peculiar vulnerability and shows peculiar problems of decline: while in Greco-Roman civilization the tension of the decline was caused by movements that represented an advance of the spirit, in Western Christian civilization the tension of the decline is caused by movements that are spiritually regressive. (*CW,* 22:135)

We have seen the reactionary impulse within the institution of the church through the adoption of dogmatic positions and the failure to respond to the reformist impulse. Furthermore, we have noticed the increasing tendency to label all sectarian movements as heretical per se. The result was a feeding of the cycle that led to the great outburst of sectarianism known as the Great Reformation.

With the linkage of the spiritual and temporal authorities under the rubric of the Gelasian doctrine, the sectarian assault upon the sacerdotal offices of the church and "against the ecclesiastical monopoly of mediating grace through the sacraments," not only constituted a threat to the church but created a political problem as well. During the Investiture Controversy, the Norman Anonymous had asserted the general priesthood of every Christian. This became a familiar assertion in the sectarian movements afterward. But, as Voegelin attests, "lay Christianity was a deadly threat to the sacerdotal and sacramental institution of the church; but it was a threat not only to the church itself. Spiritual and temporal power were closely integrated in the order of imperial Christianity; the institution could not be attacked on principle without destroying the charismatic status of rulership in the Christian order" (*CW*, 22:143).

Indeed, as we have seen, it was the idea of charismatic rulership in the imperial order that succumbed first in the eclipsing of the imperial idea. Once the idea of temporal authority was transferred from the imperial idea to the concept of the individual realm, it was largely a matter of time before universal Christianity itself would collapse under the weight of the sectarian impulse. Thus, Voegelin characterizes the "struggle between the church and the sectarian movements" as "a reversal of the process in which the church" had "overcome the eschatological, sectarian beginnings of Christianity." Furthermore, the struggle itself is characterized by Voegelin as "an unraveling of the compromises" by which Christianity had accomplished its civilizational mission (*CW*, 22:143).

The objection to the sacerdotal function of the church itself and the mediation of grace through the sacraments, of course, extends further back in history. In the examination of the Tyconian problem we noticed that the primary issue, the ultimate cause of the schism, was the Donatists' position that the sacraments were not "objective." The proper administration of grace required the purity of those who would administer the sacrament. The primary objection was against the administration of the sacraments by the priest who had committed apostasy under threat of persecution. But the Tyconian problem also illustrated what would happen in the willingness of the Donatists to use violence to compel others to accept their version of religious and spiritual truth. It was this tendency that Luther inadvertently fed through his promulgation of the doctrine of *sola fide* and the subsequent corruption of Augustinian symbolism.

Ultimately, the problem with the institutionalization of the spirit turns on the problem of apolitism that we addressed in chapter four in the context of the historical background of the relationship of the church and the nations. Voegelin notes,

> Apolitism is a permanent problem in every political culture. Institutions can do no more than stabilize and order the field of social forces that

exist at the time of their creation; even the best institutional creation is not perfect; there will always be groups and individuals who are dissatisfied with the settlement of the historical moment; and as time goes on and circumstances change, new causes of dissatisfaction will arise. An institution must be constantly engaged in the process of restabilizing itself through the solution of problems that would destroy its value and meaning if they remained unsolved. If the ruling group of an institution fails in such adaptation, an increasing number of persons will feel "left out." If the number of such persons becomes large enough in a given society, and if they express their sentiments and ideas in a philosophy of conduct suitable to persons who live with their "bodies" in a community but do not participate in it with their "souls" . . . then we have given the phenomenon of apolitism on a socially relevant scale. If, furthermore, such persons form communities and organize themselves for political action, then the situation is ripe for a revolution. (*CW*, 22:133)

Seen from this light, the Great Reformation was not the result of Luther's tinkering with the institutional order; rather, Luther's tinkering had the effect of releasing social forces that had been pent up since the end of the *imperium*. The church's retreat from the compromises of Saint Paul had made revolution almost inevitable. To be sure, the possibility continued to exist for internal reforms within the body of the church, but that is somewhat problematic given the history of the church. Voegelin hints at the problem in his assertion "that the age of Saint Paul's elementary faith was gone" (*CW*, 22:227).

In the end, however, Voegelin argues that the "most important victim" of the Great Reformation, "the symbol of the church from its beginnings" as the institutional order of the spirit, became a victim because of its own "failure of coping with the historicity of Christianity." Voegelin continues:

For the early church, the genius of Saint Paul had found the great compromise with history through the interpretation of Pagan and Hebrew civilization as precluding the revelations of divine law. In the period of Roman Christianity, the problem of a plurality of Christian civilizations had been solved, after a fashion, through the wranglings of the early councils about Christology; but the possibility of a split between Western and Eastern Christianities had become visible. Within Western Christianity, after Charlemagne, the schismatic situation could be decently covered by the relative provincialism of the Western development. But this period of relative dormancy of the problem came to its inevitable end with the enlargement of the historical horizon toward the East and the domestic complications of the West. The evocation of the Roman summepiscopate was intimately connected with the unchallenged evocation of the Western empire. With the disintegration of the imperial evocation through the internal and external changes of the historical scene, the *Romanitas* of the spiritual power could not remain an unchallenged symbol as if nothing had happened. With the finality of the imperial idea, the finality, not of Christianity, but of its Roman ecclesiastical form would pale. With the historical relativation of the imperial idea, the *Romanitas* of Christianity would become a historical accident. And the leadership of the church would be faced with the task of spiritualizing the idea of the universal church in such a manner that it would become independent of the Roman accident. (*CW,* 22:223–24)

Voegelin's presentation seems to create an air of inevitability to the destruction of the universal church that mitigates his outright condemnation of the men who would bring the end to the experiment in capturing the essence of the Christian experience in an institution.

The Forces Unleashed and the Privatization of the Spirit

The first and most obvious result of the Great Reformation was the plunging of Europe into the age of the religious wars. As Voegelin argues, "The dissociation of Christianity into a plurality of creed communities became a cause of political disturbance and of religious wars." This was largely because the "new communities continued the medieval idea of the church as the spiritual branch of the public order, to be maintained in this position by the temporal authorities whose primary function was the defense of the church" (*CW,* 23:21). Furthermore, the very nature of Christian communities as proselytizing was bound to engender conflict. It was as if the Donatists had multiplied and each different sect of the reformed Donatist church believed it had a duty to crush the unbelievers in an attempt to bend them to the will of the true church.

But the conflict between the creed communities had two very important effects upon the future development of the West both politically and spiritually. First, the violence brought on by the wars tended to discount the notion of the charismata as vested in the temporal authority of the civil government. This was true despite the fact that many of the new creed communities were able to attach themselves to kings and princes and realms in order to secure their institutional survival. Second, Voegelin writes, "The violent disorders caused by the contending spiritual movements had the general result of a contraction of public order and of a reduction of politics to the essential of preserving peace in the material sense." Thus, "in the sixteenth century does not begin, as is conventionally phrased, a separation or differentiation of politics from a religious context; what actually begins is the elimination of the life of the spirit from public representation and the corresponding contraction of politics to a secular nucleus" (CW, 23:23).

This creates a problem insofar as the spirit of human beings cannot be excised from the life of human beings generally. As Voegelin puts it, "one cannot eliminate the life of the spirit from society any more than one can the biological constitution of man" (CW, 23:22). Prior to the nineteenth century, the contraction of public order into a secular realm would be understood as a problem because the order of the soul has been understood from the time of Plato as a necessary precondition for the order of a society. However, the attempt at "substituting a humanistic substance of one variety or the other for the historical Christian order . . . have only makeshift character; the stabilizations of the moment are followed by a renewed realization of the actual disintegration of substantive order until, in the nineteenth century, the revolt begins to find its complement of substance in totalitarian eschatologies" (CW, 23:34).

The question of temporal authority is also problematic in light of the Great Reformation. Throughout the sacrum imperium, as a result of the Gelasian doctrine, the temporal authority was understood to be representative of transcendent order to the extent that the authorities temporal and spiritual were themselves manifestations of the transcendent kingdom of God in history. With the crossing of the Rubicon that was the Great Reformation, there was no turning back to the old evocation. It would be more than a hundred years before the seed of popular sovereignty planted by Salamonius would begin to bear fruit in the aftermath of the English Revolution (*CW,* 23:42–44).

In the emergence of the new entities of the nation-states, new problems arose with regard to the relations between the new autonomous units. Voegelin observes with regard to the emerging nation-states a pattern that would play itself out in the history of international relations, first under the rubric of the Christian idea of a crusade and then in terms of the secular religions of the nineteenth and twentieth centuries. According to the pattern, within a state there is a rise of a spiritual movement with the tendency to transcend borders. This is followed by the attempt to suppress the movement that might lead to wars of intervention and counter-intervention. Finally, peace is secured through the achievement of a temporary stabilization. Voegelin identifies four movements of this type beginning with the Great Reformation and the Counter-Reformation and ending with World War II (*CW,* 23:110–11). In light of the sudden implosion of the Soviet Union, one can wonder whether this categorization will continue to hold true. It is possible to define the war against fundamentalist Islam in these terms, although the outcome of that conflict remains to be seen.

The most influential attempt to harness the spiritual forces unleashed by the destruction of the Christian political order was undertaken by John Locke. In Locke's development of the idea of toleration there is an attempt to privatize the sphere of the spirit. Voegelin observes,

> The break of the great compromise by the Reformation expressed itself in the sectarian insistence on a purified church sphere and in a corresponding neglect of the secular arm. The result was not the desired subordination of the secular sphere to the ecclesiastical organization, but on the contrary the liberation of the secular sphere from the restrictions that the religious compromise had imposed. The Reform began with the program of submitting the secular sphere to the control of the saints and ended with the relegation of the saints to a corner of "a free and voluntary society." (*CW,* 25:142)

As a practical matter, the consequences of this movement are not well understood. In Voegelin's estimation, by privatizing the movement of the spirit, the remnant of Christian civilization deprived itself of the necessary tools by which to combat the new gods of the ideological mass movements that emerged in the French Revolution and into the twentieth century. One can argue that the institutionalization of the spirit is a private matter, but this approach leaves the field open to the forces of the ideological faiths that Voegelin defines as "Gnostic" in the context of *The New Science of Politics* and *Science, Politics, and Gnosticism.*[23]

23. *CW,* vol. 5.

Conclusion

✧

    Two threads run through the analysis of the problem of Christian political order: the retreat from the compromises with the world that made the institutional order of the spirit possible and the danger posed by the Tyconian problem.

    Voegelin's *History of Political Ideas* is his most comprehensive look at the problems of Christian political order as it emerged in the first community that gathered around Jesus during his life on Earth and as it expanded based upon the revelatory experience of the disciples in the days following his death on the cross. Saint Paul faced a serious political problem in constituting a community of the faithful that would live on; but through a series of compromises with the world, he was able to create a constitution of the community that would result in the expansion of Christianity throughout the world. Furthermore, Paul created the germ of an idea that would serve as a force for spiritual order throughout the Middle Ages in the *sacrum imperium*. The destruction of the *imperium* and the withdrawal from the compromises with the world by both the universal church and ranks of the sectarian Christians led to the excision of the life of the spirit from the institutional order of the new nation-states.

    The destruction of both political and spiritual orders was so complete that Voegelin characterizes the state of political theory at the beginning of the seventeenth century as "a wreck" (*CW*, 25:47). In place of the comprehensive idea of community that encompassed the immanent and spiritual life of human beings, the new political orders would generally follow Locke in the privatization of the order of the spirit, and the life oriented toward the *summum bonum* as the beatific vision of the transcendent God would be replaced by the new gods of science and progress. The carriers of the spirit would be the new creeds of sectarianism in the gnostic ideological mass movements.

For the moment, the forces of ideological sectarianism in the distinctly Christian sense have been quieted, and with the destruction of the Soviet empire the threat of an ideological mass movement in the future was thought to have passed. However, in keeping with the notion that evil never disappears, it merely changes its form, the new ideological threat to Western civilization has emerged in the form of militant Islam. But there is still an open question with regard to the "crisis of civic consciousness" that Sandoz and others see permeating American society in particular and the Western democracies generally. In part, this is caused by the closure of the realm of the spirit and the failure of the institutions of the "state" to recognize it as legitimate.

But a modicum of hope remains. In a footnote in volume IV of the *History of Political Ideas,* Voegelin asserts, with regard to the tension of decline caused by spiritually regressive movements, "this peculiarity of Western civilization should make historians hesitate to indulge in predictions with regard to the further course of Western decline. Under such conditions catastrophes of disorder without parallel are possible, while on the other hand recuperative forces without parallel are immanent to the civilization" (*CW,* 22:135n2). It is hoped that this analysis of Voegelin's study of the problem of Christian political order can be a small contribution to the recuperation of civilization.

Bibliography

Primary Works by Eric Voegelin

Anamnesis. Translated and edited by Gerhart Niemeyer. Notre Dame: University of Notre Dame Press, 1978.

Autobiographical Reflections. Edited by Ellis Sandoz. Baton Rouge: Louisiana State University Press, 1989.

The Collected Works of Eric Voegelin. Vol. 2, *Race and State.* Translation by Ruth Hein of *Raas und Staat* (1933). Edited by Klaus Vondung. Baton Rouge: Louisiana State University Press, 1997.

The Collected Works of Eric Voegelin. Vol. 5, *Modernity without Restraint: The Political Religions, The New Science of Politics, and Science, Politics, and Gnosticism.* Edited by Manfred Henningsen. Columbia: University of Missouri Press, 2000.

The Collected Works of Eric Voegelin. Vol. 6, *Anamnesis: On the Theory of History and Politics.* Translated by M. J. Hanak, based upon the abbreviated version originally translated by Gerhart Niemeyer. Edited by David Walsh. Columbia: University of Missouri Press, 2002.

The Collected Works of Eric Voegelin. Vol. 10, *Published Essays, 1940–1952.* Edited by Ellis Sandoz. Columbia: University of Missouri Press, 2000.

The Collected Works of Eric Voegelin. Vol. 11, *Published Essays, 1953–1966.* Edited by Ellis Sandoz. Columbia: University of Missouri Press, 2000.

The Collected Works of Eric Voegelin. Vol. 12, *Published Essays, 1966–1985.* Edited by Ellis Sandoz. Columbia: University of Missouri Press, 1990.

The Collected Works of Eric Voegelin. Vol. 14, *Order and History, Volume I: Israel and Revelation.* Edited by Maurice P. Hogan. Columbia: University of Missouri Press, 2001.

The Collected Works of Eric Voegelin. Vol. 15, *Order and History, Volume II: The World of the Polis*. Edited by Athanasios Moulakis. Columbia: University of Missouri Press, 2000.

The Collected Works of Eric Voegelin. Vol. 16, *Order and History, Volume III: Plato and Aristotle*. Edited by Dante Germino. Columbia: University of Missouri Press, 2000.

The Collected Works of Eric Voegelin. Vol. 17, *Order and History, Volume IV: The Ecumenic Age*. Edited by Michael Franz. Columbia: University of Missouri Press, 2000.

The Collected Works of Eric Voegelin. Vol. 18, *Order and History, Volume V: In Search of Order*. Edited by Ellis Sandoz. Columbia: University of Missouri Press, 2000.

The Collected Works of Eric Voegelin. Vol. 19, *History of Political Ideas, Volume I: Hellenism, Rome, and Early Christianity*. Edited by Athanasios Moulakis. Columbia: University of Missouri Press, 1997.

The Collected Works of Eric Voegelin. Vol. 20, *History of Political Ideas, Volume III: The Middle Ages to Aquinas*. Edited by Peter von Sivers. Columbia: University of Missouri Press, 1997.

The Collected Works of Eric Voegelin. Vol. 21, *History of Political Ideas, Volume III: The Later Middle Ages*. Edited by David Walsh. Columbia: University of Missouri Press, 1998.

The Collected Works of Eric Voegelin. Vol. 22, *History of Political Ideas, Volume IV: Renaissance and Reformation*. Edited by David L. Morse and William M. Thompson. Columbia: University of Missouri Press, 1998.

The Collected Works of Eric Voegelin. Vol. 23, *History of Political Ideas, Volume V: Religion and the Rise of Modernity*. Edited by James L. Wiser. Columbia: University of Missouri Press, 1998.

The Collected Works of Eric Voegelin. Vol. 24, *History of Political Ideas, Volume VI: Revolution and the New Science*. Edited by Barry Cooper. Columbia: University of Missouri Press, 1998.

The Collected Works of Eric Voegelin. Vol. 25, *History of Political Ideas, Volume VII: The New Order and the Last Orientation*. Edited by Jürgen Gebhardt and Thomas A. Hollweck. Columbia: University of Missouri Press, 1999.

The Collected Works of Eric Voegelin. Vol. 26, *History of Political Ideas, Volume VIII: Crisis and the Apocalypse of Man*. Edited by David Walsh. Columbia: University of Missouri Press, 1999.

The Collected Works of Eric Voegelin. Vol. 34, *Autobiographical Reflections: Revised Edition with a Voegelin Glossary and Cumulative Index.* Edited by Ellis Sandoz. Columbia: University of Missouri Press, 2006.

Order and History. Vol. 1, *Israel and Revelation.* Baton Rouge: Louisiana State University Press, 1956.

Order and History. Vol. 2, *The World of the Polis.* Baton Rouge: Louisiana State University Press, 1957.

Order and History. Vol. 3, *Plato and Aristotle.* Baton Rouge: Louisiana State University Press, 1957.

Order and History. Vol. 4, *The Ecumenic Age.* Baton Rouge: Louisiana State University Press, 1974.

Order and History. Vol. 5, *In Search of Order.* Baton Rouge: Louisiana State University Press, 1987.

The New Science of Politics. Chicago: University of Chicago Press, 1952.

From Enlightenment to Revolution. Edited by John H. Hallowell. Durham: Duke University Press, 1975.

Science, Politics, and Gnosticism. Chicago: Regnery Gateway, 1968.

Secondary Works

Aland, Kurt, ed. *Martin Luther's 95 Theses: With the Pertinent Documents from the History of the Reformation.* Translated by P. J. Schroder. St. Louis: Concordia Publishing House, 1967.

Allen, Charlotte. *The Human Christ: The Search for the Historical Jesus.* New York: The Free Press, 1998.

Anderson, Bernhard W. "Politics and the Transcendent: Eric Voegelin's Philosophical and Theological Analysis of the Old Testament in the Context of the Ancient Near East." *Political Science Reviewer* 1 (Fall 1971): 1–29.

Aristotle. *The Politics.* Translated by T. A. Sinclair. Revised and re-presented by Trevor J. Saunders. New York: Penguin Books, 1981.

Augustine. *The City of God.* Translated by Marcus Dods, with an introduction by Thomas Merton. New York: The Modern Library. 1950.

Bainton, Roland. *Here I Stand: A Life of Martin Luther.* New York: Abingdon-Cokesbury Press, 1950.

Bammel, Ernst. "Romans 13." In *Jesus and the Politics of His Day,* edited by Ernst Bammel and C. F. D. Moule, 365–384. Cambridge: Cambridge University Press, 1984.

Barrett, C. K. "Luke-Acts." In *Early Christian Thought in Its Jewish Context,* edited by John Barclay and John Sweet, 84–95. Cambridge: Cambridge University Press, 1996.

Baumann, Clarence. *The Sermon on the Mount: The Modern Quest for Its Meaning.* Macon, GA: Mercer University Press, 1985.

Beasley-Murray, G. R. *Jesus and the Kingdom of God.* Grand Rapids: William B. Eerdmanns Publishing Co., 1986.

Berman, Harold J. *Law and Revolution: The Formation of the Western Legal Tradition.* Cambridge, MA: Harvard University Press, 1983.

Bloom, Allan. "Interpretive Essay." In *The Republic,* 2nd ed., translated by Allan Bloom, 307–436. New York: Basic Books, 1994.

Blumenthal, Uta-Renate. *The Investiture Controversy: Church and Monarchy from the Ninth to the Twelfth Centuries.* Philadelphia: University of Pennsylvania Press, 1988.

Boase, T. S. R. *Boniface VIII.* London: Constable and Co., 1933.

Brendler, Gerhard. *Martin Luther: Theology and Revolution.* New York: Oxford University Press, 1991.

Buber, Martin. *The Kingship of God.* New York: Harper and Row, 1967.

Bultmann, Rudolf. *Jesus and the Word.* Translated by Louise Pettibone Smith and Erminie Huntress. New York: Charles Scribners' Sons, 1934.

Burr, David. *The Spiritual Franciscans: From Protest to Persecution in the Century after Saint Francis.* University Park, PA: Pennsylvania State University Press, 2001.

Calvin, John. *Institutes of the Christian Religion.* Edited by Henry Beveridge. 2 vols. London: James Clarke and Co., 1953.

Campion, Nicholas. *The Great Year: Astrology, Millenarianism and History in the Western Tradition.* London: Arkana, 1994.

Cantor, Norman F. *Church, Kingship, and Lay Investiture in England.* Princeton: Princeton University Press. 1958.

Carlyle, R. W., and A. J. Carlyle. *A History of Medieval Political Theory in the West.* Vol. 5, *The Political Theory of the Thirteenth Century.* Edinburgh: William Blackwood and Sons, 1950.

Chadwick, Henry. *The Early Church.* London: Penguin Books, 1967.

Chilton, Bruce. *A Galilean Rabbi and His Bible: Jesus' Own Interpretation of Isaiah.* London: SPCK, 1984.

Clifton, Chas S. *Encyclopedia of Heresies and Heretics.* Santa Barbara, CA: ABC-CLIO, 1992.

Cohn, Norman. *The Pursuit of the Millennium.* Fairlawn, NJ: Essential Books, 1957.

Collingwood, R. G. *The Idea of History.* London: Oxford University Press, 1956.

Cooper, Barry. *The Political Theory of Eric Voegelin.* Vol. 27 of *Toronto Studies in Theology.* Lewiston: Edwin Mellen Press, 1986.

Cranz, F. Edward. *An Essay on the Development of Luther's Thought on Justice, Law, and Society.* Harvard Theological Studies 19. Cambridge, MA: Harvard University Press, 1959.

Creighton, Mandell. *A History of the Papacy from the Great Schism to the Sack of Rome.* London: Longmans, Green, and Co., 1897.

Curry, Mary Mildred. *The Conflict between Pope Boniface VIII and King Philip IV, the Fair.* Washington, DC: Catholic University of America, 1927.

Dahl, Nihls Alstrup. "The Problem of the Historical Jesus." In *Jesus the Christ: The Historical Origins of Christological Doctrine,* edited by Donald H. Juel, 81–111. Minneapolis: Fortress Press, 1991.

Dawson, Christopher. *Christianity and the New Age.* Manchester, NH: Sophia Institute Press, 1985.

———. *The Making of Europe: An Introduction to the History of European Unity.* New York: Sheed and Ward, 1952.

———. *Medieval Essays.* New York: Sheed and Ward, 1954.

———. *Religion and the Rise of Western Culture.* New York: Sheed and Ward, 1950.

Douglass, R. Bruce. "Civil Religion and Western Christianity." *Thought* 55 (June 1980): 169.

———. "A Diminished Gospel: A Critique of Voegelin's Intepretation of Christianity." In *Eric Voegelin's Search for Order in History,* edited by Stephen A. McKnight, 139–54. Baton Rouge: Louisiana State University Press, 1978.

———. "The Gospel and Political Order: Eric Voegelin on the Political Role of Christianity." *Journal of Politics* 38 (February 1976): 33–37.

"The Epistle of Barnabas." In *Early Christian Writings: The Apostolic Fathers*, translated by Maxwell Staniforth, revised translation, introductions, and new editorial material by Andrew Louth, 153–84. London: Penguin Books, 1968.

Elsthain, Jean Bethke. *Democracy on Trial*. New York: Basic Books, 1995.

Eusebius. *Ecclesiastica Historia*. Translated by Kirsopp Lake. Cambridge, MA: Loeb Classical Library, 1926.

———. *The History of the Church*. Translated by G. A. Williamson. Middlesex: Dorset Press, 1965.

Federici, Michael P. *Eric Voegelin: The Restoration of Order*. Wilmington: ISI Books, 2002.

Fortin, Ernest L. "Introduction." In *Political Writings*, by Saint Augustine, translated by Michael W. Tkacz and Douglas Kries, edited by Ernest L. Fortin and Douglas Kries, vii–xxix. Indianapolis: Hackett Publishing, 1994.

Frend, W. H. C. *The Donatist Church: A Movement of Protest in North Africa*. Oxford: Clarendon Press, 1952.

Gay, Peter. *The Enlightenment: An Interpretation*. 2 vols. New York: Alfred A. Knopf, 1966.

George, Leonard. *Crimes of Perception: An Encyclopedia of Heresies and Heretics*. New York: Paragon House, 1994.

Grasso, Kenneth L. "We Held These Truths: The Transformation of American Pluralism and the Future of American Democracy." In *John Courtney Murray and the American Civil Conversation*, edited by Robert P. Hunt and Kenneth L. Grasso, 89–115. Grand Rapids: William B. Eerdmans Publishing Co., 1992.

Green, William Scott. "Messiah in Judaism: Rethinking the Question." In *Judaisms and Their Messiahs at the Turn of the Christian Era*, edited by Jacob Neusner, William Scott Green, and Ernest S. Friechs, 1–13. Cambridge: Cambridge University Press, 1987.

Guignebert, Charles. *Jesus*. Translated by S. H. Hook. London: Kegan Paul, Trench, Trubner and Co., 1935.

Hallowell, John H. "Existence in Tension: Man in Search of His Humanity." *Political Science Reviewer* 2 (Fall 1972): 162–84. Reprinted in *Eric Voegelin's Search for Order in History*, edited by Stephen A. McKnight, 101–26. Baton Rouge: Louisiana State University Press, 1978.

Halphen, Louis. *Charlemagne and the Carolingian Empire.* Translated by Giselle de Nie. Amsterdam: North Holland Publishing Co., 1977.

Hamilton, Alexander, John Jay, and James Madison. *The Federalist.* Edited with an introduction by Jacob E. Cooke. Middletown, CT: Wesleyan University Press, 1961.

Herrin, Judith. *The Formation of Christendom.* Princeton: Princeton University Press, 1987.

Heyking, John von. *Augustine and Politics as Longing in the World.* Eric Voegelin Institute Series in Political Philosophy. Columbia: University of Missouri Press, 2001.

Hollweck, Thomas A., and Ellis Sandoz. "General Introduction to the Series." In vol. I of *History of Political Ideas,* by Eric Voegelin, edited with an introduction by Athanasios Moulakis, 1–47. Vol. 19 of *The Collected Works of Eric Voegelin.* Columbia: University of Missouri Press, 1989.

Horsley, Richard A., and John S. Hanson. *Bandits, Prophets, and Messiahs: Popular Movements in the Time of Jesus.* Minneapolis: Winston Press, 1985.

Isaacs, Harold R. *Idols of the Tribe: Group Identity and Political Change.* New York: Harper and Row, 1975.

Jonas, Hans. *The Gnostic Religion.* 2nd ed. Boston: Beacon Press, 1958.

Kantorowicz, Ernst H. *The Kings' Two Bodies: A Study of Mediaeval Political Theology.* Princeton: Princeton University Press, 1957.

Kaufman, Peter Iver. *Redeeming Politics.* Princeton: Princeton University Press, 1990.

Kee, Howard Clark. *Jesus in History: An Approach to the Study of the Gospels.* 2nd ed. New York: Harcourt Brace Jovanovich, 1970.

Kendall, Willmoore. *The Conservative Affirmation in America.* Chicago: Regnery Gateway, 1963.

Kissinger, Warren S. *The Sermon on the Mount: A History of Interpretation and Bibliography.* ATLA Bibliography Series 3. Metuchen, NJ: Scarecrow Press, 1975.

Koester, Helmut. *Ancient Christian Gospels: Their History and Development.* Philadelphia: Trinity Press, 1990.

LaTourette, Kenneth Scott. *A History of the Expansion of Christianity.* 7 vols. Grand Rapids, MI: Zondervan Publishing, 1970.

Lincoln, Abraham. *Abraham Lincoln: Speeches and Writings, 1859–1865.* Edited by Don E. Fehrenbacher. New York: Library of America, 1989.

Lippmann, Walter. *The Public Philosophy.* New York: Mentor Books, 1956.

Löwith, Karl. *Meaning in History.* Chicago: University of Chicago Press, 1949.

Luther, Martin. "On Secular Authority: How Far Does Obedience to It Extend?" In *Luther and Calvin on Secular Authority,* edited and translated by Harro Höpfl, 1–43. Cambridge: Cambridge University Press, 1991.

————."To the Christian Nobility of the German Nation Concerning the Reform of the Christian Estate," translated by Charles M. Jacobs, revised by James Atkinson. In *Works,* by Martin Luther, vol. 44, edited by James Atkinson, 123–217. Philadelphia: Fortress Press, 1966.

————. "The Freedom of a Christian," translated by W. A. Lambert, revised by Harold J. Grimm. In *Works,* by Martin Luther, vol. 31, edited by Harold J. Grimm, 343–77. Philadelphia: Muhlenberg Press, 1957.

McKnight, Stephen A. "The Evolution of Voegelin's Theory of Politics and History." In *Eric Voegelin's Search for Order in History,* edited by Stephen A. McKnight, 26–45. Baton Rouge: Louisiana State University Press, 1978.

Machiavelli, Niccoló. *The Discourses.* Edited by Bernard Crick, translated by Leslie J. Walker, revisions by Brian Richardson. Middlesex: Penguin Books, 1970.

Madaule, Jacques. *The Albigensian Crusade: An Historical Essay.* Translated by Barbara Wall. New York: Fordham University Press, 1967.

Maritain, Jacques. *Three Reformers.* New York: Charles Scribner's Sons, 1940.

Marius, Richard. *Martin Luther: The Christian between God and Death.* Cambridge, MA: Belknap Press, 1999.

Millard, Allan. *Reading and Writing in the Time of Jesus.* Washington Square: New York University Press, 2000.

Montgomery, Marion. "Eric Voegelin and the End of Our Exploring." *Modern Age* 23 (Summer 1979): 233–45.

Morrissey, Michael P. *Consciousness and Transcendence: The Theology of Eric Voegelin.* Notre Dame: University of Notre Dame Press, 1994.

Morse, David L., and William M. Thompson. "Editors' Introduction." In vol. IV of *History of Political Ideas,* by Eric Voegelin, edited with an introduction by David L. Morse and William M. Thompson, 1–21. Vol. 22 of *The Collected Works of Eric Voegelin.* Columbia: University of Missouri Press, 1997.

Murray, John Courtney. *We Hold These Truths: Catholic Reflections on the American Proposition.* New York: Sheed and Ward, 1963.

Niemeyer, Gerhart. *Between Nothingness and Paradise.* Baton Rouge: Louisiana State University Press. 1971.

———. "Christian Faith and Religion in Eric Voegelin's Work." *Review of Politics* 57 (Winter 1995): 91–104.

———. "Eric Voegelin's Philosophy and the Drama of Mankind." *Modern Age* 20 (Winter 1976): 28–39.

Nineham, Ruth. "The So-Called Anonymous of York." *Journal of Ecclesiastical History* 14 (April 1963): 31–45.

O'Grady, Joan. *Heresy: Heretical Truth or Orthodox Error? A Study of Early Christian Heresies.* Longmead, UK: Element Books, 1985.

Parker, T. H. L. *John Calvin: A Biography.* Philadelphia: Westminster Press, 1975.

Plato. *The Republic.* 2nd ed. Translated by Allan Bloom. New York: Basic Books, 1994.

Pocock, J. G. A. *The Machiavellian Moment: Florentine Political Thought and the Atlantic Republican Tradition.* Princeton: Princeton University Press, 1975.

Powell, Mark Allen. *Jesus as a Figure in History: How Modern Historians View the Man from Galilee.* Louisville: Westminster John Knox Press, 1998.

Ranieri, John J. *Eric Voegelin and the Good Society.* Columbia: University of Missouri Press, 1995.

Sandoz, Ellis. "The Crisis of Civic Consciousness: Nihilism and Resistance." In *The Politics of Truth and Other Untimely Essays,* by Ellis Sandoz, 121–38. Columbia: University of Missouri Press, 1999.

———. "The Foundations of Voegelin's Political Theory." *Political Science Reviewer* 1 (Fall 1971): 30–73.

———. *A Government of Laws: Political Theory, Religion, and the American Founding.* Baton Rouge: Louisiana State University Press, 1989.

————. *The Voegelinian Revolution: A Biographical Introducton.* Baton Rouge: Louisiana State University Press, 1981.

Sawyer, John F. A. "Isaiah and Christian Origins." In *The Fifth Gospel: Isaiah in the History of Christianity,* 21–41. Cambridge: Cambridge University Press, 1995.

Schürer, Emil. *The History of the Jewish People in the Time of Jesus Christ.* Vol. 2. Edited by Geza Vermes and Gergus Millar. Edinburgh: T & T Clark, 1979.

Schweitzer, Albert. *The Question of the Historical Jesus: A Critical Study of Its Progress from Reimarus to Wrede.* Edited by John Bowden. Translated by William Montgomery, J. R. Coatts, Susan Cupitt, and John Bowden. Minneapolis: Fortress Press, 2001.

Shuler, Philip L. *A Genre for the Gospels: The Biographical Character of Matthew.* Philadelphia: Fortress Press, 1982.

————. "The Genre of the Gospels and the Two Gospel Hypothesis." In *Jesus, the Gospels, and the Church: Essays in Honor of William Farmer,* edited by E. P. Sanders, 69–88. Macon: Mercer University Press, 1987.

Stanton, Graham N. "What Is a Gospel?" In *The Gospels and Jesus,* 14–33. Oxford: Oxford University Press, 1989.

Stark, Rodney. *The Rise of Christianity: A Sociologist Reconsiders History.* Princeton: Princeton University Press, 1996.

Strauss, Leo. *The City and Man.* Chicago: University of Chicago Press. 1964.

————. *Thoughts on Machiavelli.* Chicago: University of Chicago Press. 1958.

Strayer, Joseph R. *The Albigensian Crusades.* New York: Dial Press. 1971.

————. *The Reign of Philip the Fair.* Princeton: Princeton University Press, 1980.

Talbot, Charles H. *What Is a Gospel?: The Genre of the Canonical Gospels.* Philadelphia: Fortress Press, 1977.

Thiessen, Gerd, and Annette Merz. "The Quest for the Historical Jesus." In *The Historical Jesus: A Comprehensive Guide,* by Thiessen and Merz, 1–15. Translated by John Bowden. Philadelphia: Fortress Press, 1998.

Thompson, William M. "Voegelin on Jesus Christ." In *Voegelin and the Theologian: Ten Studies in Interpretation,* edited by John Kirby and William M. Thompson, 178–221. Vol. 10 of Toronto Studies in Theology. New York: Edwin Mellen Press, 1983.

Tocqueville, Alexis de. *Democracy in America*. Translated by George Lawrence. Edited by J. P. Mayer. New York: Harper Perennial, 1988.

Tonsor, Stephen J. "The God Question: A Review of Eric Voegelin, *Published Essays, 1966–1985: The Collected Works of Eric Voegelin,* Vol. 12." *Modern Age* 35 (Winter 1992): 65–68.

Vaughan, Frederick. *The Tradition of Political Hedonism*. New York: Fordham University Press, 1982.

Vermes, Geza. "The Gospel of Jesus the Jew." The Riddle Memorial Lectures, 48th Series. University of Newcastle upon the Tyne, 1981.

Vorster, Willem D. "Through the Eyes of a Historian." In *Speaking of Jesus: Essays on Biblical Language, Gospel Narrative, and the Historical Jesus,* edited by J. Eugene Botha, 63–93. Supplements to *Novum Testamentum*. Leiden: Brill, 1999.

Walsh, David. "Editor's Introduction." In vol. III of *History of Political Ideas,* by Eric Voegelin, edited with an introduction by David Walsh, 1–26. Vol. 21 of *The Collected Works of Eric Voegelin*. Columbia: University of Missouri Press, 1997.

Watt, J. A. "Spiritual and Temporal Powers." In *The Cambridge History of Mediaeval Political Thought: c. 350–c. 1450,* edited by J. H. Burns, 367–424. Cambridge: Cambridge University Press, 1988.

Webb, Eugene. *Eric Voegelin: Philosopher of History*. Seattle: University of Washington Press, 1981.

———. "Eric Voegelin's Theory of Revelation." *Thomist* 42 (1978): 95–122.

Wilhelmsen, Frederick D. *Christianity and Political Philosophy*. Athens: University of Georgia Press, 1977.

"William of Hundlehy's Account of the Anagni Outrage." Translated by H. G. J. Beck. *Catholic Historical Review* 32 (1947): 200–201.

Willis, Geoffrey Grimshaw. *Saint Augustine and the Donatist Controversy*. London: SPCK. 1950.

Index

⚜

Abbo of Fleury, Abbot, 84
Acts of the Apostles, Book of, 44, 53, 59n33
Adam, 51, 93, 94
Alaric, 59
Albigensians, 123, 124, 156
Alexander the Great, 115–17, 118
Allen, Charlotte, 32–33, 34
Amicitia, 140–43
Amor Dei, 129
Amor sui, 129
Anamnesis (Voegelin), 34
Anchorite movement, 78
Angelo Clareno, 121
Anglicanism, 120
Antichrist, 147
Apocalyptic idea, 48
Apolitism, 115–16, 151, 157–58
Aquinas, Thomas. *See* Thomas Aquinas, Saint
Aristotle: on faith versus reason, 112; on government, 101; on *homonoia,* 19–20, 21, 23; on human nature, 20; and noetic consciousness, 13, 34; *The Politics* by, 19–20; and Thomas Aquinas, 99, 101
Artemis, 53

Asceticism, 78–79
Asia, 127, 128–29, 151
Augustine, Saint: and church, 145, 152; *The City of God* by, 59–60, 87, 129, 133; and construction of Christian history, 58–62, 81, 88, 89, 129, 134; on human nature, 64–65, 94, 136; Niemeyer on, 24; on parallel histories, 60
Augustus, 61, 72
Averroës, 12, 98, 112

Bammel, Ernst, 53
Baptism, 36, 50, 63, 67
Barnabas, 49
Barrett, C. K., 59n33
Baumann, Clarence, 56–58
Beasley-Murray, G. R., 39
Belshazzar, King, 53
Benedict, Saint, 76
Benedictine monasteries, 76–77, 154
Berith, 39–40, 51
Bernard, Saint, 79
Bible. *See* Gospels; Old Testament; and specific books of Bible
Blumenthal, Uta-Renate, 84

Boase, T. S. R., 109
Body of Christ. *See Corpus mysticum*
Boetheius of Dacia, 98
Bohemia, 123
Bonhoeffer, Dietrich, 54–55
Boniface VIII, Pope, 95, 102, 104–12, 138, 142, 146
Bultmann, Rudolf, 31, 31–32n3
Byzantine empire, 71, 74

Calvin, John, 5, 135–36, 145–50
Campion, Nicholas, 87
Carlyle, A. J., 110
Carlyle, R. W., 110
Carolingian empire, 71, 74–75
Catholic Church, 120, 148. *See also* Church; Popes
Charismata: charismatic rulership, 146, 157, 160; and *corpus mysticum* (body of Christ), 53–54, 67, 75, 105, 109, 134, 138, 139, 142; Paul on, 53–54, 67, 109, 134, 142
Charlemagne, 73, 75, 159
China, 151
Christian community: and *corpus mysticum* (body of Christ), 50–52, 53, 67; and governmental authority, 46, 52–54, 134; and law of love, 49–50; and *mana* of Jesus, 42–43; and monasteries, 5, 76–81, 120–21, 154; Paul as founder of, 13; and Pauline compromises, 2–5, 44–52, 61, 66–67, 70, 75, 86, 103, 115, 133–34, 139, 152, 153, 158, 163; and Pentecost, 44; and regulative function, 55–56; and Sermon on the Plain and Sermon

on the Mount by Jesus, 54–58, 67, 68, 151; social rules of, 49–50; and Tyconian problem, 62–64, 70, 83, 135, 145, 157; and visions of risen Christ, 43–44
Christianity: Augustine's construction of Christian history, 58–62, 81, 88, 89, 129, 134; and Calvin, 5, 135–36, 145–50; and church, 66–68; and diversity of humanity, 115, 118–19; function of, 46; and gnostic deformation of Christian symbols, 16; and living by reformation, 132–33, 142, 150–52; and Luther, 5, 135–45, 147, 157, 158; Machiavelli on, 129–32; and Pauline compromises, 2–5, 44–52, 61, 66–67, 70, 75, 86, 103, 115, 133–34, 139, 152, 153, 158, 163; and salvation, 15–16; Sandoz and Hollweck on, 28; and sectarian movements, 119–25, 135, 136, 150–59, 164; and seeds of order and disorder, 9; spiritualism of, 68; and suffering, 129–30; symbols and symbolizations of, 9, 16, 69; and Tyconian problem, 62–64, 70, 83, 135, 145, 157; weaknesses of, 1. *See also* Christian community; Christian political order; Church; Jesus Christ; Reformation
Christianity and Political Philosophy (Wilhelmsen), 12–13
Christian political order: and crisis of civic consciousness, 19–27; Gelasian doctrine of, 5, 54, 71,

73, 75, 91, 93, 100, 105, 160–
61; and Giles of Rome, 102,
106–8; and *imperium*, 3; Luther's
destruction of, 144–45, 158; and
Machiavelli, 125–32; and
monasteries, 5, 76–81, 120–21,
154; and Pauline compromises,
2–5, 44–52, 61, 66–67, 70, 75,
86, 103, 115, 133–34, 139, 152,
153, 158, 163; and Reformation,
69–70; reformations throughout
history of, 56; and reform versus
revolution, 57–58, 68, 77; and
sectarian movements, 119–25,
135, 136, 150–59, 164; Strauss
on, 12; tensions within, 68–69;
and Thomas Aquinas, 97–103;
and *Unam Sanctum* by Boniface
VIII, 95, 104–11; Voegelin's
Christian critics, 10–19, 33; and
William of Ockham, 112–14. *See
also* Christian community;
Political society; *Sacrum imperium*
Christos, 37, 38
Chronicles, Book of, 51
Church: and Anchorite movement,
78; and Cistercian orders, 78–
79, 87, 89; and Cluniac reform,
77–79; and diversity of
humanity, 115, 118–19; and
dogma, 155, 156; Donatist, 62–
63, 70, 91, 157; ecclesiasticism
of, 102, 110, 122–23, 154–55;
and Franciscans, 80–81, 90–93,
121–22; and Inquisition, 123;
and Investiture Controversy, 81–
86, 110, 156–57; and mendicant
orders, 80–81, 121; in Middle
Ages, 76; and monasteries, 5,
76–81, 120–21, 154; and

nations in history, 115–19; and
Norman Anonymous, 84–86;
and Pauline compromises, 66–
67, 75, 133–34, 139, 152, 153,
158, 163; sacraments of, 50, 63,
67, 82–83, 133, 139, 147–48,
152–53, 156, 157; and *sacrum
imperium,* 71–76; sale of
indulgences by, 137; and
sectarian movements, 119–25,
135, 136, 150–59, 164; and
simony, 82–84; as state, 103–12;
and Tyconian problem, 62–64,
70, 83, 135, 145, 157. *See also*
Christian community;
Christianity; Popes; Reformation
Church of England, 120
Cicero, 117–18
Cistercian orders, 78–79, 87, 89
City of God, The (Augustine), 59–
60, 87, 129, 133
Civic consciousness, crisis of, 19–
27, 164
Civil theology, 23–24
Civitas Dei (city of God), 60, 63–
64, 87, 133, 145, 147
Civitas diabloi (city of the devil), 63,
109
Civitas mixtum, 63–64
Civitas terrena, 60, 145
Cluniac monasteries, 77–79, 154
Cold War, 26–27
Collected Works of Eric Voegelin, 8,
28
Communist movement, 156
Community. *See* Christian
community
Conciliar Movement, 114
Concordat of Worms, 82, 86
Confucius, 151

Consensus, 22–23, 26
Conservative Affirmation in America (Kendall), 22
Constitutions of Melfi, 93–95
Corinthians: First Epistle to, 50, 51, 108, 109, 119, 138; Second Letter to, 132, 142
Corpus diaboli, 83
Corpus mysticum (body of Christ): and charismata, 53–54, 67, 75, 105, 109, 134, 138, 139, 142; and *ecclesia,* 110; Paul on, 50–52, 53, 67, 94, 97–98, 133, 134; and sacraments, 152; and *sacrum imperium,* 75, 97–98; Thomas Aquinas on, 95, 96, 98–103, 110
Cosmopolis, 117–18
Council of Chalcedon, 71
Council of Constance, 114
Counter-Reformation, 161
Covenants between God and Israel, 39–40, 51
Creighton, Mandell, 111
Crisis of civic consciousness, 19–27, 164
Crusades, 80, 123, 124, 161
Culture war, 27

Daniel, 47, 53
Dante, 90, 97
David, King, 51
Dawson, Christopher, 61, 72–73, 74, 76, 120, 121
Deborah, 40
Deculturation, 33–34
De ecclesiastica potestate (Giles of Rome), 106
Defensor Pacis (Marsilius of Padua), 111
Differentiation, 14, 18, 97

Dominicans, 81, 121
Donatist church, 62–63, 70, 91, 157, 159–60
Douglass, R. Bruce, 15, 16, 23
Dux (leader), 88, 89, 90

Ecclesia, 110
Ecumene, 10
Ecumenic Age, The (Voegelin), 2, 10–11, 33–34
Elshtain, Jean Bethke, 27
England, 103–4, 120, 123, 126, 161
Enlightenment, 33, 131n19
Ephesians, Epistle to, 50, 142n12
Ephesus, 53, 57
Epistles. *See* specific epistles, such as, Hebrews, Epistle to
Equivalence, 18
Eric Voegelin: Philosopher of History (Webb), 13
Eschatology: and history, 38, 39–40, 47–48, 81; of kingdom of God, 47–48; of Luther, 143; of Old Testament, 149–50; and Sermon on the Plain and Sermon on the Mount by Jesus, 54–56; totalitarian eschatologies, 160
Eucharist, 63, 67, 148
Eugenius III, Pope, 79
Eusebius, 31
Exodus, Book of, 39
Exousia (governmental authority), 53, 75
Ezekiel, 40

Faith: benefit of, 142n12; Calvin on, 149; and Christian community, 42–45; justification by faith alone, 142–45, 149; lack of, 131; and living by reformation, 132; Luther on, 141–45, 147, 157; Paul on, 101, 158; Thomas Aquinas on, 99–100, 112; William of Ockham on, 112–14

Federalist Papers, The, 24–25

Fides caritate formata, 140

Form criticism, 31–32

Fortin, Ernest L., 61

Fortuna, 125, 129

France, 104, 114, 124, 126, 127n16, 162

Francis, Saint, 80–81, 84, 90–93, 95, 97–98, 101, 102, 110

Franciscans, 80–81, 90–93, 121–22

Frederick II, 75, 92–95, 97–98, 102, 111, 134

Freedom of a Christian, The (Luther), 141

French Revolution, 162

From Enlightenment to Revolution (Voegelin), 28

Gallican movement, 114, 120

Gelasian doctrine, 5, 54, 71, 73, 75, 91, 93, 100, 105, 109, 156, 160–61

Germany, 123, 127n16, 137–38, 144

Giles of Rome, 102, 106–8, 142

Gnostic, 16, 162, 164

God: authority of, 52, 53; *berith* between Israelites and, 39–40, 51; creation by, 94–95; and faith, 112; friendship between humans and, 140–43; Giles of Rome on, 107; grace of, 93; of philosophers, 15; revelation of,

15, 18; timelessness of, 149; and Trinity, 88, 99; wisdom of, 108. *See also* Kingdom of God

"Gospel and Culture, The" (Voegelin), 15

Gospels: Eusebius on, 31; form criticism of, 31–32; as hagiographic, 30; as historical, 30; and historical Jesus, 30–33, 35; Messiah consciousness in, 41; purposes of, 31, 32; Voegelin on, 4, 15–16, 18, 30, 36–37; writing of, 31

Government: Aristotle on, 101; authority of, and Christian community, 52–54, 134; Calvin on, 146; and charismatic rulership, 146, 157, 160; naturalist theory of, 93–95; purpose of, 52; Thomas Aquinas on, 100, 101, 107

Grace, 93, 133, 139, 142n12, 147–48, 152–53, 156, 157

Grasso, Kenneth L., 25

Great Reformation. *See* Reformation

Great Schism, 114, 154

Green, William Scott, 37–38

Gregory I the Great, Pope, 71, 75, 103

Gregory VII, Pope, 81–82

Guignebert, Charles, 35–36

Habakkuk, Book of, 141

Hallowell, John H., 15–16, 28

Halphen, Louis, 75

Hanson, John S., 38

Heaven, 59, 69

Hebrews, Epistle to, 44, 45

Henry IV, King, 81–82

Henry VIII, King, 120
Hierarchy, 105, 107–9, 138
Historicity of Jesus, 4, 10–11, 12, 15, 18, 30–36
Historiiae Adversum Paganos (Osorius), 61–62
History: Augustine's construction of Christian history, 58–62, 81, 88, 89, 129, 134; as cyclical, 129; epochal construction of, by Augustine, 60; eschatological outlook on, 38, 39–40, 47, 81; and Gospels, 30; historicity of Jesus, 4, 10–11, 12, 15, 18, 30–36; of ideas, 7–8, 28–29; Israelite history, 18, 38–41, 46–47, 51, 61; Joachim of Flora on Third Realm, 87–90; and law of love, 49–50; Löwith on, 47, 48–49; Machiavelli on, 129; Norman Anonymous on, 85; Orosius and profane history, 61–62, 64, 98; parallel histories and Augustine, 60; Paul's compromise with, 46–50, 61, 67, 133–34; periodization of, 46–47; Trinitarian structure of, 87–89
History of Political Ideas (Voegelin): on Alexander the Great, 115–17; on Augustine, 58–62; background to, 7–10; on body of Christ (*corpus mysticum*), 50–52, 53, 67; breakthrough while working on, 8; on Calvin, 135–36, 146–50; on Christian community, 42–44, 46, 47, 52–54; and Christian critics of Voegelin, 10–19; on Christian political order, 1, 2, 4, 6, 8–9, 29, 163–64; on church and
nations in history, 115–19; on church as state, 103–11; on construction of *sacrum imperium,* 71–76; and crisis of civic consciousness, 19–27; on Franciscans and Saint Francis, 90–93, 120–21; on Frederick II, 92–95; on Giles of Rome, 106–8; on Gospels, 4, 30, 36–37; on governmental authority and Christian community, 46, 52–54, 134; on Jesus, 30–36, 42–44, 54–58; on Joachim of Flora, 87–89; on Luther, 5, 135–45, 157, 158; on Machiavelli, 125–32; on Messiah and self-consciousness of Jesus, 37–42, 43; on monasteries, 76–81, 154; on obstacles to *metanoia* and social order, 54–58; on Paul, 44–54, 66–67, 70, 75, 86, 103, 115–34; on political idea, 65–71, 133; publication of, 8; purpose of, 35; on Reformation, 134–62; relationship of, to Voegelin's later work, 27–29; scope of, 8; on sectarian movements, 119–25, 135, 136, 150–59, 164; on Thomas Aquinas, 97–103, 106–7, 140–41; on Tyconian problem, 62–64, 70, 83, 135, 157; on Western decline, 164; on William of Ockham, 112–14
History of Political Theory (Sabine), 7
History of the Jewish People in the Time of Jesus Christ, The (Schürer), 38–39
Hobbes, Thomas, 139

Hollweck, Thomas A., 28
Holy Spirit, 44, 50, 88, 89
Homonoia (concord, like-mindedness): Alexander the Great on, 116–17, 118; Aristotle on, 19–20, 21, 23; and consensus, 22–23, 26; Niemeyer on, 24; Paul on, 3–4, 117, 132–33; reformed personality and Christian *homonoia,* 132–33; Tocqueville on, 21; Wilhelmsen and Kendall on public orthodoxy, 21
Horsley, Richard A., 38
Human Christ (Allen), 32–33, 34
Human nature: Aristotle on, 20; Augustine on, 64–65, 94, 136; and Fall of Adam and Eve, 93, 94; Giles of Rome on, 107–8; and immortality of individuals, 94; and living by reformation, 132–33, 142, 150–52; Luther on, 139, 141–43; Paul on, 45, 50, 64, 111, 136; Thomas Aquinas on, 101, 136
Humbert, Cardinal, 83–85, 98
Hussite rebellion, 124

Ideas, political, 7–8, 28–29, 65–71, 133
Ideological mass movements, 2, 16, 164
Immanentism, 98–99, 134, 145
Imperial Christianity. *See Sacrum imperium*
Imperium. See Sacrum imperium
Incarnation of Jesus Christ, 11, 15, 17, 18, 61, 93, 152
Indulgences, 137
Inquisition, 123

Institutes of the Christian Religion (Calvin), 146, 147–48
Intramundane forces, 93, 99–100, 101, 111, 128, 134
Investiture Controversy, 81–86, 110, 156–57
Irenaeus, 88
Isaacs, Harold R., 26–27
Isaiah, 42
Islam, 3, 79–80, 161, 164
Israelite history, 18, 38–41, 46–47, 51, 61. *See also* Judaism
Italy, 125–31
It-reality, 18

Janus, temple of, 61
Jay, John, 24–25
Jeremiah, 40
Jesus (Guignebert), 35–36
Jesus and the Word (Bultmann), 31
Jesus Christ: baptism of, by John, 36; birth of, 61; Gospel accounts of, 4, 15–16, 30–33, 35; historicity of, 4, 10–11, 12, 15, 18, 30–36; incarnation of, 11, 15, 17, 18, 61, 93, 152; and kingdom of God, 2, 48, 54, 57; on love, 55; *mana* of, 42–43; miracles of and healing by, 36, 42; parables of, 36; Paul's encounter with risen Christ, 11–15, 17, 34, 43; resurrection of, 16–17; Saint Francis on, 92, 121–22; second coming of, 48–49, 52, 59; self-consciousness of, as Messiah, 4, 32, 36, 37–42, 43, 47–48, 93; as second Adam, 51; and Sermon on the Plain and Sermon on the Mount, 54–58, 67, 68, 150; suffering and death

of, 41, 43, 44, 93; temptation of, 36–37, 45; timing of public appearance of, 118

Jesus Seminar, 33*n*6

Jews. *See* Judaism

Joachim of Flora, 87–90, 98

John, First Epistle of, 49, 141

John Peter Olivi, 121

John the Baptist, 36

Judaism, 38–39, 49–50, 53, 119, 158. *See also* Israelite history

Judges, Book of, 40

Justification by faith alone, 142–45, 149

Kendall, Willmoore, 21–22

Kingdom of God: Augustine on, 60; and diversity of humanity, 115; eschatology of, 47–48; glory of, 52; and Jesus Christ, 2, 48, 54, 57; Löwith on, 48–49, 89; as not of this world, 122, 133; Paul on, 118; tension within construct of, 133

Kingdom of Heaven, 59, 69

Law: natural law, 49, 67, 133–34; Old Testament law, 141*n*11; Thomas Aquinas on New Law of Christ, 101

Leo I, 71

Leviathan (Hobbes), 139

Libido dominandi, 106, 141

Lincoln, Abraham, 126–27

Lippmann, Walter, 26

Locke, John, 12, 100, 135, 161, 163

Lombard kingdom, 71

Louis XI, King, 104

Love: *amor Dei*, 129; *amor sui*, 129;

of God for humans, 140–43; Jesus on, 55; Luther on, 143–44; Paul on, 46, 49–50, 55*n*28, 109

Löwith, Karl, 47–49, 61, 89

Luke, Gospel of, 54, 59*n*33

Luther, Martin, 5, 135–45, 147, 157, 158

Machiavelli, Niccolò, 12, 55, 125–32, 136

Mana of Jesus, 42, 43

Manichean heresy, 88

Marcus Aurelius, 72

Mark, Gospel of, 30, 31, 36–37, 41, 42

Marsilius of Padua, 111

Marx, Karl, 137

Masshiah, 37–38

Matthew, Gospel of, 49, 54, 55, 56, 88

McGraw-Hill publishing house, 7

McKnight, Stephen A., 18–19

Melito of Sardis, 62, 64, 72, 89

Mendicant orders, 80–81, 121

Messiah, 32, 36, 37–42, 43, 47–48, 93. *See also* Jesus Christ

Metanoia, 42, 44, 50, 54, 132, 141

Metaxy, 18

Middle class, 124

Miracles of Jesus, 36, 42

Modernity, 131, 135, 136

Monasteries, 5, 76–81, 120–21, 154

Monophysite Christology, 71

Montgomery, Marion, 16–17

Morrissey, Michael P., 10, 18, 35

Morse, David L., 136, 141*n*11

Morstein Marx, Fritz, 7, 8

Murray, John Courtney, 22–23

National Socialist movement, 156

Nation-states and nationalism, 123–24, 161

Natural law, 49, 67, 133–34

Nebuchadnezzar, 47, 53

New Science of Politics, The (Voegelin): on differentiation, 14, 97; on Gnostic, 162; on human consciousness, 13–14; on human society, 19; on modernity, 6; publication of, 7; purpose of, 2–3; on weaknesses of Christianity, 1

New Testament. *See* Gospels; and specific books of New Testament

Niemeyer, Gerhart, 11–12, 13, 15, 24, 33

Nietzsche, Friedrich, 28

Noesis and noetic consciousness, 11, 13–15, 34

Nominalism, 112–14

Norman Anonymous, 84–87, 90, 98, 156

Old Testament, 31–32n3, 141n11, 150

On Secular Authority (Luther), 144

Order: function of, 65; Plato on, 160

Order and History (Voegelin), 7, 9–11, 13, 28, 33, 35

Orosius, 61–62, 64, 89, 98

Ottoman empire, 127

Papacy. *See* Popes

Parables of Jesus, 36

Parallel experiences, 9, 60

Paul, Saint: on body of Christ (*corpus mysticum*), 50–52, 53, 67, 94, 97–98, 133, 134; Calvin on, 147; on charismata, 53–54, 67, 109, 134, 142; on Christ as second Adam, 51; compromises of, and Christian community, 2–5, 44–52, 61, 66–67, 70, 75, 86, 103, 115, 133–34, 139, 152, 153, 158, 163; and compromise with history, 46–50, 61, 67, 133–34; and diversity of humanity, 118–19; encounter of, with risen Christ, 11–15, 17, 34, 43; on faith, 101, 158; as founder of Christian community, 13; on governmental authority and Christian community, 46, 52–54, 134; on *homonoia,* 3–4, 117, 132–33; on human nature, 45, 50, 64, 111, 136; on love, 46, 49–50, 55n28, 109; on Messiah, 47–48; on natural law, 49, 67; and *parousia,* 59; persecution of Christians by, 43; on *pneumatikos* and *psychikos,* 108, 109; on relationship between God and individuals, 143. *See also* specific epistles

Pentecost, 44

Peter, Saint, 31, 147

Peter Damian, 82–83

Philip the Fair, 104

Phoenician Tale (Plato), 20, 52

Plato: on community of mutual interests, 20; on eros, 79; and noetic consciousness, 11, 13; on order of society, 160; and Phoenician Tale, 20, 52; and polis, 20, 53, 69, 77, 95; *The Republic* by, 20, 52

Platonism, 13, 65

Pneumatikos, 108, 109

Pocock, J. G. A., 81, 129
Polis, 20, 53, 69, 77, 95, 115
Political ideas, 7–8, 28–29, 65–71, 133
Political order. *See* Christian political order
Political society: Aristotle on *homonoia,* 19–20, 21, 23; and consensus, 22–23, 26; and crisis of civic consciousness, 19–27, 164; Douglass on civil theology, 23; Jay on, 24–25; Kendall on consensus, 22; Murray on constitutional consensus, 22–23; Niemeyer on civil theology, 24; Plato on polis, 20; Sandoz on civil theology, 23; Tocqueville on, 21; Voegelin on, 19; Wilhelmsen and Kendall on public orthodoxy, 21
Politics, The (Aristotle), 19–20
Polybius, 30, 129
Popes: and Franciscans, 122; and Investiture Controversy, 81–86, 110, 156–57; and Roman empire, 71–72; and *sacrum imperium,* 71–75, 79, 81–82, 84, 95, 120; schismatic papacy, 114, 154; as temporal monarchs, 103; and *Unam Sanctum,* 95, 104–11, 138, 142, 146
Poverty, 122
Praise of Virtues, 91
Predestination, 148–50
Prince, The (Machiavelli), 55, 125–26
Prophets, 39–40, 42, 43, 53, 133–34
Protestant Reformation. *See* Reformation

Psalms, 41
Psychikos, 108, 109
Public orthodoxy, 21, 23
Published Essays (Voegelin), 15

Quest of the Historical Jesus (Schweitzer), 33

Race and State (Voegelin), 50–51
Reformation: and church as state, 103; components of, 70; and conflict between creed communities, 159–60; and heretical undercurrent, 81; introduction to, 1, 2, 3, 5–6; and Luther, 135–45, 147, 157, 158; and privatization of the spirit, 159–62; and religious wars, 159, 160; results of, 159–62; and sectarian movements, 121, 135, 136, 150–59; spiritualism of, 102; and temporal authority, 160–61; and tensions within Christian political order, 69–70, 86, 114, 132–35; and Tyconian problem, 135, 145
Reform versus revolution, 57–58, 68, 77
Regulative function, 55–56
Religious wars, 2, 159, 160
Renaissance monarchy, 103–4
Republic, The (Plato), 20, 52
Resurrection of Jesus Christ, 16–17
Revelation, 15, 18, 39, 99, 112
Revolution versus reform, 57–58, 68, 77
Roman empire: and Christian community, 46, 50, 52–53; Church fathers on, 62n41; compared with *sacrum imperium,*

69; conquests of, 115; and cosmopolis, 117–18; Dawson on Hellenistic culture and, 72–73; and Jesus's public appearance, 118; Melito of Sardis on, 64, 72; Orosius on, 62, 64, 98; and popes, 71–72; sack of Rome by Alaric, 59

Romans, Epistle to, 45, 49, 52, 53, 141

Rulership: Calvin on, 146; charismatic, 146, 157, 160; Frederick II on, 93–95; Israel's kingship, 40, 51; Renaissance monarchy, 103–4. *See also* specific rulers

Sabine, George H., 7

Sacraments, 50, 63, 67, 82–83, 133, 139, 147–48, 152–53, 156, 157

Sacrum imperium: and Charlemagne, 73, 75; and Christian political order generally, 3, 66; construction of, 71–76; and *corpus mysticum* (body of Christ), 75, 97–98; end of, 3, 5, 75, 95–96, 97, 104, 114, 132, 134, 158, 163; and Franciscans and Saint Francis, 90–93, 95, 97–98, 102; and Frederick II, 75, 92–95, 97–98, 102, 134; and Gelasian doctrine, 5, 54, 71, 73, 75, 91, 93, 100, 105, 109, 160–61; and heretical undercurrent, 81; Humbert on, 83–85; as ideal type, 69; and intramundane forces, 93, 99–100, 101, 111, 128, 134; and Investiture Controversy, 81–86,

110, 156–57; and Joachim of Flora, 87–90; in Middle Ages generally, 5, 64, 66; and monasteries, 76–81, 120–21, 154; Norman Anonymous on, 84–86; and political idea in Voegelin's *History of Political Ideas,* 65–71; and popes, 71–75, 79, 81–82, 84, 95, 120; and Reformation, 69–70; and reform versus revolution, 68, 77; symbols of, 90–95; and systematic confusion, 75–76; tensions within, 68–69. *See also* Christian political order

Saeculum, 85, 88

Salvation, 15–16, 142, 145, 147

Samuel, Book of, 39, 51

Sandoz, Ellis: on civil theology, 23; on crisis of civic consciousness, 19, 26, 164; on revolutionary originality of Voegelin, 34; on roots of American order, 25, 27

Schürer, Emil, 38–39

Schweitzer, Albert, 33

Science, Politics, and Gnosticism (Voegelin), 6, 162

Second coming of Christ, 48–49, 52, 59

Sectarian movements, 119–25, 135, 136, 150–59, 164

Sermon on the Mount, 54–58, 67, 68, 150–51

Sermon on the Plain, 54–56, 68

Siger de Brabant, 98, 99

Simony, 82–84

Slavery, 57, 101

Sola fide, 145, 147, 148, 157

Soviet Union, 4, 26–27, 161, 164

Spain, 126, 127*n*16

Spiritual anthropology. *See* Human nature

Spirituals, Franciscan, 90, 91, 121–22

Stoicism, 51, 67, 117, 118

Strauss, Leo, 12, 102, 129*n*18

Suffering Servant, 40–42

Summa contra Gentiles (Thomas Aquinas), 140

Summa Theologicae (Thomas Aquinas), 86

Summum bonum, 130, 140, 164

Symbols: of Christianity, 9, 16, 69; and differentiation, 14; gnostic deformation of Christian symbols, 16; intramundane, 93; Morrissey on meaning of, 35; of order, 35; of *sacrum imperium,* 90–95; of Suffering Servant, 40–42; Voegelin on, 7–8

Tacitus, 30

Teleology, 85

Ten Commandments, 54

Third Realm, 87–89

Thomas Aquinas, Saint: on *amicitia,* 140–41, 143; and Aristotle, 99, 101; on *corpus mysticum* (body of Christ), 9, 95, 98–103, 110; on faith, 99–100, 112; on government, 100, 107; on human nature, 101, 136; and Joachitic speculation, 90; and maximum differentiation, 97; on New Law of Christ, 101; significance of, 101–2, 106–7; *Summa contra Gentiles* by, 140; *Summa Theologicae* by, 86

Thompson, William M., 13–14, 136, 141*n*11

Timothy, First Epistle of, 57

Timur, 127

Tocqueville, Alexis de, 21

Toleration, 135, 161

Tonsor, Stephen J., 15

Totalitarian eschatologies, 160

Towns, 124–25

Trinity, 88, 99. *See also* God

Tyconius, 62–64, 70, 83, 135, 145, 157

Tyrell, George, 34

Unam Sanctum, 95, 104–11, 138, 142, 146

U.S. Constitution, 24–25

Vaughan, Frederick, 126

Vermes, Geza, 32

Virtù, 125, 128, 129

Voegelin, Eric: on Alexander the Great, 115–17; on Augustine, 58–62; on body of Christ (*corpus mysticum*), 50–52, 53, 67; on Calvin, 135–36, 146–50; on Christian community, 42–44, 47, 52–54; Christian critics of, 10–19, 33; on church and nations in history, 115–19; on church as state, 103–11; on construction of *sacrum imperium,* 71–76; on Franciscans and Saint Francis, 90–93, 121–22; on Frederick II, 93–95; on Giles of Rome, 106–8; on Gospels, 4, 15–16, 18, 30, 36–37; on historical Jesus, 4, 10–11, 12, 15, 18, 30–36; on history of ideas, 7–8; on Investiture Controversy, 81–86, 156–57; on Jesus and community substance,

42–44; on Jesus as Messiah, 41–42, 43; on Joachim of Flora, 87–90; on Luther, 5, 135–45, 157, 158; on Machiavelli, 125–32; on middle class, 124; on monasteries, 76–81, 154; on obstacles to *metanoia* and the social order, 54–58; on Old Testament, 31–32n3; on Orosius, 61–62; on Paul, 11, 12–13, 14, 15, 17, 34, 43, 45–54, 66–67, 108, 109; and Platonism, 13, 65; on political ideas, 7–8, 28–29, 65–71, 133; on Reformation, 69, 134–62; religious beliefs of, 13, 15; revolutionary originality of, 34; on sectarian movements, 119–25, 135, 136, 150–59, 164; on Sermon on the Plain and Sermon on the Mount by Jesus, 54–58, 67, 68; on symbols, 7–8; on Thomas Aquinas, 97–103, 106–7, 140–41; on towns, 124–25;

on Tyconian problem, 62–64, 70, 83, 135, 145, 157; and Walgreen Lectures (University of Chicago), 7; on William of Ockham, 112–14. *See also* specific works

Voegelinian Revolution, The (Sandoz), 34

Walgreen Lectures (University of Chicago), 7
Walsh, David, 28
Watt, J. A., 109
Webb, Eugene, 13, 14
Wilhelmsen, Frederic D., 12–13, 15, 21, 33
William of Ockham, 112–14
World War II, 161

Xerxes, 127

York Tracts, 85, 113

Zeno, Emperor, 71

DATE DUE

DEMCO, INC. 38-2931